PRODUCT DEVELOPMENT
FOR THE
SERVICE SECTOR

Other Titles by Robert G. Cooper
Winning at New Products
Product Leadership

Also by Robert G. Cooper and Scott J. Edgett
Portfolio Management for New Products
(with Elko J. Kleinschmidt)

Product Development for the Service Sector

LESSONS FROM MARKET LEADERS

Robert G. Cooper

Scott J. Edgett

PERSEUS BOOKS

Cambridge, Massachusetts

Library of Congress Catalogue Card Number: 99-66436
ISBN: 0-7382-0105-7

Perseus Books is a member of the Perseus Books Group

Jacket design by Bruce W. Bond
Text design by Heather Hutchison
Set in 11-point Minion by the Perseus Books Group

1 2 3 4 5 6 7 8 9 10—03 02 01 00 99
First printing, September 1999

Perseus Books are available at special discounts for bulk purchases in the U.S. by corporations, institutions, and other organizations. For more information, please contact the Special Markets Department at HarperCollins Publishers, 10 East 53rd Street, New York, NY 10022, or call 1–212–207–7528.

Find us on the World Wide Web at http://www.perseusbooks.com

CONTENTS

ACKNOWLEDGMENTS

No project of this undertaking is possible without the support of others. This book is no exception. A number of people have contributed either directly or indirectly in the creation of this book.

We would like to provide a special thanks to: Jens Arleth, Managing Director of U3 Consultants, Copenhagen, Denmark. Jens has also provided a major European test setting for the proposed techniques profiled in this book and is a co-creator of ProBE. In addition we would like to thank Elko Kleinschmidt, a valued colleague of ours at the business school.

A number of other people and organizations have kindly helped us in writing this book. Companies and people that provided us with insightful comments and their views on new service development have included: Gary Tritle of 3M; Barry Siadat of Allied Signal; Bill Rodgers of Desyma Consulting; Dick Lee of Value Innovations; Therese Lavalle and Jean-Robert Cole of Northern States Power (NSP); Linda Applestein of PECO Energy; Tom Chorman formerly of Procter & Gamble; Kathryn Sachse and Marg Kneebone of the Royal Bank of Canada; Per Velde of Telenor Privat (Norwegian Telephone System), and Dave Erlandson of Teltech.

A final and heartfelt thanks to our families for their continued support throughout this time consuming exercise.

The Stakes Have Never Been Higher

A service organization has two choices in today's combative business environment: Succeed at developing new service products, or fail as a company.

More and more senior executives are coming to this conclusion; they have no choice. Increasing competition domestically and globally, a changing regulatory environment, the quickening pace of technological advances, and constantly shifting customer needs are all fueling the drive to design new service products and stay ahead of the competition. The stakes have never been higher.

Companies like American Express, AT&T, and Federal Express have been able to succeed with new offerings in this type of environment. Alarmingly, however, many more companies are unable to do the same; they have not figured out how to develop new services well enough or fast enough to keep pace with changing market forces. This is evidenced in less than impressive success rates for new service products: an average of only 59 percent.[1] This statistic reveals a lot of wasted resources at a time when companies can ill afford to reduce their earnings or give their competition an edge.

Meanwhile, new competitors are accelerating their efforts to bring products to market and are forcing existing companies to play catch-up. To prosper in this increasingly competitive and chaotic environment, service firms must not only constantly develop new services for their evolving markets, but also develop very successful ones—ones their customers are willing to pay for—and they must do it in record time.

Before we go any further, take a look at the situation described below. Do any of the problems facing this new executive ring a bell with you?

The retail business in a large telecommunications company is in serious trouble. The competition has successfully launched a number of new services over the past 18 months that have seriously eroded the business unit's market share. The company retaliated by launching its own series of new services, but most of them failed in the marketplace. The new executive's mandate is to fix the product development problems.

Upon investigating, she has found a number of disturbing issues. First, the business strategy calls for aggressive growth, but the existing line of services is mature. There is no strategy to implement the corporate goals for service development. Second, the people involved in service development initiatives are demoralized. They know they are not producing the results management wants but feel they are not the problem. Management has underfunded new service development for years, spending less than half the industry norms. Third, there does not seem to be a well-defined process for handling new projects. Each new idea is treated differently, and the developers of new services are reinventing the wheel for each new project. Finally, time to market is too long. An audit of the past year's new service offerings reveals that, at best, the company is fourth to market and it is very often last.

The new executive knows this business unit is in serious trouble. There is no strategy and no development process, which leads to dismal business performance results. How is she going to fix the situation? Later on, we will explain what she and others in her situation have done to address the kinds of problems described here.

We will also tell you what separates new service product winners from the losers.

Points for Management to Ponder

If you see aspects of your organization reflected in the example of the telecommunications company, this book should help you turn the situation around. Use the checklist below to take a hard look at how your product development efforts are managed. Ask yourself the following questions to honestly evaluate whether you are getting the results you should be getting:

- What is your organization's success rate at service development?
- Are you happy with this number?
- Are you reaching the market fast enough?
- For the amount of money you spend on new service development, are you getting the kind of results you should be getting?
- Do you feel that your competitors are better at service development than your own organization?
- Do you believe that your organization could do a better job of approaching the whole area of new service development?

If your answers to these questions leave you with an uneasy feeling about how your company measures up, read on. We will attempt to show you, step by step, how successful organizations approach new service development and achieve winning results.

Turbulent Times: A Rapidly Changing Business Environment

There is no question that the rapidly changing business environment of the past decade has created turbulence in the marketplace. Indeed, some would argue that the pace of change over the last decade was merely a warm-up for the upheaval to come in the next ten years. This environment places increasing pressure on managers to adapt their tried-and-true marketplace practices to suit the new conditions.[2] These conditions are as economically powerful as they are globally significant, and they can be classified according to four main categories: regulation, technology, the customer, and competition.

Regulation.   Legislative change and deregulation have removed many of the traditional barriers to entry to a number of business areas and have opened the marketplace up to increasing competition. For example, the traditional pillars of the financial services market are collapsing in one country after another. The United Kingdom changed two key legislative acts in the late 1980s that allowed financial institutions to compete in each other's arenas. The resulting changes in the industry are still being absorbed today. The United States and Canada have gradually adopted similar practices. The result has been a series of new service offerings from competitors who were previously prevented by law from entering these markets. For example, the insurance industry is increasingly under attack as other types of financial institutions begin to market insurance-related products directly to consumers. Similar market free-for-all's are occurring in other service sectors such as airlines, utilities, and telecommunications.

Although the long-term effects of these changes remain to be seen, most observers concur that the transformation is profound. If you doubt the force of the impact that regulatory changes will bring, recall the past five years of telecom wars and the effect they have had on the players in this sector.

The net effect of deregulation is to remove previous limitations on the scope of operation in individual industry sectors, thereby opening the marketplace to expansion. For many companies the changes have been an excellent opportunity for growth; for others, deregulation has led to declining market shares and tighter operating margins.

Technology.   Technology in the 1990s has probably had a more profound impact on all aspects of company operations, including new service development, than any other factor. The pace of technological change is expected to continue, leading to the creation of many opportunities that previously did not exist—for companies ready to take advantage of them. The financial industry is a prime example of how technology is driving many new service development initiatives: Some good examples are the aggressive moves made by Charles Schwab using E-commerce, or movement toward a cashless society (Mondex trials are occurring in the United States, Canada, and England). A simpler product innovation is the Canadian Imperial Bank of Commerce's experiment with Canada Post in a joint venture to have their ATMs sell postage stamps. Added to all this is the threat in all sectors of totally new competitors entering the market, for example, the possibility of Microsoft entering the banking business via the Internet.

The Customer. With the help of increased access to information, customers are becoming increasingly more knowledgeable and demanding. Witness the many service-quality initiatives that are currently in vogue. The combined effect of increasing wealth, an aging society, higher wages, higher education levels, and a younger generation that is comfortable with technology has increased pressure on companies to adapt operations accordingly.

Competition. All of these market conditions have a bearing on competition in the marketplace. As competitive pressures continue to increase, both internationally and domestically, the service organizations best able to respond to and anticipate changing regulations, technology, and consumer demands will be the ones best able to survive and prosper. Unfortunately for companies in many mature sectors, growth can be achieved only by taking market share from competitors. This means that companies able to react quickly to major transformations—and to get viable new offerings into the marketplace before the competition—will be better positioned to win the war for market share. And it is a war. The only alternative to winning is losing. The retail sector is a prime example: The strong sales gains Wal-Mart has achieved throughout the United States have very often been at the expense of other local retailers. The defeat of once-proud K mart Canada by its major competitor, Hudson's Bay Company, is another indication. Market annihilation in Canada is the price K mart paid for not changing fast enough in an extremely competitive market environment.

Consumers are constantly changing in what they require in the form of banking services. For example, though ATM banking took some time to catch on with consumers; by comparison, debit cards have caught on very quickly. This has resulted in a surge of new service offerings. But more offerings mean more choices and less consumer loyalty. Customers will quickly switch their business if they do not believe the types of services they desire are readily available from the bank they currently deal with. This makes customer retention through new services more challenging than ever.

Points for Management to Ponder

Consider the changes that are occurring in your industry:

1. How well is your company handling these changes?
2. Are you in a reactive mode that finds your project development teams constantly scrambling to develop and launch new services just to catch up to your competitors?
3. Or is your firm an industry leader, setting the pace for others to follow?

Service Development: The Competitive Weapon

Traditional manufacturing and processing companies have long recognized the need for effective product development as a competitive weapon. Companies like Proctor & Gamble, 3M, Corning, DuPont, Rohm and Haas, and Kodak all have well-conceived product development processes in place. But the service sector has been slower to adopt an aggressive stance in this area. However, each year more companies are looking to service development as a weapon in the increasingly competitive environments in which they operate. Companies like Sprint, Visa, Telenor, PECO (Pennsylvania Energy Company), and Marriott have all instituted internal processes to systematically and effectively develop and launch new services. The approaches of these and other organizations are discussed in depth later.

New Services: A Key Component of Growth

New service development is fundamental to achieving corporate growth goals. Growth in profits and enhanced shareholder value are central objectives of most firms' strategic plans. But increased profits can only come from two sources: reduced costs or increased revenue. The dilemma is that the cost- cutting side of the equation has already occurred: Companies are lean and mean, and hence there is little opportunity to squeeze extra profits from further cost-reduction efforts. At the same time, many service companies operate in mature markets, thus limiting revenue growth from increasing market size. Still, senior management demands that aggressive growth targets be met. How? Development of new services designed to *increase market share* or to *attack new markets* must be a major contributor.

The Good News. Unlike in the tangible goods industries, where new product performance norms are well known, in the services sector reliable data are harder to come by. But the evidence available strongly supports the contention that new service introductions make important contributions to companies' sales and profits:

- Service companies report that 24.1 percent of revenues came from new services introduced in the last five years,

EXHIBIT 1.1   New Service Product Success Rates by Sector

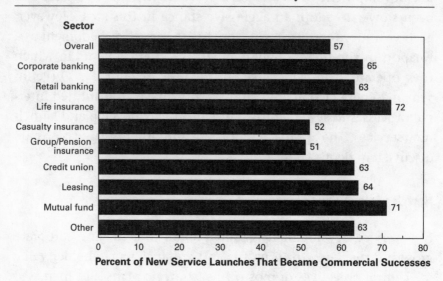

Source: Scott Edgett, "Best Practices in the Service Sector," Innovation Working Paper Series (Hamilton, Ontario: McMaster Univerisity, 1998).

according to a study published by the Product Development and Management Association (PDMA).[31] Further, 21.7 percent of company profits are derived from these new services.

- According to the PDMA study, 58.1 percent of new services launched were successful.
- According to another study, of financial institutions, new services introduced in the previous *two years* account for 10 percent of revenues.[32]
- In financial institutions in the U.S. and Canada,[33] success rates of launched new services are about 57 percent, but these rates vary by sector (see Exhibit 1.1).

Other, less quantifiable benefits have also been associated with successful new service development.[34] These can include the following:

- Enhanced corporate reputation

- Improved loyalty of existing customers
- Easier cross-selling of existing services
- Improved internal knowledge for developing future new services
- Ability to attract new customers to existing service offerings.

New services are thus fundamental to success and prosperity. Unless you have a successful service-innovation program in place, chances are you will not meet your corporate objectives. But success rates in service innovation leave much to be desired.

The Bad News. Although the above data may seem encouraging on the surface, the overall results are not. The downside to the 58.1 percent success rate is commercial failure rates of 41.9 percent. In other words, four out of ten new services fail in the market, which means that the resources expended to develop and launch these offerings have been wasted. What other part of an organization would tolerate this much failure?

If successful new services can bring nonmonetary benefits, failures can cause nonmonetary damage. The list of payoffs can just as easily become negatives. For example, failures can do the following:

- Damage the corporate brand image
- Lose customer trust and goodwill
- Make it tougher to cross-sell other services
- Lead to lost opportunities as resources are spent developing and then trying to salvage troubled new services.

Even well-known and usually successful companies can have their troubles. Consider McDonald's Restaurants, long considered a powerhouse in the fast-food industry, with over $11 billion in sales. In the early 1990s McDonald's spent millions of dollars experimenting with new menu offerings. For the most part, customers did not respond favorably. The result has been a number of marketplace flops.[35] See if you remember any of these:

1. **Carrot sticks** Currently limited to an optional item in some U.S. restaurants

2. **Fried chicken (not McNuggets)** Only available in Asia; no longer available in U.S. stores

3. **Pasta** Spaghetti and lasagna were tried; neither is available in U.S. anymore

4. **Fajitas** Never did do very well; limited to a few U.S. locations

5. **Pizza** Removed from the U.S. market, but still available in Canada

6. **McLean Deluxe** A low-fat sandwich launched in 1991 and removed from the menu in 1996

7. **Arch Deluxe** Removed from the menu in 1998.

Points for Management to Ponder

Do you know how proficient your company is at developing and launching new services? Do you track new service successes and failures? Surprisingly, many companies cannot provide solid information on how much they spend on winners versus losers, or on their rates of success and failure. Try to collect this information for the past four years in your organization. This will provide a good baseline for comparing your future results.

Some key statistics might include the following:

- Success rates versus failure rates at launch
- Proportion of resources allocated to various types of projects—both winners and losers
- The contribution that new services make to revenue and profit figures

---

What Does "New" Mean?

If we want to focus on better ways to develop and launch new services, we should be clear on exactly what we mean by "new." At first glance, "What does 'new' mean?" may seem like a simple question, but it is cause for debate and confusion in many service organizations.

The argument that true, new-to-the-world services are rare in a service environment is probably correct. Many would argue that most new services are versions of existing services or copies of competitors' products. The Mutual Insurance Group, for example, decided after a lengthy internal debate that for them, "new" means a product that, *from the customer's perspective,* represents a change; "new" is a change that affects or is noticeable to the client. Naturally, Mutual also realized this meant that there were differing degrees of new. PECO Energy has adopted a similar definition.

Other companies have found themselves debating whether or not they really have new services at all. Internally the word "service" has caused difficulty—very often it was associated with serving the customer or delivering the product. A solution has been to use the word "project." Thus the development process is seen as one to develop and manage projects that have an impact on the customer. Removed from this type of list are projects that tend to concern infrastructure, operations that are backroom in nature.

To help clarify what the term "new" means, the following definitions are offered.[36] Note that different types of "new" projects have different types of development needs and risk, from both an internal and an external perspective. Remember that "new" can be new to the company, such as a new source of revenue, or it can be new to the marketplace—or it can be both at the same time:

1. *New-to-the-world service:* These are services that have never before been offered to the marketplace. These are usually major innovations of some form. As would be expected, this type of innovation is the rarest and carries the highest level of risk. Some examples include the first television broadcast service, interest rate swaps in corporate finance, the first major on-line Internet service (CompuServe), the first automated teller machine (ATM) and the first laser eye clinic.

2. *New service line:* This type of service is one that is new to
   the organization but not to the marketplace; therefore, the
   risk is still high because the service is a new experience for
   the company. New service lines could include new business ventures, partnerships, and joint ventures. Some examples of new service lines are a hotel chain adding a new
   line of down-market hotels that caters to a business segment of the travel market (for example, Marriott's Court-
   yard); IBM's expansion into Internet services; AAA's
   partnership with the PNC Bank Corp; banks entering the
   insurance business either by developing their own insurance offerings—as did the Canadian Imperial Bank of
   Commerce—or by acquiring existing insurance companies
   (for example, Lloyds Bank's acquisition of Abbey Life).
3. *Addition to existing service line:* A service that is new to the
   company but fits into existing service lines is the most
   common type of "new" service, and such additions usually
   present less risk than the two options above. Some examples include new airline routes, call waiting or call display
   to supplement existing phone service packages, or a "new"
   chicken meal at KFC (Kentucky Fried Chicken).
4. *Improvements to existing services:* This type of "new" is really a
   replacement or update of an existing service offering. These
   projects are typically low-risk and are designed primarily to
   modernize. Very often these are presented under the banner
   "new and improved." Although these services are usually
   low-risk and produce little new revenue, they are needed to
   retain existing revenue streams. Unfortunately, many companies expend far too many resources in this category at the
   expense of other types of new services. Some typical examples include minor changes to mortgage plans and minor
   improvements to telephone banking services. Although the
   actual innovation is often small, it can sometimes be very

noticeable to the customer; for example, new uniforms or different formats for monthly bank statements.

5. *Repositionings:* This is essentially a new market or customer segment for an existing service line. The long-distance telephone service battle is a good example. Here, the same service offering is expanded into new geographic areas.

6. *Cost reductions:* These are basically modifications to services and are usually not visible to the customer. Still, they provide benefit to the company. Service changes like these are typically operations-related and cost-driven. Though market risk is low, these types of development projects use up a considerable amount of internal resources (just ask your systems people how much of their time is spent dealing with this type of change). Examples include lowering transaction cost by changing the amount of information needed from the customer, or backroom operations changes that have only a minor impact on the customer.

Most firms have a mix of these different types of service innovations. Some effort is expended on developing new sources of revenue and some is spent to ensure that existing sources are protected. Unfortunately, in many companies the balance between the two types of projects is wrong. Too much time is spent on the low-risk service modifications that do not produce enough new streams of revenue. As one executive pointed out, "I know we are doing too many low-impact projects, but the immediate pressures of the day always seem to get priority. We kid ourselves into thinking that we will work on the other projects later. Unfortunately, later never comes as there is always another crisis." A good portfolio has the right mix of new services to ensure that existing markets are protected while new opportunities are sought. More on the importance of good portfolio management in Chapter 7.

Points for Management to Ponder

Undertake a review of the new services that your organization has introduced in the past four years. Make a complete list, then categorize them according to the six types of service innovation outlined above. If possible, include the costs incurred and the revenues obtained for each new service. Next convert these figures to percentages for comparison purposes. Now ask yourself these questions:

- Is the split among the different types of new services the preferred split, or are we spending too much time on low-risk, low-impact types of service development?
- What is the breakdown by sales and profit?
- Do these percentages reflect our strategy?
- Is there a clear pattern of new revenue or is it mostly replacement revenue?
- Which types of new services have produced the best returns?
- Do our current efforts reflect where we really should be spending our time and money?
- Are we spending too much time and effort on "busy-work" projects?
- What is our success rate by type?

If you are alarmed by your answers to these questions, you are not alone. Many organizations find they are spending too much time on short-term hits that are not building new markets or streams of revenue. Instead, as one project leader said, "We are busy fools, we spend all our time on reacting to the competition instead of on the projects that will be the future of our organization".

What Does "Service" Mean?

Services Are Different Than Tangible Products

Ask anyone who works in a service industry and he or she will tell you that the service sector differs from the Proctor & Gambles and 3Ms of the world.[3] Such people will also allude to the fact that it is harder to successfully develop new service products than it is to develop new physical products. But why is this? What makes developing a new offering in a service environment more challenging than developing a new soap or a Post-It Note? Over the years, four main characteristics peculiar to services have been identified, and their impact on service development has been studied. Here is a closer look at each of these characteristics and the impact that each has on how new services are developed.

Intangibility. Unlike products, services have no physical form. This means that customers cannot see services before they buy them; nor can they take them home once they have made their purchase. This makes the service-buying decision understandably more complex than the tangible product-buying decision. It is hard to become convinced of superior quality or enhanced features before the service is paid for.

If customers cannot see or touch services, neither can the people who develop them. Design, testing, and development can become haphazard in an environment where initial capital requirements are low, where there are no physical prototypes to market-test,[9] and where qualitative rather than quantitative research is more often relied upon at the test marketing and concept testing stages.[7,11,12] All of this means that the time from idea to launch can be short, but it also means the arrival of too many ill-conceived new services in the marketplace.[4,5]

Companies often need to speed up their service-development processes because it is so easy for competitors to copy their service products.[6] Patents cannot be obtained for most services,[10] so competing firms can develop and launch new offerings at a pace that is often dizzying for both customers and operations staff. This can result in information overload and inhibition of idea generation from two important sources: front-line staff and customers.[8]

While costs of developing new services can be relatively low compared to tangible products, the cost and risk of market introductions are high,[13] because consumers cannot evaluate service offerings before actually making their purchases. This slow diffusion must be planned for, and care must be taken to speed it up.[14] One means of countering potentially slow market adoption has been generating tangibility through added features in the service design,[15] for example, price discounts in the promotional strategy, or linking the consumer's previous experience with the new service.

Another means for speeding up market adoption of services has been through linking the new service to the corporation's reputation or image.[16] But this also has an impact on establishing the company's new service-development objectives. In these cases, developers need to be sure the new service upholds the corporate identity.[17] This is an aspect of service development that usually does not apply to non-service new products, because the number of channel members in product distribution systems makes a link in the consumer's mind between product and manufacturer less likely.

The intangible nature of services also affects the way a firm measures new service-development performance.[18] Many firms report measuring success by sales volume, sales growth, new customers, and market share instead of simply by profit.[19] In some cases, new services are not even expected to earn a profit. Instead, they are used to increase sales of existing services, a form of cross-selling, or bundling.

Inseparability.   The act of supplying a service is virtually inseparable from the customer's act of consuming it. Thus, the organizational structures of service firms more seriously affect the development process than those of firms that produce tangible goods. New service development is an interactive process; it involves all departments in the company because each has a specific part to play in the ultimate delivery of the service.[20]

Staff in operations departments have been identified as particularly important to the development process, because of the critical role they play in production and delivery of the service.[21] This is why it should not be surprising that the delivery system has been identified as having significantly more importance for service firms than for goods firms in the development of successful launch strategies.[22] Short distribution channels for services mean that consumer evaluation of new offerings is directly affected by how well employees produce and deliver. The post-launch stage of the development process is also harder to evaluate than for tangibles.[23] Determining costs, and the cost-allocation process itself, can also be problematic, owing to the intermingling of the new product with other products already being offered.

Heterogeneity. Once a physical product is introduced to the market, it is taken for granted for the most part that the customer in New York and the one in Wisconsin will purchase the identical article. Thus, tangible products are considered homogeneous—all the same regardless of the market area. Services, on the other hand, generally are never delivered the same way twice—they are heterogeneous (no two people deliver a service exactly the same way). Standardization of service delivery becomes an issue, and quality control becomes a major factor in the success of the service launch: witness the emphasis McDonald's places on front-line training.

The upside of this is that, unlike that of tangible products, the service-development process presents more opportunity for customization. It is possible to develop services that differ marginally from each other, or are tailored to the customer. This offers the potential for unique selling advantages over competing service companies. Use of this advantage is particularly evident in highly innovative services.[25] Of critical importance to service introduction is the development of delivery systems that achieve a suitable degree of standardization and/or level of customization in the service.[24]

As with intangibility, heterogeneity contributes to difficulties in concept testing. Each time the service is delivered, the quality is affected by the delivery system and the people involved.[26] To overcome this variability during testing, extensive monitoring and control procedures are required. However, this leads to test results that are not an accurate reflection of the actual service, since the effects of heterogeneity that will be present in the actual launch have been removed.

Perishability. Unlike tangible products, services are produced at the time they are consumed, and they cannot be inventoried.

This leads to demand/supply difficulties and problems with production efficiency.[27] For example, an airline seat that is empty at the time of departure is a revenue opportunity that is lost forever. This perishability often necessitates further new services to fill the gap created by peaks and valleys in demand. Companies often feel pressed to develop new offerings that will help utilize service capacity in off-peak periods,[30] for example, airline seat sales or special offers to frequent fliers.

Because a new service offering must be integrated with existing ones, more planning is required for new services than for launches of physical products. This lack of flexibility in service production must be compensated for, which in turn entails a higher level of integration among operations, employee training, and marketing to develop a production and delivery system that will avoid wasted service capacity.[28] The design phase of the service development process should include consideration for the appropriate mix of human and machine/technology delivery to help offset the problems of perishability and the inseparability of supply and consumption of service.[29]

In summary, there are more questions than answers when it comes to the development process for services.[39] But we do know that services' unique characteristics (see summary in Exhibit 1.2) make it critical that they *not be treated like tangible products* when it comes to their development process. We also know the key drivers that separate new-service winners from losers. We outline these in Chapters 2 and 3. In Chapter 4, we present a service development road map that attempts to capture and deal with the peculiar traits of services.

Defining a Service

The preceding discussion applies best to what might be described as "pure" services, but in fact, a wide range of service-product mixes makes the practical definition of a service far from precise. Included in the service sector are retailers, restaurants, govern-

EXHIBIT 1.2   Traits of Intangibles and Their Effects on New Service
Development

Intangibility:
  Risk of conducting the development process too quickly
  Risk of haphazard development process (skipping steps)
  Easy for competitors to copy one's new services
  Risk of new-service proliferation
  Risk of confusing customer with too many new services
  Risk of information overload with operations staff and customers
  Difficulties in conducting R&D
  Difficulties in conducting quantitative market research
  Absence of a physical prototype to test market
  Slower market introductions
  Effect of new service on corporate image
  Difficulties in measuring success
  Difficulties in determining actual cost of new service

Inseparability:
  Need for increased interorganizational involvement
  Increased importance of delivery systems
  Higher levels of customer input
  Hard to allocate costs

Heterogeneity:
  Lack of standardized delivery system
  Quality control becomes a success issue
  Need to develop right level of standardization
  Difficulties in concept testing
  Need for more monitoring and control systems

Perishability:
  Difficulties in demand/supply management
  Need for higher levels of integration among departments
  Need to decide right mix between people and technology

ment organizations, financial institutions, telecommunications
companies, and utilities—to name a few. These diverse service
providers sometimes make it difficult to decide whether a particular organization is offering a service or a product. For example, is
IBM a service provider, or a manufacturer, or both?

In the previous section we discussed some of the unique traits
that differentiate pure services from pure products. Generally

EXHIBIT 1.3   The Tangible–Intangible Spectrum

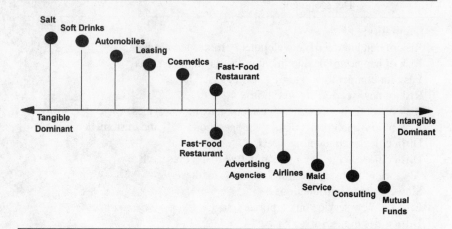

Source: G.L. Shostack, "How to Design a Service," *European Journal of Marketing* 16, 1 (1982): 49–63.

speaking, scholars have surmounted the problem of differentiating a service from a product by considering the degree of tangibility. Some offerings—like education—are pure services, while others—like the airline industry—are a mix of the tangible and the intangible. Recognition of services' complex nature has led to an understanding that goods and services can be ranked along a tangibility–intangibility spectrum[38] (see Exhibit 1.3). This spectrum demonstrates how the mix of tangibility and intangibility changes among industry sectors.

In this book we use a broad definition of services, acknowledging that in today's complex business environment there are few "pure" services or "pure" tangible goods. Instead, most companies offer some mix of tangibles and intangibles. For our purposes, we define a service company as one that tends to be on the right-hand side of the tangibility–intangibility spectrum.

Your Company Can Be a Winner in Service Development

In this chapter we have introduced the idea that new-service development is critical to the future viability of service organizations, and we have explained the unique traits of services that make de-velopment and launch more difficult. Even though much remains to be learned about refining the processes used for developing new services, there is ample evidence that specific steps can bring disci-pline to the development process and increase the chances of mar-ket success in today's increasingly tough business environment.

Some companies are beating the odds and are winning more of-ten than losing at service development. Of course, the key ques-tion is whether *your* organization will be one of these winning companies?

The next two chapters provide hard data on how organizations attack the service-development challenge. In Chapters 2 and 3 we outline best practices that companies use to develop services. Is-sues such as types of processes in use, project team structure, and the types of services being developed are discussed. We explore best practices and identify what the winners are doing differently from the losers. This way the critical success factors are isolated. These two chapters combine to provide excellent best-practice data about the development processes and the characteristics of winning projects.

Chapters 4 through 6 provide a step-by-step guide to developing a winning new service development process in your own com-pany. The game plan introduced in Chapter 4 has been proved to deliver results if designed and implemented properly. This chapter also includes some added tips and hints for making the develop-ment process work and for avoiding some of the common pitfalls. Chapter 5 is a step-by-step explanation of each stage in the devel-opment process: idea creation through launch and beyond. In Chapter 6, we introduce a number of issues that have an impact on developing a winning process: E-commerce, ways to reduce cy-cle time, and metrics.

Chapter 7 focuses on the vital issue of portfolio management—picking the right portfolio of service-development projects—and how this interacts with your development process. Here, we show you that it is no use having a great development process if you do

Reality Check

Before you move on to the next stage, you should take some time to assess your organization's new service development efforts. Provide candid answers for the following questions by answering each true or false.

	True	False
1. Our organization has a well-defined service development process in place.	☐	☐
2. We have an effective idea generation and idea capturing system.	☐	☐
3. The resources—both people and money—are allocated to ensure projects are undertaken effectively and on time.	☐	☐
4. We have effective project prioritization in place.	☐	☐
5. Project accountability issues are clearly defined.	☐	☐
6. Our culture supports service development initiatives.	☐	☐
7. Senior management is strongly committed to developing new services.	☐	☐
8. Service development performance numbers are tracked and well-known.	☐	☐

If you have responded "true" to all of the above statements, congratulations! Your company takes developing new services very seriously. If, on the other hand, you found yourself answering "false" most of the time, do not be too discouraged. Many organizations, when they make their first serious internal examination, find that they rate poorly on many of these points. It is no coincidence that these same organizations also score poorly in their rates of success. Chapters 2 and 3 provide some excellent best-practice baselines to compare your responses to.

not focus your resources on the right projects. This chapter also provides a linkage to business strategy.

The final chapter addresses implementation issues and includes topics such as the key steps in the implementation of a new service development process and portfolio management.

Altogether, these eight chapters provide you with a starting point from which to improve your organization's processes for developing new services and improving your chances of winning in the marketplace.

Some Definitions

Before we lower the microscope on how leading firms are currently developing new services, it is helpful to define the terms that we use throughout the book.

Stage-Gate* Process. This is the formal process, or road map, that firms use to drive a new-service project from idea to launch. This process typically has multiple stages, together with gates or decision points. A Stage-Gate™ process has many variants; it is also called *the new-service process*, *gating process*, or *phase-review process*. This process also contributes to effective portfolio management, because the gates are where Go/Kill decisions are made on individual projects, and where decisions are made on resource allocation.

Portfolio Review. This is the periodic review of the portfolio of all projects. It may take place once or twice annually, or even quarterly. Here, all projects—whether active or on hold—are reviewed and compared. This review often uses portfolio models (defined below) to display lists or maps of the current portfolio. The vital questions in the portfolio review are these: Are the active

---

*Stage-Gate is a trademark of R. G. Cooper and Associates Inc., a member company of the Product Development Institute. Dr. Cooper is generally considered to be the inventor of the Stage-Gate approach to product development.

projects the right ones? Do you have the right mix of active projects? Are these projects really where the company wants to spend its money?

Portfolio Models.   Portfolio models are the specific tools used to select projects and/or review the portfolio. They include scoring models, bubble diagrams and maps, various charts, financial models, and strategic approaches.[37]

Portfolio Management Process (PMP).   This is the *entire method* of project selection and portfolio management. It includes all of the components defined above.

Business Unit (BU or SBU).   This is the smallest business unit (BU) in the company for which service development is undertaken. Usually a BU or SBU is a semiautonomous, self-contained business with its own goals, strategy, and resources. A BU likely has its own development budget. For smaller firms, the BU may be the entire company.

Business Strategy.   This is the strategy for the BU. It specifies the goals, direction, and areas of focus for the BU and also fits with the company's overall business strategy.

Service Development Strategy.   This is a component of (or flows from) the BU's business strategy. It specifies the BU's development goals, direction, and areas of focus (i.e., areas where the BU will focus its development efforts). It may even specify desired levels of development spending in specific areas of focus (for example, how much to spend in certain markets or categories).

2

Critical Drivers of Success: Process Factors

Service innovations can be minor—modifying or updating an existing service—or they can be major, based on entirely new technology platforms, such as combining mobile and line-based phones into one system. Regardless of the nature of the innovation, the fact remains that rapid and successful new service development has become a vital business endeavor. The dilemma faced by management is that the need for new service development is stronger than ever, but organizations themselves do not have the tools and methods to bring new services to market.[1]

In this chapter, the three cornerstones for effective new service development are introduced: strategy, resources, and process. *Strategy*, a well-known success factor, means tying new service development to the corporate strategy and goals, identifying areas of focus for service development, taking a long-term thrust, and ensuring that the innovation strategy is clearly enunciated throughout the company. *Resource allocation* is another familiar success factor. It means having enough of the right people and adequate development financing in place.

Of the three cornerstones, *process*—more specifically, a high-quality development process that guides innovations from idea to launch—is less recognized as a critical success factor. Ironically, of the three, it is process—its nature and quality—that has the strongest impact on the business's new service performance. This chapter explores the new service development process and the ingredients that the top performers have in common. (Strategy and resources, although introduced in this chapter, are discussed in more depth later in the book.)

Cornerstones of Performance

What drives performance? Why are some companies more successful than others at developing an ongoing stream of winning new services? Recent benchmarking studies have revealed that the more successful companies do, indeed, do things differently. At the business unit (BU) level, these organizations have been found to have mastered three critical success factors that drive the performance of new services (see Exhibit 2.1). These three drivers are strategy, resource commitment, and process.[1]

Strategy.   A clear and well-communicated new service strategy for the business unit is essential. But what does this mean? It means more than setting targets and enumerating the short-term tasks required to achieve them. Many companies we visited did not have good strategies in place. Yes, targets may have been set (for example, new services are to contribute 15 percent of our new revenue). But targets by themselves do not make a strategy; rather, a target is a goal or an objective. Strategy means setting out a master plan for how a business unit will achieve its targets, and how those targets will contribute to the overall goals of the company. A well thought out new service strategy should consist of the following:

- Clear goals or objectives for the business unit's total new service effort; for example, there should be targets for revenues and profits for all new services.
- Clearly communicated information on the role that new services will play in achieving the overall business goals of the company.

EXHIBIT 2.1   The Three Cornerstones of Performance

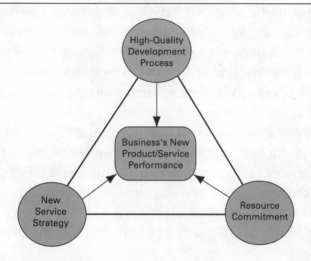

Source: Adapted from R. Cooper, "Overhauling the New Product Process," *Industrial Marketing Management* 25, 6 (1996).

- Clearly defined areas of strategic focus that give direction to the total new service effort, for example, markets and technologies.
- A long-term thrust that builds in long-term as well as short-term projects.

Resources.   Without adequate resources, an effective new service development process is nearly impossible. By resources we mean the availability and allocation of people, time, and money to conduct the research and development. To score well in resources, an organization's new service efforts should have the following:

- Senior management support for resources
- Budgets that support the necessary research and development
- Enough of the right people assigned to projects with enough time freed up to do the work required.

Process. Neither of the above two cornerstones for success can help if organizations do not have high-quality new service development processes. By high-quality processes we mean not simply a complete list of steps, but execution of those steps in a way that ensures timely completion of the project from the idea to launch. A high-quality new service development process has the following:

- An emphasis on up-front (predevelopment) activities
- Sharp, early product definition before development begins
- The voice of the customer evident throughout the process
- Tough decision points where projects are critically reviewed and, if necessary, terminated
- A strong focus on quality of execution of all the steps in a process
- Flexibility so that stages and decision points can be collapsed or skipped as indicated by the nature of the project.

The drivers of new service performance highlighted above—strategy, resources, and process—all need to be in place and working together for the realization of the superior performance results most executives are searching for. Unfortunately, many companies have not developed the internal discipline at either the project level or the decision-making level to achieve top performance. Instead, one or more of these three cornerstones is either missing or inadequately developed to respond to the challenges the company faces. In a later chapter we will discuss resource and strategy implications in more depth. Let us examine some of the norms and best practices for the new service development process.

The Ingredients of a World-Class Process

To successfully develop new services an organization must have an *effective development process in place*. Many executives say they want and need to develop new services. Unfortunately, many of these same people will also admit that their organizations are lacking an effective service development process. How common is this inconsistency? A number of best-practice reports and research studies support the assertion that many service companies are lagging behind the tangible goods industry in the effectiveness of their development processes.

Points for Management to Ponder

Consider the three cornerstones of performance: strategy, resources, and process. How does your organization measure up? Do you have the following:

- A clearly defined innovation strategy for new service development
- The resources in place to meet expectations (people, time, and money)
- A high-quality development process

If you answered no on any of these three points, perhaps it is time to consider how your company could strengthen the deficient cornerstones.

A world-class process consists of key activities from idea to launch that drive new service projects to market quickly and efficiently. Exhibit 2.2 lists activities found in a typical service development process, along with brief descriptions of what each activity involves. Exhibit 2.3 presents the results of a best-practice report illustrating that, in general, service industries lag behind manufacturing in these development activities.[2] In all eight development activities shown in Exhibit 2.3, the service sector reports performing the tasks with lower frequency than the manufacturing sector. These deficiencies are present in such key phases as concept screening, business analysis, and commercialization.

Many companies in the service sector seem to have a less-structured approach to developing new offerings than their manufacturing-based counterparts. For example, close to 60 percent of

EXHIBIT 2.2   The 13 New Service Development Process Activities

Process Activity	Description
1. Idea screening	The initial Go/No Go decision where it is first decided to allocate funds to the proposed new service idea.
2. Preliminary market assessment	An initial quick look at the market.
3. Preliminary technical assessment	A quick assessment of the technical merits and difficulties of the project.
4. Detailed market study/ market research	Marketing research, involving a reasonable sample of respondents, a formal design, and a consistent data collection procedure.
5. Business/financial analysis	A financial or business analysis leading to a Go/No Go decision prior to development.
6. Service creation/development	The actual design and development resulting in a final product/service.
7. Process development	Process (procedures) design and testing.
8. System design and testing	Systems are properly debugged.
9. Personnel training	All involved personnel are trained: training materials are prepared and people are trained in how to use and sell the new service.
10. Test market/trial sell	A test market/trial sell is conducted with a limited or test set of customers to test the plan for full launch.
11. Precommercialization business analysis	A financial analysis following development but prior to full-scale launch.
12. Full-scale launch	The launch of the service on a full-scale commercial basis: an identifiable set of marketing activities.
13. Post-launch review and analysis	The review and analysis after the new service is fully launched.

EXHIBIT 2.3   Typical Development Activities: Service Sector vs.
                Manufacturing Sector

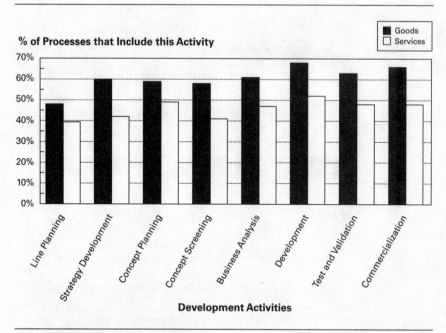

% of Processes that Include this Activity

Legend: ■ Goods □ Services

Development Activities

Source: Adapted from A. Griffin, "PDMA Research on New Product Development Practices: Updating Trends and Benchmarking Best Practices," *Journal of Product Innovation Management* 14, 6 (1997): 429–458.

the service organizations that are members of the Product Development Management Association (PDMA) identify themselves as having either no product development process or an informal approach (Exhibit 2.4).[2] Similar results are reported for financial institutions in the United Kingdom, where less than 45 percent of the companies have written guidelines for their development processes (see Exhibit 2.5).[3]

In this vein, and building upon the lessons learned from the tangible goods sectors, a number of studies have explored the links between product/service development activities and the development process itself. These studies have determined that a strong market-driven development process with thorough execution of the eight types of development activities highlighted in

EXHIBIT 2.4   Type of Product Development Process: Service vs.
Manufacturing

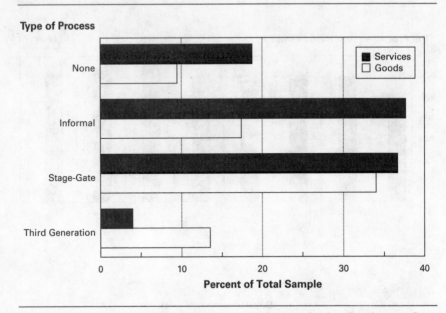

Source: Adapted from A. Griffin, "PDMA Research on New Product Development Practices: Updating Trends and Benchmarking Best Practices," *Journal of Product Innovation Management* 14, 6 (1997): 429–458.

Exhibit 2.2 does have positive impact on new service outcomes.[4] Unfortunately, a number of these studies have also shown that the theory is not being put into practice in many organizations. Instead, as Exhibits 2.3, 2.4, and 2.5 show, many companies simply do not have good processes in place.

A word of caution: The mere existence of a formal development process has not been demonstrated to have an impact on performance. There is very little correlation between the mere existence of a formal process and performance results.[4,5] The message is this: Companies that mistakenly believe they can go through the motions and "reengineer" their new service development processes (usually amounting to documenting what they are already doing) are in for a big disappointment. Merely *having* a process is not

EXHIBIT 2.5   Types of Procedures for New Service Development in U.K.
Companies

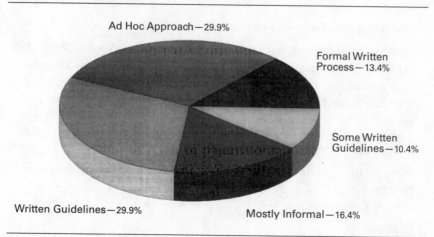

Ad Hoc Approach—29.9%

Formal Written
Process—13.4%

Some Written
Guidelines—10.4%

Written Guidelines—29.9%

Mostly Informal—16.4%

Source: Scott Edgett, "Developing New Financial Services Within UK Building Societies," *International Journal of Bank Marketing* 11, 3 (1993): 35–43.

what counts the most. This is only the starting point. What really impacts performance is the nature of the process and the quality of its execution. This means that processes have to build in best practices—activities that time and again have been shown to drive performance.

Proponents of total quality management make an argument that goes something like this: "The definition of quality is precise. It means meeting all the requirements all the time. It is based on the principle that all work is a process. It focuses on improving business processes to eliminate errors." The concept is perfectly logical and essentially simple. Most smart things are. And the same logic can be applied to developing new services.

The way to deal with the quality problem in innovation is to visualize it as a process and to apply process management and quality management techniques. Note that any process in business can be managed, and managed with a view to quality. Get the details of your processes right, and the result will be a high-quality output.

Quality of Execution: Doing It Right the First Time

Studying the Success Factors

During the past two decades, we and our colleagues—Ulrike de Brentani, Chris Easingwood, Elko Kleinschmidt, and Chris Storey—have conducted a number of studies into new product development. We have looked at companies and their development processes and performance outcomes, and the characteristics of success. Over 1,500 new service launches have been studied to determine which factors influence success. This and the next chapter incorporate many of these findings. A more complete listing of the research can be found in note 4.

Shortchanging the Process Has Consequences

Although most people seem to agree that the development process should include all of the activities shown in Exhibit 2.2, in practice many companies are found wanting. In one major study of hundreds of projects that we conducted, it was revealed that many of the commonly recommended development activities are omitted altogether from the development process.[6] Exhibit 2.6 shows how often project teams carry out specific activities. The results, summarized below, are not reassuring, given the amounts of money many of these organizations spend on developing new products and services:

- *Key activities are left out:* Commonly prescribed practices such as detailed market studies, market research, test markets, and business analyses are undertaken in less than half of the companies studied.
- *Marketing is the weakest area:* As the exhibit shows, the activities most often omitted (detailed market research, test marketing) are heavily weighted toward marketing—yet marketing activities are proven drivers of successful new service development.

EXHIBIT 2.6   Frequency of New Service Development Activities Typically
Conducted

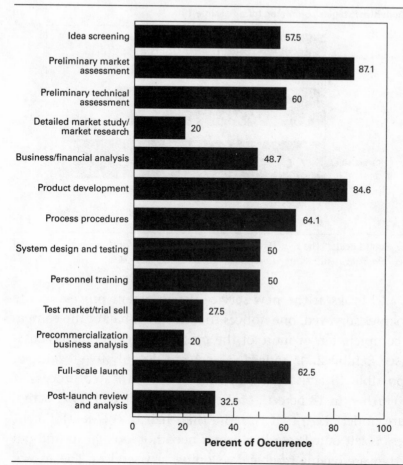

Source: Scott Edgett, "The New Product Development Process for Commercial Financial Services," *Industrial Marketing Management* 25, 6 (1996): 505–515.

- *Other activities are overlooked:* Key activities such as precommercialization business analysis and post-launch review and analysis are undertaken in less than half of the companies studied.

The picture here is bleak: Many companies have processes that are full of holes, with serious errors of omission. When one stands

EXHIBIT 2.7   Completeness of New Service Development Process

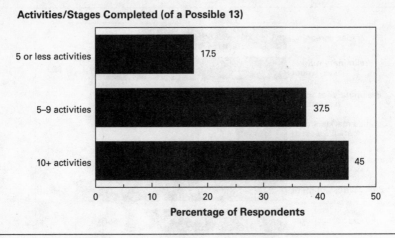

Source: Scott Edgett, "The New Product Development Process for Commercial Financial Services," *Industrial Marketing Management* 25, 6 (1996): 505–515.

back and looks at the new service development process in the companies surveyed, one notices that less than half of the companies complete ten or more of the prescribed development activities (see Exhibit 2.7).[6] Indeed, 37 percent do only five to nine of the possible 13 activities. This indicates a truncated process at best. Further, in 18 percent of the companies, five or fewer activities are undertaken; that is, more than half of the development process is left out. These companies need not look far to find out why they are having trouble developing new services. The answer probably lies in the development process itself.

What about the quality of execution? Even if an activity is carried out, is it well done? Or has the activity been undertaken in a rushed or sloppy fashion? Exhibit 2.8 is a quality index for each of the 13 key development activities.[6] The proficiency with which the tasks are performed is rated on a scale of 1 to 5. The results are not encouraging. Two conclusions can be drawn from this data:

- Two activities, *preliminary market assessment* and *product (project) development,* can be considered to have adequate quality of execution, although even here the result is not strong. These phases still rate no higher than 4 on the scale. In fact, no activity rates higher than 4. The implication is that there is a lot of room to improve the development process in many service organizations.

* Development activities are handled relatively well; it is the actions that precede and follow the development stage that are handled poorly. Particularly weak are *detailed market studies/market research, test market/trial sells,* and *business analysis*, both pre- and post-development.

EXHIBIT 2.8   Activities in the New Service Process: Quality of Execution

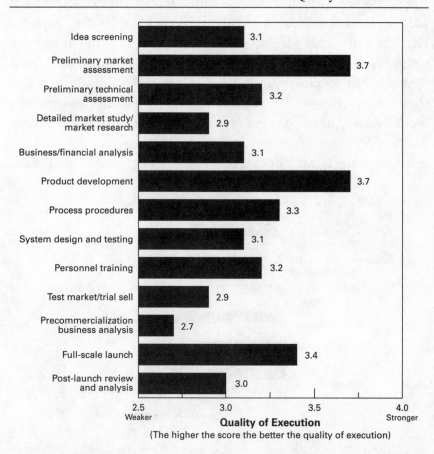

Source: Scott Edgett, "The New Product Development Process for Commercial Financial Services," *Industrial Marketing Management* 25, 6 (1996): 505–515.

When we look at these results, it comes as no surprise that the average new service success rate is reported to be only 62.5 percent. Hopefully these companies' competitors are doing no better!

Two more disturbing findings are revealed in Exhibit 2.9: First, quality of execution is not superb in any area; proficiency gaps exist. Second, there are major differences between winners and losers in terms of quality of execution. The conclusion is that the pivotal development activities—the ones that clearly separate winners from losers in Exhibit 2.9—are the ones that are not done well. In short, project teams seem to do poorly on the most important activities.

Progressive companies that have undertaken internal analyses of past projects have reached conclusions similar to the research. First, they find that success and failure hinges very much on how well key activities are performed. Second, they realize their own development processes are in need of repair. As a result, many of these companies, when overhauling their new service development process, have adopted Stage-Gate approaches from leading product developers in other industries. They have also attempted to improve the quality of execution of all project activities. For ex-

EXHIBIT 2.9   Quality of Execution: Successes vs. Failures

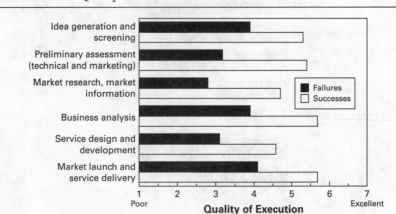

Source: Scott Edgett, "The New Product Development Process for Commercial Financial Services," *Industrial Marketing Management* 25, 6 (1996): 505–515.

ample, some companies have established action standards for pivotal tasks throughout the process (for example, what constitutes a well-done business case, or a proficiently crafted market launch plan?). These companies also build quality control checkpoints into the process. They have metrics at Go/Kill decision points to ensure projects are well executed and that substandard projects are halted. Quality of execution—doing things right the first time—has become paramount in these companies.

Focusing on the Process Brings Rewards

What about the companies that have a well-executed process in place? Do these organizations really perform better in the marketplace? The answer is yes. The same framework used in the Exhibit 2.8 sample was applied to companies achieving success rates in excess of 75 percent.[6] In Exhibit 2.10, the top third is contrasted against the bottom third in terms of quality of execution of the 13 process activities. The top performers do, indeed, score higher in terms of quality of execution. This suggests that a more thorough approach to developing new services does produce positive results.

The strongest differences between the top and poor performers are in idea screening, preliminary market assessment, detailed market studies, and post-launch review and analysis. Except for post-launch activities, the tasks that distinguish the high performers from the low performers can be classified as predevelopment. In other words, companies that have taken the time to conduct good, up-front analyses have produced better results. By spending the extra time in the predevelopment stages, these organizations ensure that new projects enter the more expensive development phases with complete information on markets, competition and financial viability. This, in turn, leads to tighter specifications for the system people to work with. This produces better end products in a more timely fashion.

Some executives express concern that emphasizing quality of execution adds time to projects, but this concern is unfounded.

EXHIBIT 2.10   Quality of Execution: Comparison of High and Low
                Performers

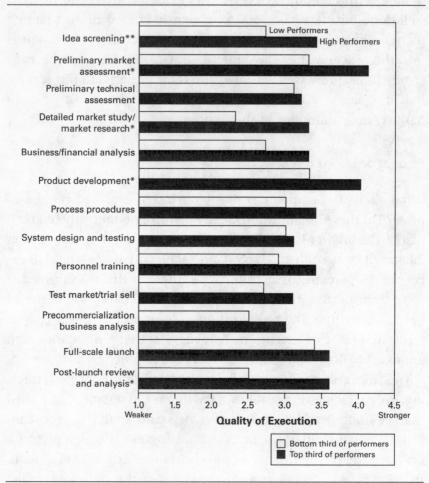

* = significant at 0.01; ** = significant at 0.05

Source: Scott Edgett, "The New Product Development Process for Commercial Financial Services," *Industrial Marketing Management* 25, 6 (1996): 505–515.

There is strong evidence that quality of execution is one of the key drivers of cycle time reduction.[7] Remember: No one is advocating postponing decisions or leaving projects in a queue awaiting perfect information; instead we are saying that successful companies take the time to do a quality job the first time through. They do not waste time recycling badly executed projects for another try.

Points for Management to Ponder

How is the quality of execution for the typical new service project in your organization? Refer to Exhibit 2.9 and ask yourself how your company would rate on the six tasks, listed below, whose performance level separates successful from unsuccessful projects.

When developing a typical new service project, does your company do well at these six tasks:

1. Idea generation and idea screening
2. Conducting preliminary technical and marketing assessment
3. Conducting necessary market research
4. Performing a rigorous business analysis
5. Service design and development
6. Launching and delivering the new service

Score yourself on the same 1-to-7 scale used in Exhibit 2.9, where 1 is poor and 7 is excellent quality of execution. How does your organization rate? Are you scoring about the same as the successes or are you closer to the typical failure? If you are not pleased with your scores, perhaps it is time to consider overhauling your new service development process.

Go/Kill Decisions: Focusing the Right Resources on the Right Projects

Most firms have far too many projects under way for the limited resources available. There is not one example in our investigations of people just sitting around with nothing to do and waiting for projects to happen. Inevitably, there are far more opportunities than there are resources to exploit them.[8]

The result of this "too many projects, not enough resources" paradigm is that funds and people are stretched too thinly. This very often means that projects take too long. Often key tasks do not get done on time or do not get done at all. And many projects suffer from sloppy work with too much corner cutting, simply because people do not have the time to do them justice.

All this means that tough choices are necessary. Service development efforts must be better focused; management must concentrate
scarce resources on the really promising projects and eliminate the
mediocre ones. First, most project ideas simply are not that good,
but management does not know how to separate the potential winners from the losers. Second, resources are too scarce to waste on
poor projects at the risk of starving the good ones. Despite this
seemingly incontrovertible logic, our studies consistently confirm
that new project evaluations are notoriously weak. Projects take on
lives of their own; there are often no serious evaluation or Go/Kill
decision points, and there are usually no criteria for rating and prioritizing projects. As one manager put it, "Once a project starts out,
it never gets stopped . . . we have a tunnel instead of a funnel." The
irony is that the profile of a winner is well understood. What is
missing is application of this knowledge to make sharper project selection decisions and achieve a better focus on the deserving
projects.

To achieve this, some firms build decision nodes or *gates* into
their development processes. The gates become Go/Kill decision
points, and better focus is achieved. Projects are subjected to increasingly rigorous criteria at successive gates, and the mediocre
projects are culled out and resources are reallocated to the promising ones.

This process management tool for product innovation is called a
stage and gate process. Stage-Gate™ builds Go/Kill decisions into
the innovation process. In Chapters 4 and 5 we take a closer look
at stage-gate schemes and how you can design and implement
them in your company.

One major bank has developed a list of qualitative evaluation criteria
based on what management believes are factors critical to success.
These criteria are applied at each of five decision points (or gates) in
the life of a project. Besides the normal financial return criteria—
"Will we make money?"—management also considers a "project
score" based on qualitative factors such as leveraging core competen-

cies, competitive advantage, and market attractiveness. Projects are rated and then prioritized on the basis of both their project scores and their financial attractiveness.

Points for Management to Ponder

Consider the challenge of focusing the right resources on the right projects. Top-performing organizations are continually striving to maintain a good balance between the available resources and the number of projects under way at any one time. To achieve this they make the decisions necessary to effectively manage their portfolio of new services.

How is your management team at making Go/Kill decisions? Do you feel you have a good balance of projects in the pipeline? Are your decision makers making the needed Go/Kill decisions in an effective and timely manner?

If you are not comfortable with your responses to these three questions, you may need to review how management is making the Go/Kill decisions for new services in your organization as projects move through the development process from idea through to launch.

Flexibility: Balancing the Need for Speed with the Need for Quality of Execution

One common pitfall some firms encounter when they redesign their development processes is to omit building in flexibility. Instead of being a template or road map, the formal process becomes a straitjacket beset with bureaucracy. This can slow things down unnecessarily. The development process should be flexible enough to handle many types of projects at varying speeds-to-market while still ensuring quality of activities.

In a flexible process, stages can be collapsed, decision points combined, and long lead time activities moved ahead. The idea is to streamline the process when it makes sense. Decisions are still made at deliberate points, rather than on the spur of the moment.

And they are made for the right reasons, with the risks of streamlining (omitting a stage or activity) weighed carefully.

The key to not sacrificing quality to speed—or speed to quality—is to be sure to provide for flexibility. Remember, the process is a risk management model: It is simply a series of steps designed to gather information to reduce uncertainty and, thereby, manage risk. Thus, adherence to every activity and decision point in the formal process depends on the risk level of the project. (Flexibility will be discussed in greater detail in Chapter 6.)

Recap

If you are thinking about overhauling your development process, remember the three cornerstones that lead to strong performance results: a clearly articulated new service strategy, commitment of adequate resources, and a high-quality development process. In this chapter we have argued that the new service development process and the activities that occur throughout the process have a strong impact on how successful the organization is at developing winning new services. However, the benchmarking results have raised a warning flag. The process itself is not the final answer; it is how the process is executed that makes the difference. Many organizations either do not have a complete process in place, or they suffer from lack of quality in execution.

Designing and implementing the new service development process is one step on the road toward more effective and timely development efforts. Many organizations are facing increased pressure to reduce cycle time and simultaneously improve the effectiveness of their new service development process. Many have successfully tackled this challenge by building into their processes the many lessons they have learned from previous successes and failures.

In this chapter we have looked from the *process perspective* at how winners develop new services. In the next chapter we lower the microscope to the *project level* and examine what the winners are doing differently from the losers on a project-by-project basis.

Conducting Your Own Audit

Before we get into more detail, this might be a good time to benchmark your own process, using the ProBE (*Pro*duct *Bench*marking and *E*valuation) test. The questions that constitute this test have been developed over the years to assess an organization's strengths and weaknesses at both the process and project level. Answering each question will help you better assess your own organization. Once you have answered the questions, refer to Exhibit A.1 in Appendix A to compare your company with those in our database. Look for areas where you have scored well and for areas where your score could be improved.

ProBE (*Product Benchmarking* and *Evaluation*) of Our Development Process

The following questions are designed to ProBE your development process for new services. Answer each question using the scale provided to characterize your organization's current process.

In our organization we use the following:

1. A formal development process, a standardized process to guide development projects from idea to launch. The process consists of stages and Go/No Go decision points.

    0 1 2 3 4 5 6 7 8 9 10
    Not at all   Very much so

2. Clearly defined stages that consist of clearly defined activities to be undertaken, e.g., "Business Case Assessment" or "Concept Development."

    0 1 2 3 4 5 6 7 8 9 10
    Not at all   Very much so

3. Activities listed and defined for each stage. For example, for the Business Case Stage, activities might be research, market analysis, cost analysis, etc.

    0 1 2 3 4 5 6 7 8 9 10
    Not at all   Very much so

4. Go/No Go decision points (or gates) defined for each stage of the project. For example, Gate 1 might be "Initial Screen," Gate 3 might be "Go to Development," and so on.

    0 1 2 3 4 5 6 7 8 9 10
    Not at all   Very much so

5. Go/No Go criteria (or exit criteria) that are spelled out (and written down) for each of the gates in the process—that is, what it takes to "pass" a gate.

    0 1 2 3 4 5 6 7 8 9 10
    Not at all   Very much so

6. Deliverables defined for each gate, that is, a fairly standard list of items that the project leader or team should "deliver," or have done, upon entering each gate or decision point.

    0 1 2 3 4 5 6 7 8 9 10
    Not at all   Very much so

7. Gatekeepers defined for each gate. The people who review the project at each gate (and make the Go/No Go decision) are a defined group, Divisional Management Team.

    0 1 2 3 4 5 6 7 8 9 10
    Not at all   Very much so

8. Our process is a *visible one:* It is written down and documented in a manual and via a flow chart.

    0 1 2 3 4 5 6 7 8 9 10
    Not at all   Very much so

9. *The process is really used.* Do most new projects really go through the process stages and decision points according to the formal scheme?

    0 1 2 3 4 5 6 7 8 9 10
    Not at all   Very much so

10. There are tough and demanding Go/No Go decision points in the process, where hard choices are made, and the project really can get killed.

    0 1 2 3 4 5 6 7 8 9 10
    Not at all   Very much so

11. Performance is measured: The outcomes of projects are determined (success/failure; ROI) and a score card of past projects is kept.

    0 1 2 3 4 5 6 7 8 9 10
    Not at all   Very much so

3

Critical Steps for Success: The Project Factors

What are the keys to developing successful new services? The previous chapter presented an overview of success factors, or more specifically, characteristics of the business's new service development process—a macro view. In this chapter we look at individual projects, their characteristics, and things project teams do—a more micro view. Here, we identify the critical success factors in day-to-day new service development. These are the activities that occur within projects that differentiate winning new services from losing ones. We explain how management can use these critical activities to improve success rates and profitability of new services.

For the last two decades, we and our colleagues have probed the question of what makes a new product a success by studying almost 3,000 new product launches in a variety of industries; some products were big winners, others losers.[1] We asked the same question each time: What are the critical factors that distinguish the winners? More recently we have targeted new services, and now have over 1,500 case histories on the development of new services in our combined databases. In this chapter some of the vital conclusions from these studies are presented along with the nine steps your company can take to improve new service performance. Some of the steps will seem obvious when you read them here, but they are not always obvious to everyone, especially to some of the managers who spearheaded the many failed projects we studied. Here are the nine steps:

1. Do solid up-front homework before the project proceeds to development.

The up-front homework—the tasks that precede the actual development phase—is vital to success. Projects that feature solid up-front homework more than double their success rates from 39 percent to 82 percent (see Exhibit 3.1). There are major differences between successful and unsuccessful projects in quality of work, most notably in the homework, or predevelopment, stages. These stages include the preliminary assessment, market research, and business analysis.

EXHIBIT 3.1   Impact of Solid Up-front Homework Prior to Development

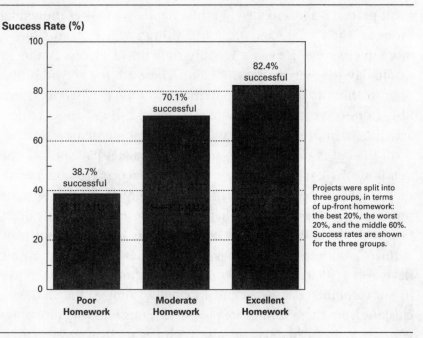

Success Rate (%)

Projects were split into three groups, in terms of up-front homework: the best 20%, the worst 20%, and the middle 60%. Success rates are shown for the three groups.

Source: Scott Edgett, "New Product Development Process in the Financial Services Sector," McMaster University Working Paper (Hamilton, Ontario: McMaster University, School of Business, 1995).

Simply stated, the steps that precede the development phase make all the difference to winning (see "Do the Up-front Homework" on pages 50–51). The first few plays of the game seem to decide the outcome. And when we study project failures, most often these failures can be traced to deficiencies in the pre-development stages. The problem is that very little time and money is spent on the up-front tasks in the typical new service. The prevailing paradigm is this: generate an idea, do a minimum of pre-work, and move it directly to development. The new paradigm should be: generate an idea, do all of the steps in the pre-development phase, then move the project to development—if and only if it still looks like it will be a winner. (See "Do the Up-front Homework" for a detailed list of steps.)

Lack of time is often cited as an excuse for avoiding the up-front detail. As one executive protested, "I'm in a hurry . . . I don't have time to do all this homework . . . let's skip the homework and get on with it . . . save some time!" Sadly, far from saving time, the end result is likely to be a less successful, more lengthy project. Why?

- First, homework improves the chances for success. There is strong best-practices evidence to support this.[2] There are basically two choices: a few thoughtful successes, or an abundance of fast failures.
- Second, homework actually reduces time to market. This is because good predevelopment work means that the project definition or specs are accurately stated. One of the greatest time wasters in development projects is that *the service specs keep changing*. This is analogous to trying to score a goal when someone keeps moving the goalposts.
- Third, homework done early allows you to anticipate problems before they become expensive or hard to fix. The worst time to be making changes to a service or to a system is when the new service is rolling out into the marketplace!

Build one or two detailed homework stages into your development process. This stage should include activities such as initial screening; market, customer, and competitive studies; technical, systems, and operations appraisals; and financial analysis. Homework results in a business case that is based on fact rather than speculation. Insist on solid up-front homework and ensure that no major project enters development missing vital information. Be sure the project definition is developed from solid information.

Do the Up-front Homework

First Stage

Up-front homework, often a missing ingredient in new service projects, means building in a "first cut" or preliminary investigation stage, involving these activities:

Preliminary market assessment: This is a quick scoping of the marketplace to assess market existence, probable market size, and expected project definition. Think of it as detective work: desk research; accessing available public and commercial databases, reports, and articles; utilizing in-house information and people; and contacting a few lead users.

Preliminary technical assessment: This is a quick appraisal that will propose a systems solution, map out a probable route, and assess development costs, times, and risks. This work is largely conceptual and uses technical literature, a vendor search, in-house systems expertise, brainstorming and creative problem solving sessions, a review of competitive solutions, and technical gurus outside the firm.

Preliminary business assessment: This is a quick financial analysis (for example, to estimate payback period) based on very rough estimates of sales, costs, and investment required. It also includes a cursory legal assessment and a quick risk assessment.

Second Stage

For larger and more complex projects, many firms build in a second, detailed investigation stage prior to development. The second stage often includes these activities:

Detailed market studies and market research:

- User needs-and-wants studies: Personal interviews with prospective customers to determine needs, wants, and preferences; performance requirements; and a definition of the customer's wish list.
- Value-in-use studies: Assessment of what economic value the new service will bring to the customer. This often involves an in-depth look at the customer's use system, the current solution, and various cost drivers.
- Competitive analysis: A detailed look at competitors' offerings, pricing, bases of competing, and performance (e.g., share and profitability).
- Concept tests: Tests of the proposed service (in concept form) to gauge interest, liking and purchase intent, and price sensitivity to estimate expected sales.

Detailed technical assessment: This is a more thorough activity to assess systems feasibility, identify likely systems solutions, deal with technical risks, and assess operations and delivery requirements (route, costs, and probable expenditures).

Detailed business assessment: These tasks define the business proposition and provide the business justification for the project, as well as dealing with potential roadblocks and risks. Tasks here can include a detailed financial analysis, business risk assessment, and legal and regulatory assessments.

Source: Adapted from R. G. Cooper, "Overhauling the New Product Process," *Industrial Marketing Management* 25, 6 (1996): 505–515.

2. Adopt a strong market orientation and build the voice of the customer into every facet of the project.

Building in the voice of the customer throughout the development effort makes a major difference to performance.[3] When marketing and market research activities are executed well, success rates rise to around 80 percent; when these marketing actions are poorly done or, worse yet, omitted altogether, success rates drop dramatically to around 20 percent. Exhibit 3.2 summarizes the impact of quality efforts in market information, research, and testing activities.[3] The efforts undertaken include preliminary market assessment, detailed market studies, marketing research, customer tests, and trial sell or test marketing.

The importance of the customer's voice is further supported in another of our studies, this time of highly successful new financial services. The factor distinguishing the top performers here is a market-driven development process, which is the number two driver of financial performance overall.[5] New service projects fare much better when customer needs, wants, and buying behavior

EXHIBIT 3.2   Impact of Marketing Activities (Includes Market Research)

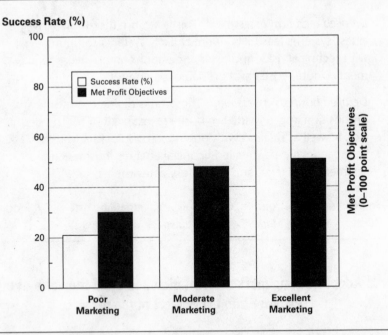

Note: Projects are split into 3 groups in terms of quality execution of market information activities: the best 20%, the worst 20%, and the middle 60%.

Source: R. G. Cooper and U. deBrentani, "New Industrial Financial Services: What Distinguishes the Winners," *Industrial Marketing Management* 25, 6 (1996): 507–515; R. G. Cooper and S. J. Edgett, "Critical Success Factors for New Financial Services," *Marketing Management* 5, 3 (1996): 26–37.

are well understood, when adequate resources are devoted to market research, when competitors' strategies and services are clearly understood, and when market research is used to test customer response to the service concept and strategy.

The lesson from this is clear: Management must build in a market orientation—the voice of the customer—throughout the entire new service development process. Here are some ways to build in the voice of the customer:

- Preliminary market assessment—a quick scoping of the market
- Market research to determine user needs and wants— in-depth personal interviews to build in the voice of the customer
- Competitive analysis—assessment of competitors' services, pricing, and performance
- Value-in-use analysis—determining the economic worth of your service to the customer
- Concept testing—gauging purchase intent long before you commit dollars to development
- Customer reaction and feedback during development—via multiple rapid prototypes and tests
- User tests and field trials—validate the commercial product
- Test market or trial sell—especially in the case of higher-risk and mass-market services
- Market launch based on a solid marketing plan.

How do you ensure that your process is decidedly market-oriented?

1. First, the key marketing tasks above should be *designed into your process*. In many businesses, they are not.
2. Second, the leadership team—the gatekeepers—must mandate that such marketing actions be undertaken in projects. If they are not, stop the project. The problem is that

in the short term, marketing actions are treated as optional or discretionary, whereas technical activities, such as writing software code, undertaking alpha tests, or testing the operations and delivery system, are normally not discretionary. Reconsider what is important.

3. Finally, make the marketing resources available to project teams. You cannot win a game without players on the field!

A payroll service company gathered customers into focus groups to help in the design and development of a new service. Scores of features (functionality items) were displayed to users, one feature at a time. Users discussed each and then, using electronic keypads, voted yes or no on each feature. The same research was conducted with salespeople. Interestingly, for about two thirds of the functionality items salespeople and customers were aligned; but for one third of the features, customers and salespeople voted differently. This reinforced the need to go directly to the customer for design input. Numerous sessions like these were held throughout the design and development phases to ensure that the voice of the customer was built into the new service.

3. Put in place high-quality teams that are truly cross-functional.

A project's organization boils down to two things: the quality of the project team, and the extent to which the project team is truly cross-functional. Both elements can have an impact on a project's outcome.

A. Characteristics of a High-Quality Project Team

- The team leader is dedicated to one project at a time (as opposed to trying to lead many projects, or having a myriad of other assignments). Very often a team leader is spread too thinly across too many projects or has too many other duties to run projects effectively. As one project leader said, "I have my real job and then I have my role as project leader for this new service. What this means is that I do not have the time to effectively lead the project team. Instead, most of my time is spent putting out fires as I manage our regular line of services."

- High-quality teams interact and communicate well and often, with frequent update meetings, progress reviews, and problem resolution sessions. The best teams have short weekly meetings to ensure that the entire team is up to speed. Short meetings require that the meetings be run effectively so that little time is wasted.

- Decisions made by outsiders (outside the team, but inside the company) are handled quickly and efficiently. In organizations where this seems to work, it is usually the result of proficient team actions. For example, the team is able to do whatever internal marketing, communication, and persuasion is necessary to get outsiders on board and to deliver quick, efficient decisions.

B. Employing Truly Cross-Functional Teams

- All projects have an assigned team of players. Many companies have heeded the call for formally designating project team members, but in some organizations it is not clear just who is on a project team and who is not.

- These assigned players are from all affected parts of the company, be it operations, systems, marketing, or some other area. In other words, the team has the required skills, and the team membership represents all the key functional areas that will influence the project's success. Hence, it is a truly cross-functional team.

- All significant projects have a defined and accountable team leader, a person who is responsible for moving the project forward. As one executive put it, "I want someone who will worry about the project and will make things happen."
- Project leaders are responsible for the project from beginning to end, as opposed to being responsible for only one phase of the project or having project leadership change hands many times during a project's life.
- The team structure is not rigid: People can be added and dropped as the requirements of the project change. But the team still has an unchanging core of responsible, committed and accountable team players from beginning to end.

When you are overhauling your new service development process, do not forget the people factor. Even the best-designed process will run into trouble if there is no team captain, if there are not enough players on the field, or if the players do not function as a true team. Ensure that every significant project has an identified team leader who is accountable from the beginning of the project to the end. Avoid the trap of spreading your best people too thinly. When assigning people to the team, try also to ensure that they are assigned the time to do the job. The result will be a better-run project with a team that is more efficient and a project that will move through the development process in a more timely manner.

4. Adopt fast-paced parallel processing to shorten cycle time.

Project teams face a dilemma. On the one hand they are urged by senior management to compress the cycle time—to shorten the elapsed time from idea to launch. On the other hand, they are urged to improve the effectiveness of new service development—to cut down the failure rate and do the project right. This desire to "do it right" suggests a more thorough, longer process.

Parallel processing is one solution to the need for a complete, high-quality process, yet one that meets the time pressures of today's fast-paced business world. Traditionally, new services have been managed by means of a sequential approach: each task performed after another, in sequence. The analogy is that of a relay race a kilometer long where each department runs with the project for its own 100-meter lap. Phrases such as "handing off," "passing the project on," "dropping the ball," and "throwing it over the wall" are common in this relay-race approach to developing new services.

In marked contrast to the sequential approach, with parallel processing many activities are undertaken concurrently. The appropriate analogy is to a rugby match rather than a relay race.[4] A team (not a single runner) appears on the field. A scrum or huddle ensues, from which the ball emerges. Players run down the field in parallel with much interaction, constantly passing the ball laterally. After 25 meters or so, the players converge for another scrum (or gate review). This is followed by another stage of parallel activities.

With parallel processing, the game is far more intense than a relay race and more work gets done in a given time period. Three or four activities are done simultaneously, each by different members of the project team. Second, in this scenario, there is less chance for an activity or task to be overlooked or handled poorly because of lack of time. Moreover, the activities feed each other (the metaphor of the ball being passed back and forth across the field). And finally, the entire new service process becomes cross-functional and multidisciplinary: The whole team—marketing, technology, systems, account management, and operations—is on the field together, participates actively in each play, and takes part in every gate review, or scrum.

Consider how you can build parallel activities into your process. Ensure that you are leveraging the strength of your team and using them to develop your new services as fast as possible.

5. Attack from a position of strength; leverage core competencies.

In this context, synergy is the ability to leverage the strengths and competencies of your organization in your new service. Thus, there is a good fit between the needs of the project and the resources, skills, experience, and core competencies of the company. The success rates of organizations that do not capitalize on their synergies are much lower—about one fourth that of the most successful organizations (see Exhibit 3.3).[5] Indeed, marketing synergy is *the number one success factor* that separates the very top-performing new services from the more modest successes.[6]

The areas where leveraging core competencies is found to be the most important are the following:

EXHIBIT 3.3   Impact of Synergy on New Service Performance

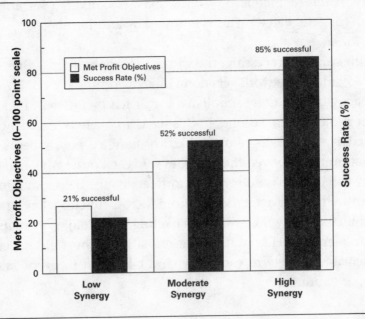

Projects were split into three groups: the 20% with the highest synergy, the 20% with little synergy, and the middle 60%. Two performance metrics are shown.

Source: Cooper and deBrentani. See Exhibit 3.2.

Marketing

- The new service fits or leverages the company's sales force and channels resources and capabilities.
- There is a strong fit with existing advertising and promotional skills and resources.
- Marketing expertise and resources are leveraged.
- There is a strong fit with in-house market research capabilities.

Operations

- The new service fits with company service delivery systems.
- There is a good fit with existing human resource capabilities.
- The new service can use or rely on existing operations facilities.

Management and Financial

- The new service leverages existing financial expertise and resources.
- The new service leverages current management expertise, skills, and preferences.

These synergy criteria should be used in the selection, rating, and ranking of projects. If a project scores low on some or most of these synergy criteria, flag it; it is probably heading for trouble. Synergies become key criteria for making Go/Kill decisions and for obtaining focus. But if synergies are lacking in some areas and the project is still a Go, every effort must be made to shore up the deficiencies. For example, you might consider a partnering relationship, perhaps with a software firm that possesses the technology or operations capability you lack. Or you might partner with another organization that owns a critical distribution channel or sales force where you might be weak. If you proceed in the face of lacking synergies—if there is a poor fit between your competencies and resources and requirements of the project—expect a much rougher road than if the synergies are there.

6. Strive for unique, superior services.

One of the top success factors is found within the new service itself: The service must truly delight the customer. Winners have *differentiated, superior services* that provide excellent value to the customer.

It sounds simple, but the fact is that me-too, ho-hum, and commoditylike new services are far more common than the truly superior ones. Note in Exhibit 3.4 the impact on two performance

EXHIBIT 3.4   Impact of Service Superiority

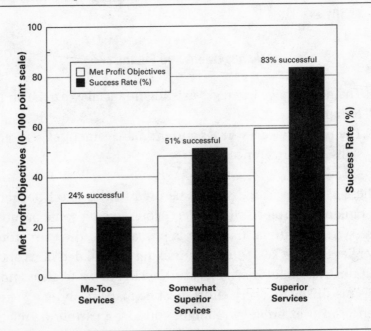

Projects were split into 3 groups: the 20% most superior, differentiated products; the 20% truly me-too; and the middle 60%. Two performance metrics are shown.

Source: Cooper and deBrentani. See Exhibit 3.2.

measures of having a superior service. These services achieve more than three times the success rate of me-too services and are much more likely to meet profit objectives.

Sometimes the ability to offer a unique service can be found in a sea of commodity services and existing technology platforms. Consider this:

One U.S. bank has developed a new and differentiated credit card for business use. The traditional leaders here are American Express and Diner's Club cards, which are positioned as travel and entertainment cards. A smaller but profitable niche lay untapped, namely, the purchase of small office items. When an office worker purchases office supplies, s/he either pays from petty cash or uses a personal credit card, and in either case is reimbursed later. Both are expensive, nuisance procedures. The new card, using Visa as the vehicle, permits designated office employees to charge small purchases, thereby eliminating both the petty cash box and reimbursement procedures. The new service, although simple in concept, required development of systems and software. So successful has the card been in this niche market that the developer has "white-labeled" the service to other banks, including foreign ones.

So who says service providers are trapped in a commodity business with no opportunity for differentiation? Commodity products and services are *a state of mind*. If you believe you cannot differentiate and gain superiority, you never will. But our studies uncovered dozens of examples where genuine differentiation was possible in spite of the many competitive, look-alike services on the market.

So what are the five ingredients of superior services that delight customers? What goes into producing services like the ones that performed so well in Exhibit 3.4? These winning services score very high because they . . .

1. deliver unique or superior benefits to customers.
2. provide better value for money than previously available services.

3. feature a better service outcome than competitive services.
4. are more reliable with fewer fail points.
5. have a higher-quality image.

Note that each one of these ingredients of superiority is defined from the point of view of the customer.

Service superiority is an obvious success factor. But it is troubling that so many companies have not internalized this fact; they are caught in a commodity mentality and continue to introduce me-too, undifferentiated services.

Here is how to build in superiority by design rather than by chance in every new service project you undertake:

1. Before development begins, figure out what a superior and differentiated service really is.
   - Undertake a detailed user needs and wants study.
   - Do a thorough analysis to determine competitors' service strengths and weaknesses.
   - Test and verify the service concept throughout development and beyond.
2. Use the five ingredients of a superior service (above) to rate and rank would-be projects through every stage of the process. After all, these are among the strongest correlates of profitability.
   - Build these items into your screening criteria at the various Go/Kill gates in your new service development process.
   - Use these criteria to pick your next project winners.
   - Insist that project teams deliver evidence of service superiority at every Go/Kill decision point.

These action items are strongly linked to positive financial performance, and they strongly reinforce the need for solid up-front homework and building in the voice of the customer.

In the development of a new Touch-Tone telephone banking service aimed at small business owners, the product manager spared no effort to determine the exact needs and wants of prospective users. She recognized that although small business owners might be similar to retail customers, they likely have unique needs as well, hence the retail telephone banking product might be inappropriate. Extensive market research—both focus groups and personal interviews—was conducted with small business owners in order to identify unique features and functionality desired by this target segment. Next, a crude working model—a *protocept*—was displayed to potential users in a controlled setting. Customer interest, liking, and purchase intent were gauged, and modifications were made. When the service was rolled out to this target audience, it delighted customers and proved to be a big winner.

7. Seek service-market fit.

Closely paralleling service superiority as a key driver of performance is service-market fit. Here are the three winning ingredients of winning fit:

1. These services clearly satisfy a customer or user need.
2. They respond to important changes in customer needs and wants.
3. They fit in with existing customer operating systems, values, and desires.

An analysis of the impact of service-market fit yields dramatic conclusions (see Exhibit 3.5). New services that feature high service-market fit—the top 20 percent on this scale—are more than five times as successful, and achieve their profit objectives much more so, than new services with poor service-market fit.[7] Many companies are particularly weak here. It is almost as though the customer is deliberately ignored in many of the new projects we studied!

EXHIBIT 3.5   Impact of Service-Market Fit

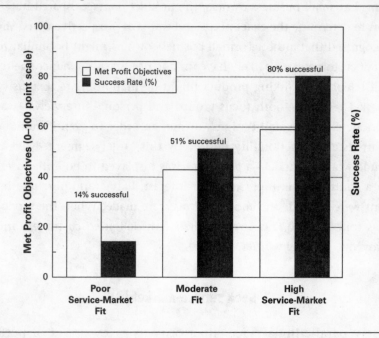

Projects were split into 3 groups in terms of service-market fit: the best 20%; the worst 20%; and the middle 60%. Two performance metrics are shown for the 3 groups.

Source: Cooper and deBrentani. See Exhibit 3.2.

This importance of fitting new services to the market cannot be stressed enough. Building in the voice of the customer, conducting the up-front homework, and constantly testing iterations of the service with the customer are necessary steps if service-market fit is to be assured. Further, like the elements of service superiority, the three components of service-market fit can also be used as screening and project rating criteria.

8. Deliver top-quality services with frontline expertise.

The expertise of the personnel who produce and deliver the service is a major key to success. Service expertise is analogous to production and product quality for physical products: It captures the degree of professionalism and training of personnel who will deliver the service. It is vital for two reasons:

1. Service production and consumption occur simultaneously, unlike the process for physical products. As a result, service quality, delivery quality, and expertise of personnel are virtually synonymous. A poorly trained or uninformed frontline person will ruin the experience for the purchaser and thus destroy the sense of quality, from the customer's point of view, of an otherwise well-conceived service.
2. Services are intangible, and it is more difficult to assess the "goodness of the product" before purchase. It is frequently the firm's service expertise and image that the customer buys. Customers base their purchase decisions less on service functionality or attributes than on the perceived expertise of the frontline personnel.

New services that are rated highly in terms of service expertise are ones that company experts play an important role in producing and delivering. They are also the ones in which frontline and operations personnel are highly trained or skilled.

High service expertise is generously rewarded: The top 20 percent of new services in terms of service expertise have 3.6 times the success rate as those lacking expertise. Among the very top-performing (the most profitable) new services, *superb customer service* is the number 4 driver of performance. Very profitable new services are ones through which the customer is served in a prompt, friendly, efficient, and courteous manner, by knowledgeable staff.

Frontline and the behind-the-scenes operations personnel very often *are* the service. Professionalism and expertise, training, and knowledge are absolutely critical to success. Make this element a vital part of your market launch plan: No service goes to market without the right frontline and operations people, the right skills, and the right training in place.

9. Remember to follow through with the last play of the game: a quality launch effort.

New services featuring a superb launch—the top 20 percent—have a stellar success rate of 81 percent.[8] By contrast, services with poor launches—the worst 20 percent—have only a 30 percent success rate (see Exhibit 3.6). Indeed, launch quality is the number two driver of the most successful services.[9] We measured the ingredients of well-executed launches and correlated them with project success and profitability. Here is what we found:

- First, top performers have marketing launch plans that are carefully crafted and very detailed. A formal promotional and marketing communications program with sufficient resources backing the initiative is part of this plan.
- Second, all staff understand and fully support top-performing new services. The services have been extensively marketed internally before launch to both frontline and field sales people to ensure their full buy-in.
- Third, customer contact staff possess the necessary knowledge, marketing, and selling skills before launch. Frontline service personnel receive extensive training on the service.
- Finally, the winning new service has been thoroughly tested for design problems prior to launch.

Too often, these vital launch ingredients are missing. Many new services are rolled out without adequate frontline personnel training; in some cases key personnel are barely aware of the service. Often there is no formal marketing, communications, and advertising plan, and often the service has bugs or defects at launch time. The results are predictable: a misfire in the marketplace.

EXHIBIT 3.6   Impact of a Quality Launch

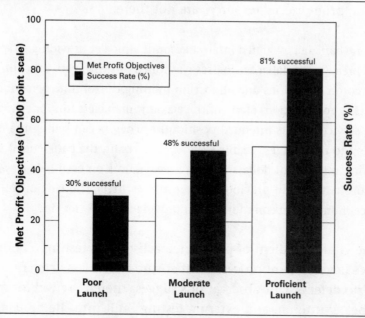

Projects are split into 3 groups: the 20% with the best launch, the 20% with the worst launch, and the middle 60%. Two performance metrics are shown.

Source: Cooper and deBrentani. See Exhibit 3.2.

The marketing plan is a key part of the new service development process, and it must begin early in the life of a project. In one major electric utility, the rule is simple: No project goes to development unless there is a preliminary marketing plan on the table. The marketing plan must be approved and supported by senior management, ensuring that there is alignment among all functions, including field sales and operations people. If key frontline personnel have not been trained, or if they lack enthusiasm for the new service, do not expect it to be a winner.

The marketing plan must deal with all facets of the launch (advertising, promotion, training, and communications), and it must encompass both external and internal marketing. Finally, the launch must be adequately resourced. Too often, well-developed services are left to limp into the marketplace, simply because selling and promotional resources are not there.

> In one bank, a new tiered interest account aimed at providing a "special break" for smaller businesses was rolled out with very little internal communications and almost no training of frontline personnel. Lacking information, many of the account managers misunderstood the service and its intended positioning. They began selling the offering to their largest clients instead. As a result, the bank ended up paying millions of dollars in interest payments on cash balances in accounts that had previously been interest-free. The lack of sales-force training and communication provided a costly lesson.

One vital ingredient of pre-launch activities is testing. Your new service development process must ensure a seamless delivery effort with no defects. Our observations suggest there is a need for more and better internal and external testing built into the pre-launch stage. This could be called a "validation stage." Does your process include a validation stage?

Recap

In this chapter, we have laid out nine critical steps that project teams need to undertake if they are to develop winning new services. This advice is based on years of research in thousands of companies, both service organizations and tangible goods producers. We have laid these out here as steps toward developing a successful new service.

The development of new services is the crucial corporate challenge for companies as we move into the next millennium. Technology charges ahead at a breakneck pace, opening up myriad new possibilities: banking and insurance on the Internet, new information products for retail and business clients, and new electronic delivery channels, to name a few. Customer needs are changing, too,

Summary of Critical Steps for Success

1. Do solid, up-front homework before the project proceeds to development.
2. Take a strong market orientation and build the voice of the customer into every facet of the project.
3. Put high-quality teams in place that are truly cross-functional.
4. Use fast-paced parallel processing to shorten cycle time.
5. Attack the market from a position of strength—seek synergies.
6. Strive for unique, superior services.
7. Seek service-market fit.
8. Deliver top-quality services with expertise, as judged by the customer.
9. Remember to follow through with the last play of the game: a quality launch effort.

as businesses and consumers deal with the realities of a more competitive, faster-paced, chaotic, information-intensive world.

Companies that succeed at developing new services—at seizing the market and technological opportunities presented—will be the ultimate winners. Those who choose to ignore service development, or who seem unable to get innovation right, will be left behind. Consider the nine critical steps for success outlined in this chapter and ask: Have you built these into your new service development methods? Where and how? Most often, our studies reveal major deficiencies.

In the next two chapters, a Stage-Gate™ approach is mapped out that has been used successfully in many industries and is now being adopted in service companies (see Exhibit 3.1). This approach is a proven route to incorporating critical success factors into the way you develop and launch new services. Stage-Gate methods promise to drive new services to market quickly and successfully.

4

Developing a Winning New Service Development Process

There are two fundamental ways to win at developing new services. One way is to pick the *right projects:* If you are particularly astute at how you invest your development and marketing resources, chances are your business will end up being a winner. The other approach is to *do projects right.* Given the slate of projects you wish to invest in, what's the best way—the right way—to drive these to market? Doing the *right projects* introduces the topics of project selection and portfolio management. *Doing projects right*, on the other hand, has more to do with managing the innovation process. A stage-and-gate approach, the topic of this chapter, tries to do both:

- It helps you select the right projects—doing the right projects
- It guides teams as they bring projects to market—doing projects right

The desire to drive new services to market quickly and efficiently, and at the same time incorporate the critical success factors into a process by design rather than by chance, has led many firms to adopt stage-and-gate or gateways systems. What is a stage-and-gate process and how can it be implemented in your business? Begin by viewing new service development as a process, a process that starts with an idea and ends with a successful new service on the market. Indeed, all work is a process, and any process can be redesigned to be more efficient and effective. Make sure your business processes are right, and the result will be improved performance.

Many tangible goods companies have designed and implemented systematic new product processes in the form of Stage-Gate™ systems. In fact, 60 percent of product developers in the U.S. have adopted a Stage-Gate new product process, according to a best-practices study by the Product Development Management Association.[1] And the top performers have even moved to more sophisticated versions of Stage-Gate.

To find out exactly what stage-and-gate processes are and how they can apply to your business, read on.

The Stage-and-Gate Processes: A Quick Overview

What Are Stage-and-Gate Processes?

Stage-and-gate processes are roadmaps or guides for driving new services from idea through to launch and beyond successfully and quickly.[2] They map out the key activities in a typical major project. These activities—often several hundred in number—are then collapsed or clustered into stages. Most often, a five- or six-stage model is the result. Each stage contains the mandatory best-practice activities that should be part of a well-executed project.

Each stage is preceded by a decision point, called a *gate*, at which you decide whether or not the project is still in the game. At these gate meetings, management makes the Go/Kill and resource allocation decisions. Thus, gates can be seen as opening or closing the road ahead for the project.

How Do Stage-Gate Processes Yield Better Results?

Stage-Gate processes yield better results because in the process of mapping out the various stages one builds in the current best practices, which are the items outlined as critical success factors in the last two chapters. These best practices include undertaking solid up-front homework; building in the voice of the customer; sharp, early, and stable project definition; the quest for service-market fit; service quality; a focused funneling approach; a superb, well-planned launch; and so on.

A Stage-Gate process also builds in quality-control checkpoints. These are the gates, which subject the project to a thorough review:

- Is the project unfolding as it should—on time, on budget, and in a quality fashion?
- Is the project a good one—should we continue to invest?
- Is the path forward—the plan of action and resources requested—sound?

The gates provide the essential Go/Kill and prioritization decision points in the process. They are where the tough choices are made, where lackluster projects really do get killed. The gates provide focus and make the funneling scheme work. For each gate a set of required deliverables, a list of Go/Kill and prioritization criteria, and a set of outputs (for example, an approved action plan with required deliverables for the next gate) are specified.

An illustration of a working Stage-Gate process is given in Exhibit 4.1. This particular Stage-Gate model is used for new service development by the Business Banking Division of the Royal Bank of Canada (RBC), a major financial institution in North America with assets in excess of $100 billion and over 50,000 employees worldwide.

EXHIBIT 4.1   Royal Bank of Canada's Stage-and-Gate Process

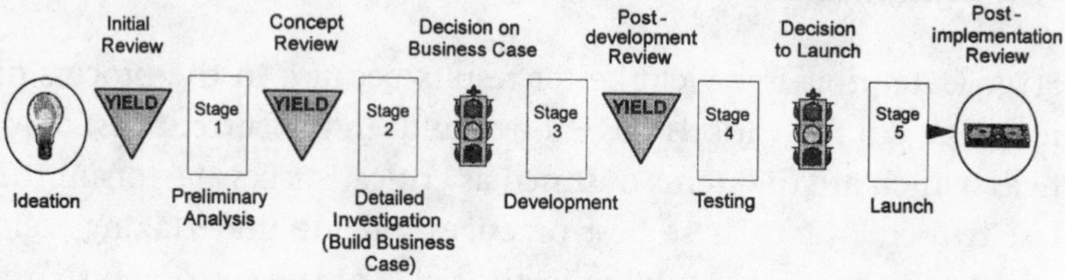

RBC's process has five stages and five gates. Stages are shown as boxes, gates are Yield signs or traffic lights (critical gate).

Consider the flowchart in Exhibit 4.1 and note some of the characteristics of this bank's Right Projects Right, or RPR,* new product process:

- There is an active idea generation and capture system, with a special emphasis on customer-derived ideas.
- The first gate, the Initial Review, is done by product managers, some field people, and technical experts from Systems and Technology as well as Operations and Delivery.
- There are two homework stages. The first is the Preliminary Analysis 1, a "quick-and-dirty" homework stage, which yields a very preliminary and inexpensive "first cut" or "scoping" of the project. Stage 2, the Business Case, is much more detailed, involving rigorous market studies and technical investigations. A completed Business Case is the result of Stage 2. One deliverable to Gate 3 is a fully de-fined project on paper as part of the Business Case.
- The third gate is Decision on Business Case, also called the "money gate," and is tended by senior people in the bank.

---

*RPR: Right Projects Right is a trademark of the Royal Bank of Canada. Used with permission. Thanks to Ms. Kathryn Sachse, Senior Group Manager, Product Development & Processes, Royal Bank of Canada.

This gate opens the door to full-scale development. After this point, it is increasingly difficult to kill the project.

- Stage 3, Development, is where, for example, the development of software and systems is done. Stage 3 is also the time for internal, or alpha, testing. The deliverable at the end of this stage is an internally tested new service, ready for field trials.
- Stage 4, Testing, validates the project. Tasks here include extended in-house testing, customer field trials and preference tests, trial operations and delivery, and sometimes even test marketing in one geographic region.
- The final gate is the Decision to Launch.
- Stage 5 is Launch: Operations start-up and market roll-out begin.
- Six to 12 months after launch, a Post-implementation Review is undertaken to assess performance versus expectations: Was the project and new service really a winner? And what can we learn in order to do the next one even better? The project team, a cross-functional group, remains accountable for the project's results right into the post-launch stage and until the Post-implementation Review.

This bank's Stage-Gate process is also built for speed. For example, clearly defined decision points and visible decision criteria mean more timely decision making and fewer recycles—less going back to obtain the "right" information. The process emphasizes the voice of the customer and solid up-front homework, so that there are fewer glitches in the project as it approaches commercialization. The cross-functional team approach with dedicated project leaders also helps speed projects to market. Finally, the process is flexible: Lower-risk and minor projects can be fast-tracked through the process by collapsing stages and combining gates.

The results: higher success rates, fewer last-minute glitches, faster to market, and better focus.

So You Want to Overhaul Your New Service Process!

Let us imagine for a moment that you and your management team want to move ahead and revamp your service development process. You have benchmarked other companies with processes similar to the one shown above, and you have become convinced about the merits of designing and implementing a Stage-Gate approach for your own business. You have this nagging feeling that all is not well in many of your new service projects—that they take too long, or things do not happen as well as they should, or when they should. Or perhaps you lack focus—you try to do too many projects, or you are doing the wrong projects.

Before charging ahead to overhaul your innovation process, consider what the key ingredients of a well-designed new service development process are—what it must be and do.

We strongly contend that there is a big difference between merely having a development process and having *a high-quality, world-class innovation process*. Our many benchmarking studies reveal that simply having a process—stages or phases followed by gates or review points—does not improve new service performance at all. Rather, the nature of that process—what is built into it, and how it is implemented—is what distinguishes the top performers.

So before you move ahead to set up a task force and design your new service process, think hard about the critical elements of a well-conceived process. We urge you to go back and review the success ingredients in Chapters 2 and 3 before you proceed. The sad truth is that most businesses miss the mark here. Our benchmarking studies of winners and losers—both project teams and businesses—provide the key elements you need to build into your winning game plan.

The Structure of the Stage-Gate Process

Stage-Gate is a conceptual and operational model for moving a project from idea to launch.[3] It is a blueprint for managing the innovation process to improve effectiveness and efficiency. Stage-Gate methods break the innovation process into a specific set of stages and gates. Each stage consists of a set of prescribed, cross-functional, and parallel activities. The entrance to each stage is a gate. These gates control the process and serve as the quality and Go/Kill check points. This stage-and-gate format leads to the name Stage-Gate.* Stage-gate methods are predominant in new product development among manufacturing firms in the United States, and now they are also being adopted by an increasing number of service companies.

The Stage-Gate method is based on the experiences, suggestions, and observations of a large number of managers and firms—data collected through our own and others' research in the field. Indeed, observations of what happened in over 60 case histories laid the foundations for the approach.[4] Since this Stage-Gate method was first described in print, it has been implemented in whole or in part in thousands of leading firms worldwide, many of which have provided an excellent "laboratory setting" to further refine and improve the process. For example, Stage-Gaters have periodic benchmarking sessions among themselves, where they compare notes and learn from each other, and we are often asked to attend these sessions.

The Stages

The Stage-Gate process breaks a project into discrete identifiable stages, typically four, five, or six. Exhibit 4.2 shows another typical Stage-Gate model, not unlike the Royal Bank of Canada's Business Banking Division RPR process, shown in Exhibit 4.1:

- Each stage consists of a set of parallel activities undertaken by people from different functional areas within the firm.

---

*Many other names are used besides Stage-Gate, including PDP (Product Delivery Process), PIP (Product Innovation Process), NPP (New Product Process), Gating or Gateways system, and Product Launch System.

EXHIBIT 4.2   Typical Stage-and-Gate Process

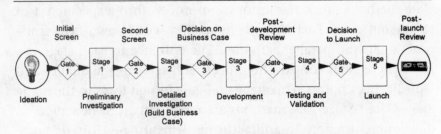

Most firms' Stage-Gate processes set forth a list of pre-scribed or highly recommended actions and best practices for each stage:

- Each stage is designed to gather information needed to progress the project to the next gate or decision point.
- Each stage is cross-functional, and no stage is owned by a single functional area or department: There is no "systems stage" or "marketing stage."

In the early part of the process, each stage costs more than the preceding one. The process is one of incremental commitment. For example, Stage 1 might cost $5,000; Stage 2 costs $50,000; Stage 3 costs $500,000; and so on. As the amount of money at stake increases, risk is managed by ensuring that the uncertainties of the project decrease. Note that risk is some combination of amounts at stake and uncertainties. The process is deliberately de-signed to drive uncertainties down at each successive stage, so that by the time you have completed Stage 2, you are much wiser than you were at the completion of Stage 1. Each stage, then, can be viewed as a set of tasks whose purpose is to gather information to drive down uncertainties and manage risk.

The Gates

Preceding each stage is a *decision point* or *gate*. Gates are critical to the Stage-Gate process: as the gates go, so goes the process. These gates are review meetings, which serve as Go/Kill and prioritization decision points. The gates are where poor projects are weeded out, and where resources are allocated to the truly meritorious projects. Thus, gates are the *quality-control checkpoints* in the process.

The structure of each gate is similar. Gates consist of the following:

- *A set of required deliverables:* These are what the project leader and team must bring to the decision point. An example of deliverables would be the results of a set of completed activities. Typically, for each gate there is a standard menu of deliverables, and they define precisely what is expected from the project leader and team. Expectations are made crystal clear!
- *Criteria against which the project is judged:* This checklist of criteria include must-meet and should-meet questions. Each should-meet question is scored (a point count). The questions are used by the gatekeepers at the gate meeting to score projects, and they become important inputs to the Go/Kill and prioritization decision.
- *Outputs*: Each gate has specific outputs—a decision (Go/Kill/Hold/Recycle), an approved action plan for the next *stage* (complete with people required, estimated money and person-days budget, and time schedule), and a list of deliverables for the next gate.

Gatekeepers

Gates also define who the decision-makers or gatekeepers are—the locus of decision making. Note that all relevant decision makers attend the gate meeting, and they make the decision together; there is alignment among the functional heads. This is a subtle but important point. It is clear who needs to make the decision, and time spent seeking and/or waiting for lengthy and multiple approvals from various senior people is eliminated.

Who are the gatekeepers? They typically own the resources required for the project to move ahead. They have the authority to approve spending decisions and resource allocations. Thus, they are management; from Gate 3 onward (see Exhibit 4.2) they are most often the leadership team of the business .

The Game Plan: Stage-Gate™

Let us walk fairly quickly through the Stage-Gate process in order to gain insights into what the process is and does. We use the Royal Bank's process in Exhibit 4.1 as the example, since it is a fairly typical model. Also, theirs is judged to be a good process, and an excellent example of how one major company has tailored the general Stage-Gate scheme in Exhibit 4.2 for its own business. Exhibit 4.3 shows the first few stages of the Royal Bank's process so that you can follow along as we begin our walk-through. (Note that in the next chapter, we look in much more depth at a general Stage-Gate model as shown in Exhibit 4.2—at one that you might adapt for your business.)

Ideation

The first stage, even before the process begins, is submitting an idea. Ideas are entered into an idea bank, a database repository of all ideas that is a central on-ramp to the new service process.

EXHIBIT 4.3   The Front End of RBC's RPR Process

Ideation from everyone in the organization is encouraged, from field sales and account management, from systems and operations, from product management and other areas. Ideas are recorded and submitted via an idea submission form, either electronically or on paper, and are guaranteed a quick evaluation with feedback. The idea bank is available on-line for review.

Gate 1: Initial Review

A team of gatekeepers reviews the idea submissions each month. At this meeting, all crucial functional areas are represented: product management, systems, operations, and sales.

This first gate, Initial Review, is a flickering green light whose spirit is as follows: "This idea appears to have merit. Let's spend a little more time fleshing it out to see if we really do want to spend a lot more time and money on it." This is not a major decision to commit significant resources, so Gate 1 does not have to be a perfect decision.

Ideas are screened using objective, visible criteria. This bank uses four must-meet criteria followed by four should-meet questions. The must-meet, knock-out questions concern issues such as strategic alignment and technical feasibility, and serve to remove from discussion any projects that are obvious nonstarters. The should-meet questions are used to rate ideas on the basis of desirable characteristics such as degree of strategic fit, competitive advantage, and market attractiveness. Ratings on these criteria produce an attractiveness score useful for project prioritization.

Stage 1: Preliminary Analysis

This first stage after ideation provides a quick, high-level, and inexpensive scoping of the proposed project to determine its feasibility and commercial potential before any heavy spending occurs. The time frame is limited to something like one month, and the cost, to a total of 5 to 20 person-days of work.

Stage 1 includes the following:

- A preliminary market investigation consisting largely of desk research, although feedback from selected customers and account managers may be sought even at this early stage.
- A preliminary technical investigation, conceptual work to map out the probable technical solutions and define development costs, timing, and risks.
- A preliminary branding/legal/copyright analysis, to check up on freedom to operate.
- A project diagnostic—an assessment of the project's strengths and weaknesses, undertaken using the New-Prod™ 2000 model.*
- A risk/reward assessment.

Gate 2: Concept Review

The second gate opens the door to a more extensive and expensive investigation, so the Concept Review is a little more rigorous than the initial idea screen. As with the first gate, the gatekeepers are representatives from the various involved functions, with some more senior people attending.

As at all gates, the project is evaluated by the gatekeepers on a set of visible criteria. The must-meet criteria, listed below, remain the same from gate to gate, and serve to knock out any obvious loser projects:

- Strategic alignment: Does the project support the bank's missions and objectives?

---

*NewProd 2000, a diagnostic tool, is a registered trademark of R. G. Cooper & Associates, a member company of the Product Development Institute. Some companies use diagnostic analysis, undertaken by the project team and knowledgeable outsiders, to assess the project's strengths, weaknesses, likely risks, failpoints, etc. before the project begins. The NewProd 2000 diagnostic is often used to pinpoint the key uncertainties and issues that need to be dealt with and helps the team chart the best path forward. See Appendix B for more information on NewProd 2000.

- Technical feasibility: Is the project doable (systems and op-erations)?
- Marketing feasibility: Does it satisfy a need? And are the selling/distribution resources available?
- Opportunity: Will it yield sales and margins that make it an attractive opportunity?

Should-meet questions are also used here to help rate, rank, and prioritize the project. Six should-meet criteria are employed at the Concept Review: strategic fit, synergy (leverages core competencies), competitive advantage, market attractiveness, customer reaction, and payback period. Projects are scored on each of the six, and they must clear a hurdle on each. The scores are weighted to yield a prioritization score.

Stage 2: Business Case

The purpose of this stage is the preparation of a detailed business case; this is the vital input to the major spending decision (Gate 3). The purpose is to define the requirements and specs for a winning new service, to justify spending on the project, and to map out the path forward. This map is a detailed plan of action for development, and also contains high-level plans for launch and implementation.

Stage 2 involves multiple cross-functional activities, including the following:

- Preparing a detailed market analysis, including customer and competitive analyses.
- Undertaking market research such as user needs and wants studies and concept tests with users.
- Undertaking a detailed technical assessment to evaluate all aspects of the technical development work required. This evaluation results in a high-level technical spec, a detailed technical development plan, and a 90 percent confident development cost and time estimate.

- A branding/legal/copyright assessment
- Developing preliminary action plans:
    - –technical systems plans
    - –operations plan
    - –quality assurance plan
    - –market launch plan
    - –sales plan
    - –risk plan (contingencies)
- Evaluating financial impact—details on costs, volumes, pricing, revenues, trade-offs, development costs and resources required—all resulting in a figure for NPV (net present value), IRR (Internal Rate of Return), and sensitivity analysis.

The key deliverable here is the business case: a definition of the service, the project's justification, and the actions plan for the steps ahead.

Gate 3: Decision on Business Case

The third gate, denoted by a traffic light in Exhibit 4.3, is the important money gate. This is the last point at which the project can be halted before incurring heavy costs. It also marks the end of the homework phases and the beginning of serious project work. This third gate is staffed by senior people in the bank, including the vice-presidents in charge of the areas that are asked to commit resources to the project. The gate meeting is chaired by the senior executive of the bank's Business Banking Division.

The key agenda items focus on the must-meet and should-meet criteria from Gate 2 (these are revisited to ensure that the project continues to "pass"), as well as on the quality of information presented (this company stresses fact-based decision making) and the financial attractiveness of the project. The final part of the gate meeting deals with the proposed action plans and resource allocation to the project. Portfolio management and resource allocation across projects is very much an issue at this gate.

Stage 3: Development

The purpose of this stage is to implement the development plan approved at the previous gate, and also to finalize the various launch plans. Stage 3 could be a lengthy stage, hence multiple milestones are usually built in. Key actions include the following:

- The actual development of the service (for example, the software code and system)
- Development of the operations manual
- Function and systems testing (alpha tests)
- Continued monitoring of the external situation, ensuring that the market assumptions and product acceptance remain positive
- Development of test plans (for the next stage)
- Refinement of action plans:

    –market launch plan: Strategy, pricing, channels and service, marketing communications, launch control

    –training plans: Documents/materials for sales staff and customers, and service staff training

    –sales plan: Sales estimates

    –operations plan: Implementation, service training, user documentation, acquisition of equipment

    –quality assurance plan: An update of plans
- Update of the financial analysis (as in Stage 2, but with better data)

The key deliverables at the end of this stage are the constructed service (internally tested), the revised financial analysis, and the various action plans for subsequent stages.

Gate 4: Post-development Review

After Stage 3 we move to the back end of the Stage-Gate process, shown in Exhibit 4.4. With Gate 4 the emphasis shifts from "Should we be doing this project?" to "How well is the project progressing?" This gate in Exhibit 4.4 marks the end of development and the beginning of commercial activities, starting with testing the new service with customers. It is a *sanity and consistency check*; it ensures that Stage 3 activities—notably the development and alpha testing—were successfully completed, that the project remains an economically attractive one, and that the proposed path forward to launch is sound. The gatekeepers are the same executives who approved the project for development.

Because of the shifting emphasis at the Post-development Review, the criteria for Go also shift. The original must-meet and should-meet criteria are once again revisited to check for major changes, but now the emphasis is on the fact that Stage 3 was completed in a satisfactory manner, that the deliverables are in good shape, and that the project remains an economically attractive one.

Stage 4: Testing

This stage, just prior to launch, tests and validates the entire project. Its purpose is to ensure that the software and systems function properly under live field conditions, that the operational facets of the service (for example, at branches and in user premises) func-

EXHIBIT 4.4   The Back End of RBC's RPR Process

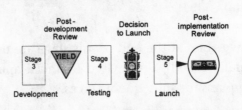

tion well and are user-friendly, and that the new service itself is commercially viable.

Stage 4 activities may include the following:

- Systems tests
- Business acceptance testing—outputs versus expected results
- Production acceptance testing at branches:

  –external tests (with clients)

  –beta tests with customers

  –pilots with customers

- Test market or trial sell (sales to beta-test customers to verify pricing and purchase intent)
- Updating of plans and materials: all launch plans (see Stage 3)
- Updating the financial analysis

The main deliverables to the Launch gate are a fully tested service with test results, finalized launch plans, and a final financial justification for full launch.

Gate 5: Decision to Launch

This is the final gate in the process and it is a vital one. Here, the emphasis shifts to a check on the deliverables (does the service really work? does it delight the customer?) and a review of the appropriateness of the action plans and resources requested. Gatekeepers remain the same executive group as at the previous two gates.

The gatekeepers once again revisit the original must-meet and should-meet criteria. Next, the gate meeting focuses on the deliverables: Were the testing stage tasks completed in a comprehensive and quality fashion? The project's financial attractiveness is reviewed for the final time, and the soundness of the launch plan is checked.

Stage 5: Launch

The Launch stage sees full implementation of the finalized market launch, and operations and quality assurance plans. Although the Launch stage is often implemented by people who are not team members (for example, account managers and branch personnel), the project team and leader remain accountable for results, and they are responsible for ensuring that the launch plans are implemented effectively.

As might be expected, Launch stage activities include the following:

- Briefing and communication with those involved in implementation:
- Implementing the various launch plans
    - –market launch plan, sales plan, risk plan
    - –operations plan, quality assurance plan, training plans
- Monitoring the progress of the launch—fixing, adjusting, and changing as needed
- Preparing for Post-implementation Review

Following the Launch stage, the key deliverable is a total review of the project and results achieved.

Post-implementation Review

This is the final checkpoint in the process and serves to terminate the project. This phase occurs once the launch implementation is completed and running smoothly. The review meeting is attended by the executive gatekeepers who approved the project at the last three gates.

The focus of the Post-implementation Review meeting is on results achieved and lessons learned. The project's performance is compared to projections made at the two traffic-light gates (see Exhibits 4.3 and 4.4) on important metrics: times, costs, revenues, margins, profit. Variations from the predictions and reasons for them are noted. Next, a total postmortem on the project—what happened, what we can learn, and how we can do the next one better—is conducted.

A "pass" at this point ends the project. It means that the project team and leader are no longer accountable for the project, and that the service offering becomes a "regular service" in the bank's product mix. Success is celebrated!

* * *

There you have it—a bird's-eye view of a real development process in a real company. According to senior management, it is a superb process and is yielding positive results. But this is only an example of one company's method. If you are interested in using such a process yourself, in the next chapter we drill down into the stages and gates and get into the operational details of a process that is generally applicable to different types of service businesses.

Which Projects Go Through the Stage-Gate Process?

We have now mapped out a road map for development from idea to launch and beyond. But the question remains, which types of development projects does this road map apply to? This is a controversial and often problematic question, but one that you cannot avoid.

In their desire to keep things simple, some companies demand that only "major" projects—defined by expenditure level or person-days of work—be put through this process. In these companies, smaller projects are handled separately. In other companies, only new service projects go through the process, while other projects—improvements and fixes, process improvements, platform and infrastructure projects, etc.—are handled in other ways.

The problems with these approaches should be obvious. First, all of these projects compete for the same resources. If the Stage-Gate process is a decision model that helps allocate resources via the Go/Kill decision points, then surely all competing projects should be in the process. How can one have a resource decision model where many of the resource-consuming projects are outside the decision process? This point consistently causes problems:

> Product managers at a major bank complained that there were insufficient systems resources to develop the new services that they needed to keep pace with competition. A closer review revealed numerous projects initiated from a variety of sources outside the bank's stage-and-gate process. Most of these were small projects, but they were consuming almost 60 percent of the total available systems and development resources. Approval decisions for these small projects were made by a number of different senior people, often informally and without recognition of the impact that their casual approvals were having on the totality of the development effort. The end result was pipeline gridlock. Nothing seemed to get done very fast.

Handling projects outside the process raises a second issue: For these projects, the approval process may be perceived as less rigorous, hence, easier to get through. Thus, the shrewd project leader sees this as the route to easy project approvals, and is motivated to circumvent the process. In effect, by setting up two categories of projects—those that go through the stage-and-gate process and those outside it—you reward project leaders for circumventing a best-practices approach.

> One company established an expenditure limit of $250,000 for projects that needn't go through their stage-and-gate process. A cursory review of the portfolio of projects two years later revealed a remarkable number of projects in the under $250,000 range. Furthermore, many project leaders had simply subdivided larger projects into clus-

ters of smaller ones, each under the $250,000 limit. Project leaders had figured out how to get funding for their projects without formal approvals.

Increasingly, we recommend that all new and improved service projects be put through the process, regardless of their size. We define a new or improved service as any change to the customer deliverable that is visible to the customer. This might include some fairly simple, low-cost projects such as extensions and additions of features. But it is important that these smaller projects be given similar scrutiny as larger ones, since collectively they can consume a high proportion of available resources. These projects, too, must be considered in the total portfolio of projects competing for resources. Hence, they must pass through the Go/Kill gates.

This does not, however, mean that smaller, less costly, and lower-risk projects should be required to pass through a complete five-stage, five-gate process. Imposing this requirement in your company will cause even the most dedicated adherent of the process to seek ways to circumvent it. Rather, develop fast-track versions of your process—perhaps a three-stage or two-stage version (as shown in Exhibit 6.2)—to handle these straightforward lower-risk projects.

What about projects that are not new services or improvements—should they go through the process? Such projects—say, process improvements, infrastructure projects, or platform developments—compete for the same resources as new services, and for them we offer two options:

1. Modify your Stage-Gate process to handle these types of projects (discussed more fully in the next chapter).
2. Or agree to handle these projects outside the process. But decide in advance what proportion of resources will go to these other types of projects. This way, once the a priori split in resources is made, these other projects do not compete for the same pool of development resources as

new/improved product projects. (More on this splitting of resources—which we call the *strategic buckets approach*—in Chapter 7.)

Built-in Success Factors

The logic of a well-designed new service process, such as the Stage-Gate process in Exhibits 4.1 and 4.2, is appealing because it incorporates the critical factors and lessons vital to success and speed that were highlighted in the previous two chapters:

1. The Stage-Gate process places much more emphasis on homework, or predevelopment activities. Stages 1 and 2— the Preliminary investigation and the Business Case (detailed investigation) stages—are essential steps before the door to development is opened at Gate 3.
2. The process is multidisciplinary and cross-functional. It is built around an empowered, cross-functional project team. Each stage consists of technical, marketing, operations, and even financial activities, necessitating the active involvement of people from all of these areas. The gates are cross-functional too: The gatekeepers are from different functions or departments in the company; they are the senior people who own the resources needed for the next stage. Thus, alignment among senior managers and across functions is assured.
3. Parallel processing, by means of a "rugby game" approach, speeds up the process. Activities in each stage are undertaken concurrently, rather than sequentially, with much interaction between players and actions within each stage. Compared to the "relay race" approach, many more activities are done in a given time period, and time compression is the result. One caveat: Projects must be resourced properly in order for this rugby approach to work.

4. A strong market orientation is a feature of the process. Marketing inputs begin in the idea phase, even before Stage 1, and remain an important facet of every stage from beginning to end of the process. Stage 2 sees extensive marketing research and customer information as vital inputs to the design of the service and justification of the project. Even during the lengthy Development stage (Stage 3), there is constant customer input and feedback as the service starts to take shape.

5. A project-definition step is built into the process at Stage 2, Detailed Investigation. It is here that the project and service are both defined and justified. This definition is a key deliverable to the third gate, "Decision on Business Case"; without it, the project cannot proceed to Stage 3, Development.

6. There is an emphasis on delivering a superior, differentiated service—one that offers customers unique benefits and superior value for money. The actions in Stage 2, with an emphasis on user needs-and-wants studies along with customer feedback throughout the process, do not guarantee superiority, but they certainly improve the odds. And gate criteria that demand superiority help weed out mediocre, ho-hum projects and reallocate resources to projects that promise to deliver services that delight the customer.

7. There is more focus. The process builds in decision points in the form of gates. These gates weed out poor projects early in the process and help focus scarce resources on the truly deserving project so that good projects are accelerated to market. With their defined criteria, gates also ensure that you do the right projects: ones that are strategically aligned and important, that enable you to leverage (build on and maximize) your core competencies, that target more attractive markets, and that promise to deliver unique, superior services.

8. There is a strong focus on quality of execution throughout. The recommended activities within each stage lay out a road map for the project leader and team so that there is less chance of critical errors of omission. The gates provide the critical quality-control checks in the process. Unless the project meets certain quality standards, it fails to pass the gate.

9. The process is flexible and designed for speed, but without loss of discipline. Activities with long lead times can be moved forward; gates can be combined and stages collapsed; and lower-risk projects can be fast-tracked. But these departures from the prescribed process are conscious ones, decided at the previous gate, with full knowledge of the risks involved. They are approved by you, the gatekeepers.

10. Finally, the international dimension can easily be accommodated by the process, should you chose to do so. Note that this international component was not a feature of the bank's process described above, but you can build it into your own. The Stage-Gate process in some multinational companies is a transnational and universal one, used around the world by all business units. Activities at each stage can include international checks, international involvement, and marketing and market research actions in multiple countries. Gate criteria can be designed to favor global, not strictly domestic, ones. Project teams and gate meetings are also international.

Move Toward a World-Class Process

Many service companies are only now beginning to experiment with and implement Stage-Gate methods. Leading firms in telecommunications and banking are relatively new to Stage-Gate processes. By contrast, physical product companies, such as Corning, DuPont, Lego, Northern Telecom, Polaroid, Procter & Gamble, and many others began to use Stage-Gate approaches in the mid- to late 1980s. According to benchmarking studies, enviable results have been achieved: faster times to market, earlier detection of failures, higher success rates, more projects on time and within cost targets, better cross-functional communication, and greater customer satisfaction. Service companies have been somewhat slower to adopt Stage-Gate approaches, but a number of telecommunications companies, energy companies, and financial institutions in the United States, Canada, and Europe have made the move and are seeing improvements in their new service performance.

Indications thus far from a handful of early users among financial institutions and telecommunications companies are that results here are just as positive as they have been for product companies. Over the next few years, we expect to see a number of financial institutions, telecommunications companies, deregulated power companies, and other service providers begin to benchmark outside their own industries, and to see the benefits realized in other industries of a high-quality, systematic new product process. Service companies increasingly recognize that stage-gate approaches not only make sense but have become a necessity, given the increasing complexity of service development and the need to speed new services to market.

Designing a Stage-Gate process and building in best practices and critical success factors into the process on paper is the easy part. Implementation is far more difficult. Even well-managed firms, such as Corning, Procter & Gamble, and Exxon, took some years to successfully implement Stage-Gate processes. Note that Stage-Gate processes, when properly implemented, yield very positive results, according to independent studies. But implementation takes time, so be prepared to hold the course once you start. These are the three steps you need to take:

Step 1 is doing the homework and defining the requirements for your process. This usually means internal assessment, problem detection, undertaking a handful of retrospective analyses of past projects, conducting a thorough literature search, and perhaps even some external benchmarking with other firms inside and outside your industry.

Step 2 is designing the new process on paper. This is conceptually and operationally much more difficult than it looks. Merely lifting a model from another organization (like the Royal Bank of Canada's in Exhibits 4.1) is not the answer. Remember: New service development is probably the most challenging and difficult endeavor in the modern corporation, so designing the development process is logically also the most difficult and challenging process redesign you will encounter.

Step 3 is implementation. Implementation has already begun in Step 2, if you handle it properly. Implementation amounts to a number of key activities, including internal communications, ensuring that everyone is on board, training, bringing existing projects into the system, setting up gate reviews, securing a process owner or manager, establishing metrics, creating a database system to enable management of the portfolio of projects, and so on. (There will be more on this pivotal topic of implementation in Chapter 8.)

Recap

The development of new services is the crucial corporate challenge for your business as you begin the third millennium. Technology charges ahead at a breakneck pace, opening up myriad of new possibilities: banking and insurance on the Internet, new information products for retail and business clients, and new electronic delivery channels, to name but a few. Customer needs are changing, too, as businesses and consumers deal with the realities of a more competitive, faster-paced, chaotic and information-intensive world. The firms that succeed at developing new services—at seizing the market and technological opportunities presented—will be the ultimate winners. Those who choose to ignore service development, or who seem unable to get innovation right, will be left behind. Consider the critical success factors that separate winners and losers in new services outlined in Chapters 2 and 3, and ask yourself: Have you built these into your development methods? Where and how? Most often, our studies reveal major deficiencies here.

A Stage-Gate approach, used successfully in many industries, and now being adopted in service businesses, was mapped out in this chapter as one route to incorporate critical success factors into the way you develop and launch new services. In the next chapter, we show in detail how you can apply this process to your own new service development process. Stage-Gate methods can help your business drive new services to market successfully and quickly.[6]

How to Build a Winner: From Idea to Launch, the Process in Detail

In this chapter we take a closer look at the Stage-Gate process and gain a solid idea of what's involved at each stage and gate. Later in the chapter, we lower the microscope on some key issues, such as which projects should be put through the process, how to handle alliance and outsourced projects, and the special case of platform developments. Players—the project team and gatekeepers—and their roles are also discussed in this chapter. Finally, how gates should work and the "rules of the game."

The Stage-Gate Process

For now, let's just go through the model, which you can follow stage by stage in Exhibit 5.1.[1]

Stage 1: Idea Generation (Ideation)

Ideas are the feedstock or trigger to the process, and they make or break it. Do not expect a superb new service development process to overcome a deficiency in good new ideas. The need for great ideas coupled with

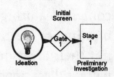

EXHIBIT 5.1   An Overview of a Typical Five-Stage, Five-Gate Stage-Gate
Process

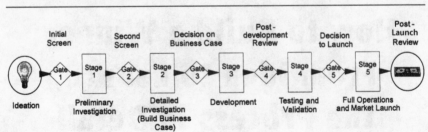

their high attrition rate means that the idea generation stage is pivotal: You need quality ideas and lots of them. Many companies consider ideation so important that they handle this as a formal stage in the process and build in a defined, proactive system for idea generation and capture, or ideation.

Four components of an idea generation and capture system that you can implement are these:

1. *Establish a focal point.* The problem is that in most companies, idea generation is everyone's job and no one's responsibility. No one particular person is charged with making ideas happen, and there is no one to send a good idea to for action. The first step is to assign one person the responsibility of stimulating, generating, and handling new ideas—a person to act as a focal point or lightning rod for ideas.

2. *Identify the sources.* Where do good ideas come from? And where should they be coming from? The second step is to make a list of possible sources of new ideas.

3. *Grease the path.* The third step is to stimulate and facilitate the flow of ideas from these sources. For example, suppose you have identified your sales force as a potential but underutilized source of ideas. Greasing the path might involve having a sales force idea contest, featuring idea generation at your next annual sales force meeting, or creating an easy-to-use idea kit so salespeople can submit their ideas quickly. Exhibit 5.2 lists some ways to grease the path and get good new ideas.

EXHIBIT 5.2   Twenty Ways to Grease the Path and Get Great New Ideas

1. Run pizza-video parties, informal sessions where groups of customers meet with company technical people to discuss problems and needs, and brainstorm potential solutions. Kodak developed and perfected this method for their products, but it also applies to service industries.
2. Make a customer brainstorming session a standard feature of your facility tours by customers.
3. Run focus groups with your customers; let them "experience" your products and identify problems and desires.
4. Set up a customer panel that meets regularly to discuss needs, wants, and problems that may lead to new ideas.
5. Survey your customers: Find out what they like and dislike in your and competitors' offerings.
6. Use Product Value Analysis in which customers interact with facets of your services, and then express their views, concerns, and difficulties.[2]
7. Undertake "fly-on-the-wall" anthropological research with customers, as does Hewlett-Packard. Do "day-in-the-life" research, where you spend a day or two at the customer's premises.
8. Observe your customers using (or misusing and abusing) your services.
9. Identify your lead users—your innovative customers—and work closely with them. This is the approach suggested by MIT's Eric von Hippel.[3]
10. Use iterative rounds: In one room a group of customers focuses on identifying problems; in the next room, a group of your technical and marketing people listen and brainstorm solutions. The proposed solutions are then tested immediately on the group of customers.
11. Hire sales and technical support people who can recognize potential new services. Train, encourage, and motivate them to do so.
12. Routinely survey your competition. Analyze their services, strategies, and business successes.
13. Set up a key word search that routinely scans trade publications in multiple countries for announcements, news, etc. of new services/products.
14. Insist that your technical or development people visit customers with salespeople at least once per month, and not just on trouble-shooting visits.
15. Treat trade shows and conferences as intelligence missions, where you view all that is new in your industry under one roof.
16. Have your technical and marketing people visit your suppliers and spend time with their technical people. Find out what is new with them.
17. Set up an idea suggestion scheme or contest in your business. Promote it widely, and offer prizes and awards for good ideas.
18. Run some group creativity sessions—brainstorming or synectics—in your business.
19. Set up an idea vault, and make it open and easily accessible. Allow employees to review the ideas and add constructively to them.
20. Try an "immersion technique" as suggested by marketing leader Procter & Gamble: Pick a business category, and have several people devote themselves full time to immersing themselves in that area. Have them visit prospective customers, attend trade shows and conferences, talk to experts, read every report and publication. After six months or so, use creativity techniques to harvest the ideas from this immersion group.

4. *Set up an idea capture and handling system.* Support the system with IT (information technology) support. The system in Exhibit 5.3 is a good example, and boasts the following features:

- Idea submissions should be easy to prepare and can be submitted via a simple one-page e-mail form.
- In some companies, ideas are public (for example, on Lotus Notes or Intranet) so that others can see them and make comments and suggestions.
- Set up an idea-screening group who function as the Gate 1 (Initial Screen) gatekeepers and meet monthly to review ideas. Timely decisions are important.
- Make sure this Gate 1 group uses a consistent list of published criteria, so that decisions are fair and feedback is provided to the submitter (with reasons why the idea was rejected or accepted).
- Feedback to the submitter must be timely and in writing—a good reason to use gate criteria and a scoring sheet.
- Go ideas move to Stage 1, so empower the Gate 1 gatekeepers to allocate resources and people at the gate meeting.

EXHIBIT 5.3   An Example of a Systematic Idea Capture and Handling Process

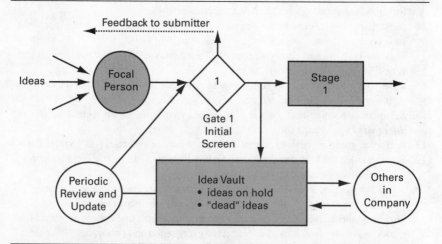

Hold and dead ideas enter an idea vault, which is open to others in the company.

- Establish an idea vault for Kill and Hold ideas (again, group software makes it possible for this vault to be public, so that others in your business can augment ideas in the vault).
- Consider giving some kind of recognition to successful idea submitters whose ideas progress past Gate 1.

Gate 1: Initial Screen

Initial screening is the first decision to commit resources to the project: The project is born at this point. If the decision is Go, the project moves into the preliminary investigation stage. Thus, Gate 1 signals a tentative commitment to the project: a flickering green light.

Gate 1 is a "gentle screen" and amounts to subjecting the project to a handful of key must-meet and should-meet criteria. Combined, these criteria often concern strategic alignment, project feasibility, magnitude of opportunity and market attractiveness, competitive advantage, synergy with the business's resources, and fit with company policies. Financial criteria are typically not part of this first screen. A checklist for the must-meet criteria and a scoring model (weighted rating scales) for the should-meet criteria can be used to help focus the discussion and rank projects in this early screen.

GTE's Network Systems Division in Boston has implemented a process where the initial gate has seven must-meet yes/no criteria:

- *Strategic alignment:* Is the proposed project aligned with the division's strategy and vision?
- *Technical feasibility:* Is there a reasonable likelihood of technical feasibility—can we develop and deliver it?
- *Competitive rationale:* Does a competitive reason exist to undertake the project? Is it necessary from a defensive or strategic position?

- *Leverage:* Does the project leverage (or build from) the division's core competencies?
- *Legal, ethical:* Does the project meet legal and ethical requirements?
- *Value to the division:* Is there potential for profit or positive financial impact, or is the project a strategic initiative?
- *Show stoppers:* Absence of evident show-stoppers or potential "killer variables" at this point?

Here, the gatekeepers include both technical and business (marketing) people. At this Gate 1 or Initial Screen meeting, project ideas are reviewed against these seven criteria using a paper-and-pencil scorecard. The questions are answered yes or no; a single no kills the project.

Stage 1: Preliminary Investigation

This first and inexpensive stage after the Initial Screen has the objective of determining the project's technical and marketplace needs. Stage 1 is a quick scoping of the project, often done in less than a month, and with 5 to 20 person-days of work. Key activities in Stage 1 include the following:

1. Preliminary Market Assessment.   A relatively inexpensive step very early in the life of a project is a quick scoping of the marketplace designed to assess the existence of a market for the service, probable market size, and market acceptance and also to flesh out the idea into a defined concept. This is largely detective work, and might involve desk research; a library and key word search through various trade magazines, commercial databases and reports; utilizing in-house information and people; contacts with a few key accounts or lead users; a few focus groups with users/customers; and even a quick concept test with a handful of potential users.

Royal Bank of Canada builds in a "quick-cept" test—a quick and inexpensive concept test—into Stage 1 of their process. The new service idea is described in a paragraph or two, and along with a standard 5-question questionnaire gauging interest, liking, and customer purchase intent, is e-mailed to about 10 selected salespeople. The salesperson answers the questionnaire, and is requested to share the concept with a few key commercial customers for their answers too. Thus, for minimal cost, feedback on the concept is received very quickly from 10 salespeople and up to 30 customers.

As an alternative, try running periodic focus groups of business users or retail customers (consumers) and prospects to screen and review a number of new concepts. The cost of a focus group is obviously higher than the quick-cept test described above, but when used to review five to ten concepts, the cost per concept is more acceptable.

2. Preliminary Technical Assessment. This is a quick technical appraisal to propose a technical solution, map out a probable route, and assess technical costs, times, and risks. This work is largely conceptual: technical literature search; utilizing in-house technical expertise; brainstorming and creative problem-solving sessions; reviewing competitive solutions; drawing on technical experts and vendors outside the firm.

3. Preliminary Business Assessment. This is a quick financial assessment to, for example, calculate the payback period, on the basis of very rough estimates of sales, costs, and investment required; make a cursory legal assessment; and make a quick risk assessment.

4. Alliance/Vendor Assessment. The need for a partner or alliance is identified. Your department that oversees your business alliances can help to identify possible partner candidates and undertake a preliminary screening of candidates. Your alliance process should begin here, if you have one. Build-versus-buy options are assessed (preliminary assessment only), and potential suppliers identified (names of manufacturers, suppliers, and vendors).

Stage 1 thus is the opportunity for gathering both market and technical information—at low cost and in a short time—to make possible a first-pass financial analysis as input to Gate 2. Because of the limited effort, and depending on the size of the project, very often Stage 1 can be handled by a small team (perhaps from marketing and a technical group) in less than one month.

Gate 2: Second Screen

The project is subjected to a second and somewhat more rigorous screen at Gate 2. This gate is essentially a repeat of Gate 1: The project is reevaluated in the light of the new information obtained in Stage 1. If the decision is Go at this point, the project moves into a heavier spending stage.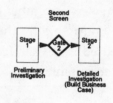

At Gate 2, the project is again subjected to the original set of must-meet and should-meet criteria used at Gate 1. Here additional criteria may be considered, dealing with sales force and customer reaction to the proposed service, and potential legal, technical, and regulatory "killer variables"—all the result of new data gathered during Stage 1. Again, a checklist and scoring model facilitate decision making at this gate. The financial return is assessed at Gate 2, but only via a quick and simple financial calculation.

PECO (Pennsylvania Energy Corporation) uses a proven set of criteria for making Go/Kill and prioritization decisions at Gate 2 of "Gateways," their new service process.

First the project is subjected to a set of must-meet questions:

- *Deliverables check:* Are all deliverables here and in good enough shape to proceed?
- *Strategic alignment:* Is the proposed project definitely aligned with PECO's strategy and vision?

- *Legal, ethical, core values:* Does the project meet legal and ethical requirements? Do any barriers exist?
- *Show stoppers:* If potential show stoppers ("killer variables") have been identified, can they be dealt with?

These four must-meet criteria must yield "yes" responses; a single consensus "no" kills the project.

Next the project is rated on a set of desirable characteristics, or should-meet questions, on a scale of 1 to 5. High scores on these help to identify the really attractive projects:

Company fit:
- Strategic alignment
- Company capability

Product/service advantage:
- Uniqueness/differentiation
- Customer appeal

Market attractiveness:
- Market potential
- Relative competitive strength

Economics:
- Return (profitability)
- Risk

These should-meet criteria scores are weighted and totaled to yield a project score, which is used to prioritize projects for Stage 2.

Stage 2: Detailed Investigation (Build the Business Case)

The business case opens the door to development. Stage 2 is where the business case is constructed. It consists of a detailed investigation that clearly defines the service and verifies the attractiveness of the project prior to heavy spending. It 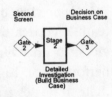 is also the critical homework stage. Exhibit 5.4 shows the major activities and events in this pivotal stage. Here are the key actions:

EXHIBIT 5.4   The Key Activities in Stage 2: Detailed Investigation (Building the Business Case)

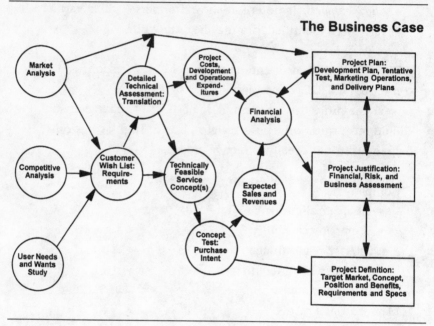

1. A *user needs and wants study* helps flesh out the idea into a winning new service definition. This market research must entail in-depth surveys or face-to-face interviews with prospective customers and users to determine customer needs, wants, and preferences; likes, dislikes, and order-winning criteria; performance requirements; and a definition of the customer's wish list.

2. A *value-in-use study* provides an assessment of the customer's economics—what economic value the service will bring to the customer (this often involves an in-depth look at the customer's use system, the current solution, and various cost drivers).

3. *Competitive analysis* is also a part of this stage. Here the project team investigates direct and indirect competitors and their services, to uncover their strengths and weaknesses; their business performance, to gain insights into how well each is doing, and their strategies and bases of competition. This helps you to understand how each competes, what works and what does not.

4. *Concept testing* is needed here. This means showing a representation of the service to prospective users to gauge customer interest, liking, and purchase intent (and to make an estimate of expected sales and price sensitivity).

Though the new service is not yet developed, this concept test is vital because it helps you spot deficiencies when they can still be corrected, and also gauges purchase intent, a key input into the determination of expected sales volumes. Price sensitivities can also be measured here, although this must be done with caution.

5. *Detailed technical assessment* focuses on the technical solution and feasibility of the project. Customer needs and wish lists are translated into a set of requirements and high-level specifications. The likely technical solution—one that is technically and economically feasible—is identified; development costs and times are defined; and technical risks, along with legal and regulatory issues, are assessed and dealt with.

6. *Vendor assessment* is undertaken. If the development project is to be outsourced, or a third party, such as a software supplier, is to be used, an assessment of this solution and route must be undertaken here:

- Make-versus-buy analysis
- Sources of supply and their capabilities (contact and work with vendors)
- Assessment of degree of customization of the "off-the-shelf" package required to suit your needs and/or be integrated into your system
- Costs, terms, and timing

Here, the project team prepares the requests for proposals (RFPs), and vendors' proposals are assessed. Appropriate confidentiality agreements are put in place. Usually a recommended vendor is part of the business case, a key deliverable to the next gate.

7. An *operations appraisal* is part of building the business case, where issues of operations, delivery mechanisms, operations and

delivery costs, and investments required are investigated. This work involves bringing your operations and/or service delivery people into the process. Additionally, if facets of the operations are to be outsourced, then as noted above, the make-versus-buy analysis is done here, along with vendor qualification.

8. *Project justification* is part of the business case. A detailed financial analysis is conducted as part of the justification facet of the business case, typically involving a discounted cash-flow approach (NPV and IRR or ROI percent), complete with sensitivity analysis to look at possible downside risks. Most businesses agree on a standard compiled spreadsheet and use that for all Gate 3, 4, and 5 financial analysis deliverables.

9. The *life cycle plan* is mapped out. This is especially important in the case of platform projects, or where the current service is expected to be the first of a series or suite of related offerings. The project team maps out the future plan for this service and subsequent variants, spin-offs or releases, creating a product road map.[5] This specifies the next versions, additional functionality and features to be available in subsequent versions of the service, and the timing. Some life cycle plans go as far as specifying the exit plan and date.

10. *Alliance development* proceeds. You continue to move through your alliance process. Note that many companies now have such a process or procedure in place, one that includes a number of both legal and relationship-building tasks. A more thorough screening and review of potential partner candidates is undertaken, and relationship establishment begins. The project team prepares the proposed memorandum of understanding (MOU): how the relationship will work, who does what, etc.

The Business Case.   The result of Stage 2 is a business case for the project. The business case comprises three crucial elements: the "what and for whom," the "why," and the "how, when, how much, and by whom."

1. *What is the service and whom will it be sold to?* The *service definition* is developed and agreed to. Recall from Chapter 3 the importance placed on sharp, early product definition prior to the start of development work. The product definition goes well beyond a technical definition (specifications), and includes the following:
   - Specification of the target market: exactly who the intended users are
   - Description of the service concept and the benefits to be delivered
   - Delineation of the positioning strategy (including the price point)
   - A list of the service's features, functionality, requirements, and high-level specs, prioritized as "must have" and "would like to have"

2. *Why invest in this project?* A thorough *project justification* is developed. This includes the strategic rationale for the project, the financial analysis, and a business risk assessment. The financial sensitivity analysis provides useful inputs to the risk assessment by addressing a set of "what if" questions.

   The life cycle plan also forms part of the business case, and in particular helps to justify the expenditures for this first project in a possible series of projects.

3. *How will it be undertaken, when, and by whom, and how much will it cost?* A project plan is developed. The general rule is that, at each gate, senior management wants to see a detailed plan of action for the next stage—in this case, a detailed Development plan—and also a tentative or throw-away plan through to launch, with extraordinary expenditure items highlighted.

Stage 2 involves considerably more effort than Stage 1, and requires the inputs from a variety of sources. Stage 2 is best handled by a team consisting of cross-functional members, who are the core group of the eventual project team.

Gate 3: Decision on the Business Case

Gate 3 is often called the "money gate." This is the final gate prior to the development stage, the last point at which the project can be killed before entering heavy spending. Once past Gate 3, financial commitments are substantial. In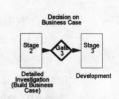
effect, passing Gate 3 means "go to a heavy spend." Gate 3 also yields a sign-off on the project definition. Because of Gate 3's importance, the Gate 3 gatekeepers are usually the leadership team of the business.

The qualitative facet of this evaluation involves a review of each of the activities in Stage 2. It checks that the activities have been undertaken, the quality of execution is sound, and the results are positive. Recall that gates have a predefined list of deliverables, and as a gate quality controller, the gatekeepers' role is to review these deliverables to ascertain that they are of high quality. Exhibit 5.5 shows a fairly typical list of deliverables for Gate 3; this is the one used at Northern States Power (NSP), an electric and gas utility. Every one of your gates should have a similarly detailed list.

Gate 3 once again subjects the project to the set of must-meet and should-meet criteria used at Gate 2, but now they are more rigorously applied. Finally, because a heavy spending commitment is the result of a Go decision at Gate 3, the results of the financial analysis are an important part of this gate decision.

If the decision is Go, Gate 3 sees commitment to the project definition and agreement on the project plan that charts the path forward: The development plan and the preliminary operations and marketing plans are reviewed and approved at this gate. If the project is to be outsourced (or a technology solution is to be purchased off-the-shelf), the proposed agreement is reviewed and approved here. The full project team—an empowered, cross-functional team headed by a leader with authority—is designated. The resources, both people and money, are committed. And a list of deliverables for the next gate is agreed to.

EXHIBIT 5.5   Sample Deliverables to Gate 3 (the "Go to Development" Gate)

Project recommendation: Go/Kill/Hold/Recycle

Deliverable to Gate 3: A completed Business Case

1. Executive Summary:
   - Description and value of project
   - Goals and objectives
   - Critical success factors
   - Major milestones and resource requirements
2. Business Case Details:
   - New service/product definition
     - description of new service
     - target market
     - features, functions, and benefits
     - positioning strategy
   - Strategic alignment:
     - strategic fit
     - synergies
     - impact on existing operations
     - impact of external factors
   - Market assessment:
     - market opportunity
     - market trends
     - market share
     - target market and segmentation
     - demographics
     - customers' needs and wants
     - buying influences
     - competitive environment and analysis
     - SWOT analysis
     - new service positioning
     - competitive advantage of new service
     - distribution strategy and channels
   - Technical assessment:
     - technological foundation for project
     - patent issues
   - Operational assessment:
     - infrastructure
     - fulfillment
     - impact on existing operations
     - skills required
     - contingency and exit plans
   - Financial projections:
     - new service costs
     - pricing
     - revenue, gross margin, net profits, and cash flows
     - NPV, IRR, ROI, EPS
     - sensitivity analysis
   - Action plan:
     - schedule
     - resource needs
     - derailed development and testing plan, including funding needs
     - launch funding needs and outline for launch

Source: Adapted from Northern States Power *Ready for Innovation* manual.

Stage 3: Development

Stage 3 is the implementation of the development plan. Some in-house (alpha) testing of
the system or software usually occurs in this
stage as well. The main deliverable at the end of

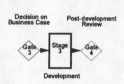

Stage 3 is a developed product—one that has been tested in-house
and also has undergone some preliminary customer tests: Feedback
from customers has been received.

The development plan, which is signed off at Gate 3, is the road
map for Stage 3. It consists of the following:

- A chronological listing of activities, actions, and tasks
- A timeline showing beginning and end points of these actions
- Resources required for each action or task, notably personnel, person-days, and money
- Milestones to be achieved throughout the development
  phase.

The timeline is a critical element in the plan. The plan is developed, complete with the tasks to be done and the deadline dates.
It must be aggressive, causing team members to stretch a bit. But it
must also be realistic. Furthermore, deadlines must be regarded as
sacred if speed is the objective. By sacred deadlines, we mean that
a predetermined date is adhered to as a guideline for planning,
with no excuses. Delays are dealt with via extra input of effort and
resources, not postponement.

The emphasis in Stage 3 is on technical work, which is done to
pin down the detailed technical specifications for the service and
to begin development work itself. In the case of some services (for
example, software-based), prototypes are developed quickly in order to seek early feedback from a few customers before development of the final service. Also, alpha testing of the fully developed
service, system, or software occurs to ensure that the service functions as specified.

Marketing and operations activities also proceed in parallel to technical work in Stage 3. For example, market-analysis and customer-feedback work continue concurrently with the technical development, with constant customer opinion sought on the service as it takes shape during development. These activities are back-and-forth (*iterative*), meaning that each development result—for example, rapid prototypes, some sample computer screens, a crude working model, etc.—is taken to the customer for assessment and feedback.

Meanwhile, detailed test plans, market launch plans, and operations plans, including facilities requirements, are developed. An updated financial analysis is prepared, while regulatory and legal issues are resolved.

Lengthy Projects. In the case of projects with a long timeline, numerous milestones and periodic project reviews are built into the development plan. These are not gates per se: Go/Kill decisions are not made here. Rather, these milestones provide for additional project control and management, checkpoints along the way where the team checks to make sure that the project is on schedule and on budget. One rule of thumb is that if several milestones in a row are missed, the project is flagged, and the project leader must call for a full review of the project (in the flow model in Exhibit 5.1, the project cycles back to Gate 3, so that the gatekeepers can reconsider the wisdom of continuing with this project, now in trouble). In this way, milestone points can be used to identify projects that are heading off course before the problem becomes too serious.

Projects Involving Third Parties or Vendors. Where third parties or vendors are involved, the Development stage may amount to little more than finalizing and signing the contract. In the case of outsourced or contracted development efforts, this stage is where your project team should work closely with the vendor's people, ensuring that they follow the timeline, meet the milestones, and follow the prescribed practices listed above for internal developments.

For Partnering or Alliance Projects. Stage 3 sees you continuing to work through your alliance process. This is the time to define how best to undertake the partnership: roles, responsibilities, expectations, deliverables, timing, etc. The cooperative work is initiated: service creation, development of test and launch plans, etc. The pilot agreement for the next stage is negotiated and the proposed Letter of Intent prepared.

Gate 4: Post-development Review

The Post-development Review is a check on the progress and the continued attractiveness of the project. Development work is reviewed and checked, ensuring that the work has been com-

pleted in a quality fashion and that the developed service is indeed consistent with the original definition specified at Gate 3. This gate also revisits the economic issues via a revised financial analysis based on new and more accurate data.

  By Gate 4, the decision emphasis has shifted from the main question at the earlier gates, "Should you invest in this project?" to "How well is the project unfolding? Is it on track?" The Go/Kill criteria at Gates 4 and 5 reflect this shift. Certainly, the Gate 3 criteria that deal with strategic fit and financial performance are revisited, but now most of the gate questions focus on the successful completion of tasks, and the fact that positive results are being achieved—that the deliverables are in place and positive.

  Gate 4 sees the test or validation plans for the next stage approved for immediate implementation, and the detailed marketing and operations plans reviewed for probable future execution. Capital expenditure decisions are often approved at Gate 4 as well.

Stage 4: Testing and Validation

This stage tests and validates the entire commercial viability of the project: the service itself, the operations and delivery process, customer accep-

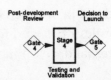

tance, and the economics of the project. A number of activities are undertaken at Stage 4:

- *Alpha tests: In-house tests.* Extended internal tests to check on quality, reliability, and performance under controlled conditions.
- *Beta tests: User tests and field trials.* To verify that the service functions under actual use conditions, and also to gauge potential customers' reactions to the service—to confirm purchase intent and market acceptance.
- *Pilot tests: Trial, limited operations and delivery.* To test, debug, and prove the operations and delivery process, and to determine more precise delivery costs and capacity.
- *Market test: Pretest market or trial sell.* A mini-launch of the service in a limited geographic area or single sales area. This is a test of all elements of the marketing mix, and gauges customer reaction, measures the effectiveness of the launch plan, and determines expected market share and revenues. Note that a test market or trial sell is both expensive and time consuming, and the information it yields can sometimes be obtained via other methods, hence it is not appropriate for every project.
- *Finalization of launch plans.* All launch plans—market launch, operations, delivery, post-launch—are based on test results in Stage 4.
- *Revised financial analysis.* To check on the continued economic viability of the project, based on new and more accurate revenue and cost data.

Just before launching a new combined client service and credit card, the development team at one financial institution decided to conduct a beta test to ensure that everything was working as planned. To conduct the test without launching the card to the public, company employees were asked to volunteer to try out the card, which they used for one month. The development team monitored the technical aspects during this period to ensure everything worked as planned.

They also interviewed users to determine how the interface was working and to spot any changes that might be needed. This relatively inexpensive beta test enabled the development team to test the card under real-life usage conditions and to gather valuable marketing information at very little cost.

For alliance projects, in Stage 4 the project team continues to work their way through the alliance process. Here you negotiate a full-scale agreement for the Launch stage.

Gate 5: Decision to Launch

This final gate opens the door to full commercialization: market launch and full operations start-up. It is the final point at which the project can still be killed. Although some managers  consider this gate largely a formality, note that this gate is important because it signifies that the leadership team of the business is 100 percent aligned and in support of the commercial launch of the service.

At this gate, gatekeepers scrutinize the quality of the activities at the Testing and Validation stage and their results. Criteria for passing the gate focus largely on expected financial return and appropriateness of the launch and operations start-up plans. The operations and marketing plans are reviewed and approved for implementation in Stage 5.

Some businesses' senior management also prefer post-launch plans to be in place and approved here. The post-launch plan can be short term, dealing largely with monitoring the launch (what performance metrics will be measured and how?), and incorporating needed fixes along the way.

Note that the life cycle plan, concerned with the long term and with new releases of the service, has been submitted as part of the business case and is updated during each stage.

Stage 5: Full Operations and Market Launch

The final stage involves implementation of both
the marketing launch plan and the operations
and delivery plan. Other supporting plans, such
as the quality assurance plan, are also executed.
The post-launch monitoring plan kicks in early in
the Launch stage: The project's performance is gauged on key metrics, and the project team responds with necessary action. Finally,
some elements of the longer-term life cycle plan begin to be implemented—for example, needed improvements and new variants
or new releases of the service.

No project ever runs perfectly during the Launch phase. But
given a well thought out plan of action and backing by appropriate resources—and of course, barring any unforeseen events—
it should be clear sailing for the new service . . . another big
winner!

Post-launch Review

At some point following commercialization (often
6 to 18 months later), the new service project must
be terminated. The project team is disbanded, and
the service becomes a "regular service offering" of
the company. This is also the point where the pro-
ject's and the service's performance is reviewed. The latest data on
revenues, costs, expenditures, profits, and timing are compared to
projections in order to gauge performance. Gaps or variances between actual performance and projected performance are identified, and reasons for these gaps are explored. Finally, a post-launch
audit is carried out: This is a critical assessment of the project's
strengths and weaknesses, what you can learn from this project,
and how your business can do the next one better. This review
marks the end of the project. Note that the project team and leader
remain accountable for the success of the project through this

post-launch period, right up to the point of the Post-launch
Review.

The Post-launch Review is a critical review point in the project,
but in too many cases it does not take place. Rather, the project
team members go their own way, while the new service itself drifts
into the history books. This is wrong, for a number of reasons:
First, there is lost accountability. Insist that the project team report back to the Gate 3, 4, and 5 gatekeepers, with a full account
of what they achieved versus what they promised. Second, no one
knows whether or not the project was really a success or not.
Third, there is no organizational learning.

Some businesses split this Post-launch Review into two parts.
The first mini-review is held relatively soon after launch to bring
the gatekeepers up-to-date on results thus far, and to seek approval
and resources needed for quick course corrections. The final review takes place, much as described above, after all the business
results are known.

The Players

Too often the roles and responsibilities of the various players in
the new service process are vaguely defined. This is a constant
complaint of project team leaders. Consider now the various players in the Stage-Gate process, their roles and responsibilities.

- Projects are undertaken by *cross-functional teams*, led by a
  team leader.
- Gates are tended by decision-making groups called *gatekeepers,* who are the senior managers or executives in the
  business. They "own" the resources required for the next
  stage in the project. They become the project's bankers,
  mentors, and executive sponsors.
- The *process manager* is the facilitator, referee, and coach—
  the "keeper" of the process. His/her job is to see that the

process is working and that project teams are making good progress.

Teams and Leaders

The use of cross-functional teams is critical both to the project's success and to its speed to market. Having a cross-functional team means much more than simply assigning people to the project randomly. For successful commercialization, the right project team members assigned at the right time is essential. Truly cross-functional teams should exhibit the following characteristics:

- *The right people, the right functions:* Team members are from the right areas, including marketing, systems (or technology), operations, and even the sales force. Be sure to include people who are central to the commercialization phase (salespeople and operations) early in the process.
- *Empowered and accountable:* Teams are able to make appropriate decisions on their project and are responsible for the outcomes. Thus, they are accountable for certain deliverables, and accountable for the final results of the project.
- *Dedicated and focused:* Members are not spread over too many other activities and projects. This means not only that people are assigned to teams, but that specific time commitments—how many person-days this month—are made for each person. Note that the gatekeepers "own" the resources and are required to sign off on these time commitments.
- *Committed:* Members are passionate about achieving the objectives of their project. This means they are true team members, and not just functional representatives who show up for a few meetings.

For larger projects, a core team approach is used. The core team is a relatively small but dedicated group (at most, five to seven people). There may also be peripheral players on the team who provide resources, inputs, and help on a part-time basis. There may also be players who report to some of the core team members within a given function.

The project team leader is vital to success, and must be carefully selected. The team leader may be from any function: The nature and focus of the work decides from what part of the company the team leader is drawn. Note that people skills and personality traits may be more important than technical skills (most companies make the mistake of choosing team leaders on the basis of their technical skills alone). Look for project team leaders who . . .

- have a passion for the project and a high energy level
- are charismatic and can impart this passion to others
- are willing to persevere, even when the going gets tough
- have people skills—are good communicators, listeners, and conflict managers.

Then look for the technical skills:

- Project management skills
- A knowledge of the technology
- Customer knowledge or intimacy with the marketplace.

Groom your project leaders. Project leadership is an acquired skill. The first time a person is a project leader, he/she may make many mistakes, but the second project will work better. There is a learning curve. So if you spot an able project leader, make it worth his/her while to want to remain a project leader by means of rewards, recognition, and perks. Sadly, in some companies, project leadership is a one-time only job, a mere stepping stone to something better.

One more point: In the case of major projects, ideally the leader spends 100 percent of his/her time on this function. Certainly the leader should not be spread across too many projects—two to three projects per leader is the maximum.

Continuity of team members and the leader over the life of the project is the rule. There are no project hand-offs and no disconnects. The composition of the team may change over time (from stage to stage), and the team size may vary. But there is continuity of players—the majority of the team remains in place from stage to stage—particularly the key knowledge holders. Circumstances may dictate the need for a change in team leadership over time, but the initial team leader should also remain on the team to ensure continuity.

Team membership is confirmed at each gate, and all the team members for the next stage are identified and their release times indicated and agreed to by the gatekeepers. Additional team members may be added as needed during the stages.

The Gatekeepers

Who are the gatekeepers who make the Go/Kill and resource allocation decisions and who are essential to making the process work? Obviously, the choice of the gatekeepers is specific to each business and its organizational structure. But here are some rules of thumb:

- The first rule is simple: The gatekeepers at any gate must have the *authority to approve the resources* required for the next stage. They "own" the resources.
- The gatekeepers must *represent different functional areas,* to the extent that resources will be required from different functions—for example, from systems, technology, marketing, operations and perhaps sales, purchasing, and quality assurance. There is not much sense in having a gatekeeper group from just one functional area.
- The gatekeepers usually *change somewhat from gate to gate.* Typically, at Gate 1, the Initial Screen, the gatekeepers are

a small group, perhaps three or four people, who need not be the most senior in the organization. The spending level here is quite low. By Gate 3, however, where financial and resource commitments are substantial, the gatekeepers typically include more senior managers; for example, the leadership team of the business.

- There should, however, also be some *continuity of gatekeepers* from gate to gate. The composition of the gatekeeper group should not change totally; this would lead to a total start-from-the-beginning justification of the project at each gate. For example, some members of the leadership team— the heads of marketing and technology for example— might be at Gate 2, with the full leadership team at Gate 3.

Critical projects, those with major strategic implications, often involve the senior gatekeepers at earlier gates—even at Gate 1 in some businesses. Senior people argue, "We do not want any projects starting that may ultimately involve millions of dollars in expenditures without our early approval!" In other businesses, the leadership team is happy to review projects at Gate 3 and onward, leaving the earlier gate decisions to a more junior group, but they do want to be informed of early gate decisions.

Projects of varying magnitude require varying levels of gatekeeper groups in some businesses. For example, the Business Banking Division at Royal Bank of Canada has two levels of gatekeepers after Gate 3: a senior gatekeeping group for larger, riskier projects, with total cost in excess of $500,000; and a middle-level gatekeeping group for lower-risk and/or smaller projects. This middle-level group also handles Gate 2 decisions for both large and smaller projects.

A final issue is whether the same gatekeeping groups should be used for all projects, or whether each project should have its own individual group of gatekeepers. At Telenor, the Norwegian telephone company, each project has its own gatekeeper group, but a downside of this approach is that the gatekeepers can quickly turn into steering committees and cheerleaders for "their" particular project, so that no projects are ever killed. The company has, subsequently, revised its gatekeeping methods, and has moved toward "standing gatekeeper groups" that review all Gate 3, 4, and 5 projects and really do kill weak ones.

The Process Manager

The Stage-Gate process requires a process manager to shepherd the process. No process, no matter how good or logical, has ever implemented itself, and so a process champion must be in place to make it happen. Experience suggests that process facilitation is a critical ingredient of success. If your company does not have this

EXHIBIT 5.6   Job Description—Stage-Gate Process Manager

The process manager . . .
- leads the implementation effort of the new service process throughout the business
- is responsible for maintaining the process upon implementation
- provides for training and trains new employees
- acts as a focal point for feedback on the process (e.g., feedback received at gates and at the Post-Launch Review), making necessary improvements to the process
- develops and maintains the process database and metrics
- uses portfolio analysis techniques to provide data for portfolio analysis and gate meetings
- tracks each new project throughout the process; measures performance and ultimate success
- establishes practical and consistent guidelines for deliverables (e.g., templates)
- facilitates the gate meetings
- acts as a coach to project teams
- serves as a resource to project teams to help remove roadblocks and blockers
- develops and maintains process documentation (manuals, guides, booklets).
- promotes the use of the process at every opportunity, seeking buy-in from key people.

person in place—preferably as a full-time job—do not expect your process to work.

The process manager has many duties, among them attending every gate meeting, ensuring that senior people are prepared, ensuring that the team's deliverables are in place, ensuring that the meeting runs according to the rules of the game, and making sure that a decision is made. The manager is also responsible for mentoring project teams and helping to remove roadblocks and blockers. This person keeps score and is keeper of the database essential to providing performance metrics and inputs to portfolio analysis. Typically the process manager is a staff position that reports directly to a senior executive. His/her specific roles are outlined in Exhibit 5.6.

Designing the Gates

How should your business go about designing and implementing effective gate meetings? In this section we look at the purpose of gates and the requirements for a good gating system, and then move to the design of gates: structure, criteria, roles, and gate procedures ("rules of the game").

Purpose of the Gates

Gates provide various points during the process where an assessment of the quality of the project is undertaken. They ensure that your business does the right projects, and does them right. Gates deal with three main issues: quality of execution, business rationale, and the quality of the action plan.

Quality of execution: Have the steps in the previous stage been executed in a quality fashion? Have the project leader and team members done their jobs well?

Business rationale: Does the project continue to look like an attractive one from an economic and business standpoint?

Action plan: Are the proposed action plan and the requested resources (both money and people) reasonable and sound?

These are separate issues, and should be debated separately. Take the situation where a project team does a superb job but has its project put on hold simply because there are better projects to do. Unless the debate on "quality of execution" is separated from "business rationale," the team may have the impression that the discontinuation of their project means they are being chastised by senior management for doing a poor job. Not true!

The Structure of a Gate

A little structure of gates and also gate meetings goes a long way to improving the effectiveness and efficiency of your leadership team's decision making. Well-designed gates and gate meetings have a common format with three main components (as discussed in Chapter 4):

Deliverables.   Too often, project leaders do not understand the expectations of senior management. Hence they arrive at gate meetings lacking much of the information that senior management needs in order to make a timely Go/Kill decision. So gates must define visible deliverables in advance. These are what the project leader and team must deliver to the gate. They are the results of actions in the preceding stage. The list of deliverables for a gate becomes the objectives of the project leader and team. A standard menu of deliverables is specified for each gate. A typical menu of deliverables for Gate 3, the vital "money gate," is shown in Exhibits 5.5 and 5.7.

Criteria.   In order to make good decisions, your leadership team needs decision criteria that are actually used at gate meetings, are visible, and are clearly understood by all gatekeepers. These criteria are what the project is judged against in order to make the

EXHIBIT 5.7   Typical Deliverables for Gate 3 (the "Go-to-Development" Gate)

- Results of detailed market analysis
- User needs, wants, and desired benefits defined (based on customer interviews)
- Concept test results and purchase intent data
- Competitive analysis (who, market shares, pricing)
- Preliminary marketing plan (one page)
- Results of technical analysis
- Probable technical route; risks identified
- New service definition: target market, positioning, price point, product requirements
- Estimates of likely development costs, timing, and resources
- Probable operations and delivery requirements
- Estimates of operations costs, equipment, and capital requirements
- Legal and regulatory assessments
- Financial analysis (IRR, NPV, EPS, sensitivity analysis)
- Plan of action for next stage (in detail)
- Tentative plan through to launch (with extraordinary items flagged).

Go/Kill and prioritization decisions. These change somewhat from gate to gate, but there is usually a standard list of criteria for each gate. They include both financial and qualitative criteria and are broken down into required (must-meet) characteristics versus desired characteristics (should-meet).

Outputs.   Gates must have clearly articulated outputs. Too often, project review meetings end with a vague decision. Outputs are the result of the gate meeting, and they include a decision and a path forward (an approved project plan, and a date and the list of required deliverables for the next gate). There are only four possible decisions from a gate meeting (Go/Kill/Hold/Recycle); the decision cannot be to "defer the decision."

- *Go* means the project is approved and the resources, both people and money, are committed by the gatekeepers.

- *Kill* means "terminate the project"—stop all work on it and spend no more time or money here.
- *Hold* means that the project passes the gate criteria but that better projects are available and resources are not available for the current project. A Hold decision is a prioritization issue.
- *Recycle* is analogous to "rework" on a production line: Go back and do the stage over again, and this time do it right. Recycle signals that the project team has not delivered what was required.

Types of Gate Criteria

Each gate has its own list of criteria for use by the gatekeepers. These criteria are what the gate decision is based on, and can be of two types: Go/Kill and project prioritization criteria:

- *Must-meet:* These are yes/no questions; a single no can signal a Kill decision. Checklists are the usual format for must-meet items.
- *Should-meet:* These are highly desirable project characteristics, but a no on one question would not kill the project; rather, these questions are scored and a point count or project score is determined. Scoring models handle the should-meet questions well.

Note that criteria can be quantitative (for example, IRR exceeds 22 percent) as well as qualitative, meaning the criterion captures issues such as the strategic alignment of the project.

The must-meet criteria typically capture strategic issues, feasibility questions, and resource availabilities. Examples:

- Does the new project fit the strategic direction of the business?

EXHIBIT 5.8   Typical Must-Meet Questions at Gates 1, 2, 3.

- Strategic alignment (fits the business's strategy)
- Existence of market need (minimum size)
- Reasonable likelihood of technical feasibility
- Service/market fit (meets customers' needs; a potential market exists)
- Meets LER (legal, ethical, regulatory) policies
- Positive return versus risk
- No show stoppers ("killer variables").

- Is its development technically feasible?
- Do you have the resources required to undertake the venture?

A no to any one of these questions (for example, a lack of strategic fit) is enough to kill the project. A typical list of must-meet criteria is shown in Exhibit 5.8.

Answers to the should-meet questions indicate the relative attractiveness of the project. Examples:

- How large is the market?
- How fast is it growing?
- To what degree can the new service utilize existing equipment and technology?
- To what extent does the new service have sustainable competitive advantage?

Low scores on any one of these should-meet questions certainly would not kill the project. But enough low scores may indicate that the project is simply not attractive enough to pursue. Sample should-meet criteria are shown in Exhibit 5.9.

Gate criteria are designed to be used by the gatekeepers at the gate meeting. After the project is presented and debated, the criteria should be discussed one by one, scored, and a decision reached. Progressive companies use scorecards or computer-

EXHIBIT 5.9   Should-Meet Prioritization Criteria at Gate 3
(Scored 0–10 or 1–5)

---

1. Strategic:
   - Degree to which project aligns with the business strategy
   - Strategic importance of project to the business
2. Competitive advantage: extent to which the new service . . .
   - Offers unique benefits to users/customers (not available on competitive offerings)
   - Is a higher quality service than competitors' (however the customer measures quality)
   - Fits the customer better than competitors' services (service/market fit: customer needs, use system, etc.)
3. Market attractiveness:
   - Market size
   - Market growth rate
   - Competitive situation (tough, intense, price-based competition is a low score)
4. Synergies (leverages core competencies):
   - Leverages our business's marketing, distribution, and selling strengths/resources
   - Leverages our technological know-how, expertise, and experience
   - Leverages our operations and delivery capabilities, expertise, and facilities
5. Technical feasibility:
   - Size of the technical gap (small gap is a high score; e.g., technological solution readily available)
   - Complexity of the project, technically (less complex is a high score)
   - Technical uncertainty of outcome (high certainty is a high score)
6. Risk versus return:
   - Expected profitability (magnitude: NPV in $000)
   - Percent return (IRR or ROI percent)
   - Payback period—how fast you recover your initial expenditure/investment (years)
   - Certainty of return/profit/sales estimates (from "pure guess" to "highly predictable")
   - Degree to which project is low-cost and fast.

These should-meet items are scored (e.g., on a scale of 1 to 5 or 0 to 10) and added (weighted or unweighted) to yield six factor scores.

Each factor score must clear a hurdle for a pass. They are also added (again, weighted or unweighted) to yield the project score. This project score must pass a minimum hurdle for a pass, and is also used to rank projects against each other.

Points for Management to Ponder

Gates have three main components:

- A menu of deliverables (defined for each gate)
- Criteria on which the Go/Kill and prioritization decisions will be based
- Outputs: Go/Kill/Hold/Recycle and resources approved

Consider using a set of must-meet questions in a checklist format as culling questions, followed by a list of should-meet questions in a scoring format to help determine relative project attractiveness. Be sure to use these criteria at your gate meeting, discussing each question and reaching closure on it. If you do this, chances are your gatekeeping group will make more objective, more reasoned, and better decisions.

---

assisted scoring at gate meetings, so that scores can be displayed and differences debated.

Making the Gates Work

Gatekeeper Roles and Responsibilities

The critical role of gatekeepers is to facilitate the rapid commercialization of the best projects. It is their job to ensure that projects receive a timely and fair hearing, that objective and consistent decisions are made, that resources are allocated and commitments kept, and that roadblocks are removed. Good gatekeepers achieve these goals by doing the following:

- *Making timely, firm and consistent Go/Kill decisions:* Too often gatekeeping teams cancel gate meetings, or fail to make the decision in a timely fashion. Yet they are the first to complain about long cycle times and projects that take too long to reach the marketplace.

- *Prioritizing projects objectively:* Projects must be prioritized at gate meetings and these prioritizations must be made on the basis of objective, visible criteria, supported by facts, not just the opinions of the gatekeepers. There is no room for politicking and "opinioneering" at gate meetings.
- *Establishing visible deliverables for successive gate meetings:* Deliverables are based on a standard menu for each gate. But each project is unique and may deviate from the standard deliverables list. The gatekeepers must agree to a list of needed deliverables for the project in question and ensure that the project leader understands what is required.
- *Committing necessary resources and ensuring their availability:* Resource commitments must be made at gates. There is no sense having a gate meeting and deciding on a Go but failing to assign the needed resources. Recall that the gatekeepers are the people who "own" the resources required for the next stage. Hence, they are in a position to make the resource allocation decision right at the gate meeting.
- *Mentoring and enabling project teams:* The traditional notion of a gatekeeper as judge and critic is obsolete in progressive businesses. Rather, the gatekeeper is very much an enabler, helper, and mentor, providing resources and assistance, facilitating the rapid execution of the project.
- *Setting high standards for quality of execution of project tasks:* Gatekeepers are also the quality assurers in the process, ensuring that projects unfold as they should. To make the point, one senior executive stated, "As a member of the executive and also a key gatekeeper, I view my role not so much as judge and critic, but more as a quality assurer."

Gate Procedures

Most business leadership teams develop and agree to procedures for gate meetings. These might sound like a bit of a nuisance, and not the most exciting task you face, but at best, gate meetings are tricky affairs to make work well. It is important that the leadership team take the time to review and develop these gate procedures.

Gate procedures typically deal with how the project information will be presented, how the project will be evaluated or scored, and how the decision will be made. Note the importance of these gate decisions. Some structure to promote effectiveness is a desirable element. The following is a typical gate procedure:

The Right Procedure to Ensure High-Quality Gate Meetings
Before the Meeting

The deliverables are submitted and delivered to gatekeepers approximately one week ahead of the gate meeting. Consider using a standard format for deliverables.

If major questions and show stoppers have arisen in the course of the work done at that stage of the process, gatekeepers should contact the gate facilitator or the project team leader in advance of the meeting.

Hold the meeting! Cancellations or postponements are unacceptable unless the deliverables are not ready. And hold the meeting even if the project team recommends a Kill decision. This achieves closure; you agree on the lessons learned and you celebrate success, namely, a "correct Kill" decision. If gatekeepers cannot attend, they must use video or teleconferencing from whatever city they are in.

The entire project team should be present, where physically possible and convenient. (Some businesses only invite the project leader to gates; this may be efficient, but communication to the entire team is hampered). Other attendees should be limited—no cheering sections and gate-crashers!

Some businesses nominate a head gatekeeper for each gate meeting—a rotating position. One of her roles is to follow up with the project team leader on any outstanding items or "loose ends" following the gate meeting. This eliminates the need for the entire gatekeeping team to reconvene, and helps speed up the process.

At the Meeting

The project team has 15 uninterrupted minutes to do its presentation. Give the team a chance to finish their presentation before you dive in with questions! Next follows a question-and-answer session by the gatekeepers. Then the gate facilitator walks the gatekeepers through the list of criteria. The must-meet checklist is gone through, and then the should-meet items are scored by gatekeepers, ideally using a scorecard. The scores are recorded on an overhead projector, and differences debated. Consensus is reached and a decision is made: Go, Kill, or Recycle.

Next, a prioritization level is established: The project in question is compared to the existing projects in the pipeline as well as to projects that are on hold, to establish its priority level. Various portfolio models and displays are used to achieve this prioritization (portfolios models are discussed in greater detail in Chapter 7). (The project team members may be asked to leave the room while the gatekeepers have a frank discussion on difficult issues). The end result is a decision to resource the project immediately (Go) or to put the project on hold, awaiting resources. If Go, the gatekeepers make an immediate commitment of resources: people, their time, and money.

The proposed action plan is discussed and modified if necessary. Agreement is reached on the action plan and the deliverables for the next gate. A date is set for the next gate meeting.

If the project team has been asked to leave the room, they are brought back into the gate meeting now. They are informed of the decision and reasons for it.

Effective Gatekeeping Performance

Your leadership team must work toward becoming an effective gatekeeping group if you want to see new services prosper in your business. Recent research has revealed the secrets to success for members of effective gatekeeper teams in leading companies. This research was undertaken in business units of major firms. Effective gatekeepers and gatekeeping teams were questioned about what made them perform so well; here is a summary of their responses:[6]

Consensus: Gatekeepers must work together as a team to reach consensus decisions. Once the decision is taken, all gatekeepers agree to support the decision. Agreement among the members of

EXHIBIT 5.10 Typical Gatekeeper "Rules of the Game"

1. Gatekeepers must hold the meeting and be there. Postponed or canceled meetings are not an option. If you cannot attend, your vote is Yes or you can designate a proxy to vote for you.
2. Gatekeepers must have received and read relevant information and be prepared for the meeting. Contact the gate facilitator or project team if there are show stoppers or killer variables; no surprise attacks at the gate meeting.
3. Gatekeepers cannot request information or answers beyond that specified in the deliverables: no playing "I gotcha." Gates are not a forum to demonstrate your machismo, political clout, or intellectual prowess.
4. Gatekeepers cannot "beat up" the presenter. Give the project team an uninterrupted period to present. The question-and-answer session must be fair, not vicious.
5. Gatekeepers must make their decision based on the criteria for that gate. Gatekeepers must review each criterion and reach a conclusion. Each gatekeeper should use a scoring sheet.
6. Gatekeepers must be disciplined: no hidden agendas; no invisible criteria; decisions based on facts and known criteria, not emotion and gut feel.
7. All projects must be treated fairly and consistently. They must pass through the gate with no special treatment for executive sponsored or pet projects; all are subjected to the same criteria and the same rigor.
8. A decision must be made within that working day. If the deliverables are there, you cannot defer the decision. This is a system built for speed.
9. The project team must be informed of the decision immediately and face-to-face.
10. If the decision is Go, the gatekeepers support the agreed-to action plan, they commit the resources (people and money), and they agree to release times for people on the project team. (Note: No one gatekeeper can override the Go decision or renege on agreed-to resources.)
11. If the decision is Hold, the gatekeepers must try to find resources. The project cannot remain on Hold for more than three months. Up or out! (This rule puts pressure on gatekeepers to make tougher decisions—some real Kills—or to commit more resources).

the leadership team is vital. It makes no sense to have the head of marketing strongly supporting the project while the head of technology is against it, and refuses to commit the needed resources.

Strategy and criteria: Gatekeepers must reach agreement on several key items in advance. They must agree on a business strategy and the arenas of strategic focus. They must also agree on the criteria against which the project will be assessed and commit to making decisions based on these criteria.

"Rules of the game": Effective gatekeeping teams develop "rules of the game" and agree to live by them. These rules cover expected behaviors of the members of the gatekeeping group and are clearly visible to each gatekeeper as well as to project teams and leaders. Exhibit 5.10 is a sample set of rules of the game based on those we have gathered from various companies over the years. Review these and see how many your leadership team will endorse.

Prioritization method: Gatekeepers must also agree to a prioritization process for projects (more on the topic of prioritization and portfolio management in Chapter 7). And since resources must be committed at gate meetings, the gatekeepers need a solid understanding of commitments already made—the priorities of active projects and the resource commitments made to them, as well as projects on hold and awaiting resources.

Understanding the process: Finally, gatekeepers must possess a solid understanding of their company's service development process: what activities are expected within the different stages, and in particular what the required deliverables are for each gate.

Outsourced Projects and Alliances

Involving third parties is one route to accelerating the development process. Third parties can provide more efficient and cost-effective developments in several ways, and they may even make possible new services that previously were simply not feasible.

Outsourced Projects.   Often there are reasons not to undertake all facets of a project in-house. A vendor may be able to supply an off-the-shelf system or software that provides the basis for your new service. For example, telephone companies rely heavily on vendors of software and hardware such as Nortel, Lucent, Siemens, Ericsson, and others to provide the technology and operations capability to yield new telephone services. In effect, telephone companies (telcos) have become integrators of hardware and software, and marketers of the resulting services. So the vendor's role in the telco's development process is crucial.

Vendors are also called upon to provide custom-tailored solutions—in effect, to do the company's development work under contract. For example, when a financial institution relies on a contractor to develop the software for a new on-line loan system, much of the traditional technical work (writing software code) that the institution used to do itself is outsourced. Even facets of the operations and delivery of the service can be outsourced. This may be a particularly effective way to develop or deliver services, particularly when the vendor has superiorexpertise/experience/capacity in this area and when your own resources are limited. In addition, some smaller outside vendors seem to be able to get things done a little faster than your own organization, perhaps because they are smaller and more entrepreneurial.

Alliances.   Alliances imply a much closer relationship than the usual vendor-customer dyad described above. This type of joint venture, called partnering, is yet another route to speed new services to market.

> An electric utility company proceeds to develop a new service, Premium Power. The concept is to guarantee electrical power to clients 100 percent of the time, avoiding power outages totally. Certain clients—hospitals, banks, data management centers, telephone companies—incur huge costs if their electrical power supply fails. But to offer such a service, the utility must ally itself with two other parties: an equipment supplier (who supplies the diesel engine or turbine and generator) and a contractor (who installs, operates, and maintains the backup power supply system). None of the three parties operating on their own could have provided the service.

Many companies have in place both a *procurement process* (for dealing with outside vendors) and an *alliance process* (for dealing with potential partners). If you do not have such processes, policies, or guidelines in your company, we strongly urge you to develop these. Note that procurement and alliances are pervasive activities throughout your company, by no means limited to new service activities. For this reason, general advice on how to develop such procurement and alliance processes and procedures lies outside the scope of this book.

Still, we recommend that you build vendor relationship and alliance guidelines into your Stage-Gate process. Borrow from your procurement methods and from your alliance process those steps and procedures that are specifically relevant to new services, and integrate them into your stage activities and gate deliverables. For example, in the detailed process described earlier in this chapter, you probably noted some sections that were specific to alliance projects or projects where vendors play a key role. There were specific tasks in every stage where dealing with vendors or alliance partners was the focus.

Finally, if you do no physical product development yourself, but rather purchase off-the-shelf solutions as the basis for your own new service, perhaps you need an abbreviated development process—a simpler version of the full model in Exhibit 5.1—for example, the model in Exhibit 5.11. This is a combination of a generic procure-

EXHIBIT 5.11   Modifying the Stage-Gate Process for Outsourced Products

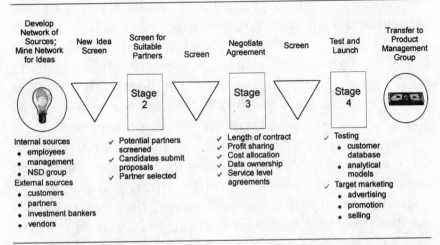

Source: Adapted from Council on Financial Competition, *Beyond Commodity Status* (Washington, D.C.: The Advisory Board Company, 1997), p. 253.

ment process model and the Stage-Gate process. Versions of this abbreviated process have been successfully employed in firms that undertake no technical development work themselves.

Platforms: A Base from Which to Operate

The PDMA (Product Development Management Association)
handbook defines a platform as "design and components that are
shared by a set of products in a product family. From this platform, numerous derivatives can be designed."[4] The original notion
of a platform was very much physical product-based. For example,
Chrysler's engine-transmission assembly from its K-car was a platform that spawned other vehicles, including the famous Chrysler
minivan.

Many businesses look to platforms as a way to accelerate projects, reduce development costs, and execute strategic thrusts, so
the notion of platforms has since been broadened to include *technological and operations capabilities*. For example, Iridium is a technology or capability platform that is yielding many new product
and customer bundles in the telecommunications industry.

The analogy is that of an oil well drilling platform in the ocean.
The initial cost of building the platform is high; but once in place,
one can drill many holes relatively quickly and at low cost. The
platform thus leads to many related new service projects in a
timely and cost-effective manner. A bank may invest heavily in
developing a new deposits system, which functions as a platform
because it then enables the bank to launch a number of new deposit products, each aimed at different customer segments.

The notion of platforms is appealing. Invest heavily in a platform, and then harvest the benefits for years, developing and
launching one new service after another from that platform. As
one senior executive in a major telco stated: "In a few years, product development will amount to turning a switch on the platform—the service will be instantly developed and immediately
available for launch."

We view a platform as follows:

A platform is an enabler. Building a platform means investing in a capability, hardware, software, or technology that then leads to a series of *commercial entities* or *deliverables*. These can be new, improved, or enhanced services or improved or new backroom processes or operations.

The advent of platforms raises three new issues in new service development:

1. Platforms are typically much more costly to develop or purchase than individual new services and have a broader and longer-lasting impact on the business. Thus, poor decisions on platform developments have much more severe repercussions than inadequate decision making in a conventional new service project.
2. Often the projects or services that will be spawned from a platform are vaguely defined or simply not known when the decisions regarding the platform are being made. Thus, defining the specs for the platform and even justifying the platform investment are difficult.
3. Platforms can spawn more than just new services. Many different types of projects could be spawned from a single platform. For example, in addition to new or improved services and extensions, a platform can also lead to improved operations processes, or more cost-effective delivery systems.

Having considered these three issues, we offer the following suggestions:

1. *Make your decisions on platforms more rigorously.* Decisions on platforms are usually far more important than decisions on single new service projects. Thus the decision to invest in a platform must be handled in a far more rigorous fashion. In practice, these platform decisions often are not made with much rigor: Platforms

often seem to proceed through the decision process on the basis of unsubstantiated visions of the future. This is one reason why we recommend that you develop a Stage-Gate process specifically for platform projects, and consider platforms as part of your development portfolio. Admittedly, the criteria for Go may be more qualitative and strategic (and less quantitative and financial), but they are defined criteria and they must be applied.

2. *Make the justification and specs for the platform as precise as possible.* In order to sharpen the definition and justification of the platform, try to identify the first one or two commercial entities that the platform will spawn (see Exhibit 5.12). Use these two as the basis to undertake your market research, to build your business case, and to develop your financial justification. Do not rely on blind faith and some "executive vision" regarding the merits or design of the platform. Then, be sure to anticipate additional services that the platform could yield. These additional entities might be somewhat vaguely defined at this early stage, but make assumptions and build these into your business case anyway, to help shape and justify the platform development. In short, the

EXHIBIT 5.12   The Platform Spawns Many Projects

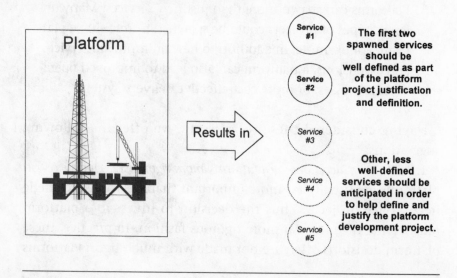

platform cannot usually be justified or specified on the basis of the first two spawned services, but pinning these down, with the anticipation of more to come, helps to sharpen both definition and justification.

3. *Recognize that there is more than one kind of platform.* This makes the situation more complex—like apples and oranges in the same basket. A recent benchmarking session of several telecom companies and financial institutions on new service innovation identified three types of platform projects:

- Platform Type 1: Designed to deliver new services, or new features and functionality on existing services, to external customers. An example is the new deposits platform described above, from which numerous new deposit services can be offered to different customer segments.
- Platform Type 2: Provides support for customer-destined services. An example is a new customer billing system.
- Platform Type 3: Provides a system for internal business management; for example, a new information system to assist salespeople.

Types 1 and 2 can be handled by a development process that resembles the generic Stage-Gate process outlined in Exhibit 5.1, but some of the important details of the process need to be modified. Platform Type 3, often called an internal infrastructure project, is quite a different type of project, and likely requires its own, custom-tailored development process. We suggest that you strip these Type 3 infrastructure projects out of your regular new project portfolio: Create a separate "bucket" of resources for these and handle them in their own tailored process.

Handling Platform Projects

What changes are required to the generic development process of Exhibit 5.1 in order to handle platform projects, especially the Type 1 and 2 platforms identified above? Processes designed to develop new platforms are somewhat newer than product development processes, and companies are still experimenting with these. On the basis of work to date, we recommend the following for Type 1 and 2 platform projects (designed to deliver new/improved services or a support system for a service offering):

1. Use a modified Stage-Gate process for these platform development projects (see Exhibit 5.13).
2. Keep the same stage and gate structure as that shown in Figure 5.1, and use the same stage and gate names, so as not to confuse the user. Merge this process with your standard development process, as shown in Exhibit 5.13.
3. Modify some of the activities within stages to accommodate platform projects. Examples:
   - In Stage 2, require that the project team envision two concrete new services or products resulting from the platform and that they perform market research for these two envisioned services: user needs and wants studies, competitive analysis, and concept tests.
   - In Stage 2, insist that the life cycle plan include some visioning regarding future services beyond these two. Develop a product road map for the platform that shows future new services, their functionality, and their timing.[5] Make this life cycle plan a key deliverable to Gate 3.
   - In Stage 2, revise the financial analysis method to reflect the fact that sales projections, margins, and costs are not well defined for all the services/products that the platform might spawn. Sensitivity analysis (what if . . .) and development of alternate scenarios (if this platform results in the following new services, then . . .) might be used here.
   - In some companies, the final stages of the platform project start to blend into the initial stages of the development process, with several new service or other projects running in parallel (Exhibit 5.13).

EXHIBIT 5.13   Platform Development Process

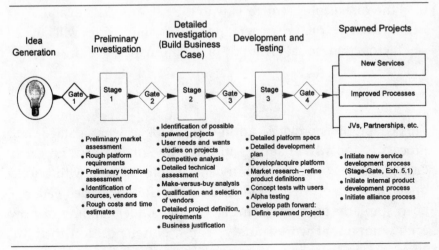

- In Stage 2, build in some activities that investigate answers to the question: If we do not invest in this platform now, what are the consequences?

4. Modify the gate criteria. Clearly, with future services less well defined, financial projections are based on fuzzier data and hence are less reliable. The critical criteria to move ahead with a platform *should not be strongly based on financial criteria*, but rather on strategic criteria. Simply stated, calculating the NPV for a platform and using this NPV as the main input to the Go/Kill decision is naive in the case of platforms. Strategic criteria are more relevant: the strategic importance and strategic impact of the platform, and the strategic leverage to be gained from the platform (for example, what services it might yield, their competitive advantage, their sustainability). These are much more qualitative criteria, which certainly make gate-keeping and gates a greater challenge.

5. Organizationally, the process is likely to cut across several business units. Whereas a new service process is often self-contained within one business unit, platforms may affect several BUs. Moreover, it may take the envisioned services

from several BUs to justify investing in the platform. Thus, the gatekeeping structure (who the gatekeepers are) and the team structure (where the players come from) will cut across traditional organizational boundaries.

Recap

This chapter has provided an in-depth look at what a Stage-Gate process is and what happens in the individual stages and gates. Each stage has been profiled in detail to provide you with a solid understanding of what activities occur in the stage; each gate has been similarly profiled. Gaining a better understanding of how each component works puts you in a better position to think about designing your own process. The difficult issue of alliances and partnerships has also been discussed. If your business uses these types of arrangements, you will need to consider how you are going to build this into your process.

The people side of the process has also been explored. Companies lacking effective process leadership and stewardship have had great difficulty in trying to make a new process stick in their organization. A good process is the first step, but you also need to consider the people factor. After all, the process is supposed to make people's jobs easier while at the same time helping an organization achieve its new service objectives. We also spent some time discussing the gates and gatekeepers, the role they play, and how they work. Successful companies have found that strong support for the process at the top is a necessary precondition.

Before you begin to redesign your development process, let's move on to the next chapter, where we discuss several selected topics that can also have a big impact on your process in today's business environment.

6

Issues and Challenges: New Approaches in the Innovation Process

We live in turbulent times. The world around us seems to change at a dizzying pace. And so it is with the methods, practices, and techniques we must employ to be successful in business. This pace of change is particularly evident in the field of innovation. As innovation moves ahead faster and faster, the methods we use to manage the innovation process must change.

This chapter focuses on four key topics that have emerged as critical to new service success in the future. No book on service development would be complete without a look at these topics:

1. *Internet and electronic commerce (e-commerce)* has taken the business world by storm. The impact of e-commerce on the way you conceive, develop, and launch new services is the first topic in this chapter.
2. Next, we go *beyond the Stage-Gate method* that was described in the last two chapters. Top performers have now moved to the third-generation development process, according to the most recent PDMA best practices study.[1] We look at the six F's of our third-generation process, and how it differs from the method outlined in Chapters 4 and 5.

3. *Speed has become the new competitive weapon*—the ability to move quickly to market. Cycle time reduction is our third topic. We discuss proven ways to dramatically reduce the time your project takes from idea through launch.

4. "What gets measured gets done" is an old adage. Not only are metrics—measuring your results and gauging how well you are doing at service development—fundamental to successful innovation, but *metrics are also fundamental to change*. They are necessary to making improvements in your innovation process and practices.

Topic #1.
The Impact of E-commerce on Your Development Process

The Internet and electronic commerce have introduced many new possibilities in the service sector, but they also present major challenges. The obvious opportunities are in the roll-out of the new service (launch) through the use of an e-commerce channel. But there are other less obvious and potentially higher-impact marketing and distribution implications:[2]

More Direct Delivery Routes. The supplier can now sell directly to the end user or ultimate customer. The traditional intermediary can be cut out or "dis-intermediated."

An estimated 22 percent of autos in the United States are sold via the Internet. What does this mean to General Motors, whose traditional strength has been its dealership on every corner? On-line sales by Dell Computers and Gateway are posing major threats to other PC makers who use traditional channels (HP, Compaq). Charles Schwab launched its on-line stock purchase service, and now well over half of the company's trading is via this channel.[2] Other brokerage companies are worried. Meanwhile, Amazon.com is redefining the business of selling books.

The bottom line is that market launch, channel, and marketing options are much different today than they were a few years ago.

Some of the products/services sold over the Internet include banking services, investment brokerage, insurance, mobile and other telephone services, small package delivery, and travel and tourism, to name a few. If your new services have the potential to be sold via the Internet, then chances are your competitors are already working on their launch.

An important point to understand is that because services are intangible, they are *particularly well suited for Internet sales*. When you buy a tangible product—a new dress, a new suit, or even a new car—chances are you want to experience it before you make your decision: try it on, or take it for a test drive. But customers are accustomed to buying new services without trying them first. Hence, services are particularly amenable to "sight-unseen, long-distance buying," or e-commerce.

Here is what e-commerce means to your new service launch plans:

- At minimum, you must consider e-commerce and the Internet as a serious option in your new service development. The good news is that this opens up all kinds of new channel possibilities for you that can potentially lead to competitive advantage and increased sales and profits. The bad news is that your traditional channel strategies may be obsolete for your next launch.

- You may have to radically rethink your traditional marketing plans. For example, for some categories the Internet has become a real-time auction, and this means that your pricing strategies may have to change. One might envision a service launch where pricing is fluid—where customer demand (or lack of it) can cause real-time pricing adjustments during the launch phase. To accomplish this, you might have to build a real-time, on-line pricing learning model into your launch.

- Your advertising and promotion must change. Traditionally, you controlled the advertising through mass media and direct mail. But the Internet changes all that. Now customers have more control over the amount and type of information they see. With the click of a mouse, the customer can switch from your message to a competitor's. Even more unsettling is that people and businesses are turning to the Web for product information, which means that traditional media are increasingly taking a backseat. In 1999, Procter & Gamble, one of the world's largest advertisers, expects to spend 2 to 3 percent of its advertising dollars on Internet advertising. Within a few years, the figure is expected to increase by a factor of ten.

No More Geographic Monopolies.   There are no geographic monopolies anymore. The fact you are the only bank or travel agent in town, or the major brokerage company in a metropolitan area, no longer guarantees you a market or customer loyalty. Via e-commerce, service providers in other parts of the country, or even other countries, can invade your market domain. And you can access their markets too. This opens up a myriad of new market opportunities for the innovator.

ING, a Dutch Bank, has mounted a major marketing initiative via the Internet to attract customers in Canada. Via television advertising and a Web page address, in a short time the bank has picked up sixty thousand retail clients who previously banked at domestic Canadian banks.

The implication is this: The removal of geographic boundaries means a much higher potential for profit for the successful innovator in the service sector. Traditionally, service businesses were restricted to the areas that their offices or outlets covered, but no longer is this so. Geographic freedom multiplies the potential market size for your new product by orders of magnitude. It also means that you may have to innovate more often and more quickly because now your competition can be from anywhere.

Instant Custom Design.   With e-commerce, services and products can be custom-designed for customers almost instantaneously. Witness the example of Dell computers. Via the Internet, the consumer can custom-tailor a new computer by specifying memory size, processing and modem speeds, and types of drives. This is a far cry from the "take what we have" offering of a handful of standard models available in most retail computer outlets.

The implication is this: E-commerce makes it possible for service suppliers to offer a much wider range of service packages with an infinite array of features. Ideally, the customer designs his/her own product or service. The market segment has become *a single customer*. If you can service the single customer, it gives you enormous competitive advantage over the "fixed package" approach aimed at a broad segment as practiced by competitors.

A customer recently visited the private banking service of a major North American bank to inquire about high-end service offerings. A service package option was suggested, for which an extra fee was charged, that covered a wide variety of services. The salesperson stressed that the customer could get guaranteed personal loans up to a large dollar maximum. The customer explained that he currently had no loans, and typically does not borrow money. The business he owned provided a constant positive cash flow. The banker went on to explain how this Private Banking Service package offered preferred interest rates on loans. The customer again explained he did not want to borrow money, and that he wanted investment counseling and investment services, especially in international markets. The banker admitted this service package did not cover that. The potential customer left.

This bank had come up with a "fixed design" service offering, likely based on extensive market research. The trouble is, the bank had designed a service offering aimed at the "average person" in this target market. What they had missed is the fact that no one is average. Now, imagine that you are a bank that can offer your small business clients an infinite array of product features—you "put product design in the customer's hands." The customer chooses (and pays for) only the features and options she really needs. What a deal for the customer. And what an advantage for you!

Ultimately one may be able to launch services and modify them on the fly, literally designing the service in real time. For example, the approach might be to launch Version 1 of the new service and let the customer make choices on options via the Internet. Some of the options shown on your Web page may not even be available yet, but by recording the number of "customer votes" for certain features or options, the fast-paced developer can design and release Version 2 to suit these customer requests. This real-time development offers significant advantages in terms of responding to market needs.

"Virtual" Market Testing.   E-commerce means that customer requirements can be gauged and concept tests can be done with "virtual products." One advantage of Internet technology is that the developer can seek customer input or feedback on service/ product design *without actually having the service available*! Recall the user-needs-and-wants studies and the concept test outlined in Stage 2 in Chapter 5. Both are critical activities, but they are resource- and time-intensive. Imagine the day when you can conduct both these studies electronically. That day is here:

> SAP, the German software company, is developing a Web-based market research page designed to solicit input from its current customer base. Customers are invited to provide their design input via the Internet. The Web page offers a number of possible suggestions, features, and functions that might be possible in the next-generation SAP product. It seeks customer input as to how important or relevant each feature is. In this way, SAP is able to gauge customer needs and wants before it begins development. The advantage is much broader customer input (from multiple markets, segments, and countries)

than would be available via traditional market research, and it is undertaken more quickly and less expensively.

Concept tests are also possible via the Web, by means of a *virtual product:* One develops the service concept and displays it to prospective users via e-mail or the Internet. But it is a "pretend service"—no development has taken place yet. Potential customers can then indicate their degree of interest, liking, and purchase intent. They could also indicate what features they like best, and what they do not like. The advantage here is a cost-efficient and quick concept test before the service has even been developed. The virtual concept is much less expensive and quicker to develop than a real service/product. Of course, a disadvantage is that your potential new service is now public, providing the competition with advance notice.

A word of warning: There is no fool-proof way to ensure that those customers accessing the Web page are representative of your company's client base. For example, one might speculate that people who have a lot of time on their hands, or who like to surf the Web, would be more likely than others to access a company's research Web page. Even worse, competitors might feed disinformation to the Web page! Some checks can be built in to control access or to monitor the respondents' profiles. But, unlike with traditional survey market research, with Web-based research, the customer and not the company controls who provides input.

Modifying Your New Development Process for the World of E-Commerce

What does e-commerce mean to the way you conceive, develop, and launch new services—to the development process we laid out in the last chapter? One major bank has already mapped out the stage-by-stage impacts that the Internet will have on their development process. In Exhibit 6.1 we take their input and some of our own to show the impact on the generic Stage-Gate model of

EXHIBIT 6.1   Impact of E-Commerce on the Stage-Gate Process

	Stage 1 Preliminary Investigation	Stage 2 Build Business Case	Stage 3 Development	Stage 4 Testing	Stage 5 Launch
Customer-centered	Customer communities	Real-time surveys	Prototype design	Custom pilots	Segment tracking and on-line monitoring
Iterative Development	Customer design input	Proof of concept and "live prototypes"	Configuration management	Version management tools	Rapid distribution and selling
	Partner opportunity identification	New venture considerations	Collaborative design tools	Performance management	Rapid product fixes (on-line)
					Real-time pricing (via learning systems)

Source: Deloitte & Touche Consulting Group, Toronto.

Exhibit 5.1—what new tasks, possibilities and opportunities e-commerce and the Internet add to each stage. Below are listed some of the new opportunities and key tasks if you move to an Internet-based development process and service delivery system:

Stage 1: Preliminary Investigation. *Customer communities.* Customer communities such as a chat-line, mailbox, or bulletin board, where your customers can communicate with each other, are now an option. Amazon.com, the on-line bookseller, makes it possible for customers to send in their comments and reviews of books they have read. This is the beginning of a network of customers. Monitoring what your customers are saying to each other provides clues about what is required in that next new service.

Customer design input. Here the goal is to undertake the preliminary market research on specific requirements via the Internet. Recall what SAP is doing: Establish a Web page for your current customer base in which you can solicit information as to what features, bundles, and functionalities they want in the next release.

Partner opportunity identification. Feedback from customer communities may indicate the need for complementary services or service packages beyond your own capabilities. Potential services or suppliers might even be suggested. And customer communities can expand beyond just customers. You can also begin to include complementary suppliers in the network.

Stage 2: Detailed Investigation (Build Business Case).

Real-time market surveys. Market surveys can be sent directly to your prospective customers via the Internet. Much like traditional mail surveys in design, they offer many advantages over the old way: great graphics; point and click answering; hypertext options (the next questions that appear depend on the answers given); instant returns; and the data are already coded and entered. Incentives to users can also be displayed more vividly to induce a high response rate.

Proof of concept and "live prototypes." Imagine being able to test your next new service with the customer without actually having developed the service. This is possible with "virtual services": concepts displayed over the Internet. For example, a limited demonstration of the live protocept—a travel, tourism, or restaurant service—could be displayed via a short video clip. The possibilities for presenting concepts to users to gauge interest, liking, and purchase intent are endless.

Stage 3: Development.   *Prototype design.* In Stage 3 the concept is translated into a working prototype. Some services, such as financial services (banking, insurance, investment services) and information services, will be ultimately delivered via e-commerce, so why not also undertake initial prototype testing with customers over the Internet? The Internet helps you obtain quick feedback from selected customers during the development stage. Other ser-

vices may be marketed over the Internet but delivered traditionally (travel, tourism, restaurants, telephone services, etc.). During the development of such services, constant iterations—rapid prototypes and tests—with the customer can be conducted over the Internet.

Stage 4: Testing and Validation. *Custom pilots.* Custom-tailored prototypes can be developed for select beta-test customers and delivered over the Internet. And results of the test—usage rates, patterns of usage, functions and features used most often—can be monitored electronically.

Performance measurement. One purpose of a customer trial (or beta test) is to gauge the service's performance under live field conditions. If the beta version has been delivered electronically, then it is relatively easy to build in performance and satisfaction measurement tools to monitor performance.

> Picture a new Internet loan being beta-tested on a handful of small business clients. The functional performance can be measured by traditional measures (number of fail points and shutdowns, speed of operation). Also built into the offering could be a number of satisfaction questions, asking the test customers about their reactions to the service (the concept, each computer screen, the instructions, and operation) as they walk through the loan procedure.

Stage 5: Launch. *Market Segment tracking.* One can undertake real-time tracking of purchase rates by market segment via Internet delivery of the product. Traditionally, it takes weeks, sometimes months, to get data on how fast the service is selling, who is buying it, and whether the positioning at the intended target segment is right. With on-line selling and distribution, and by building in a user profile questionnaire, real-time tracking is possible, making fast-paced fixes to the marketing plan feasible.

Rapid product fixes. If there are glitches in the service/product, fixes can be made on-line. And most important, design improvements can be made on the fly. For example, build in a "features and functionality options" list, and measure customer votes. You will soon see which features are missing and which ones must be built into the next release. And that next release can be delivered effortlessly to the customer.

Real-time pricing. You can build in a learning model to make real-time pricing adjustments. Monitor demand (purchase rates), and if demand is less than expected, implement a price decrease and monitor the increase in demand. Measure the price elasticity (price sensitivity) in real time and adjust your price accordingly.

Topic #2. Beyond Stage-Gate: The Third-Generation Stage-Gate Process

What lies beyond the Stage-Gate process described in the last chapter? Companies that have successfully installed a Stage-Gate process (what we call a second-generation process) are now moving towards our *third generation version* of the process, according to the latest PDMA survey of best practices.[1] Here is the evolution:

First generation processes were the phased-review processes that appeared in the 1960s. They were largely technically driven and featured laborious checkoffs at each review point to ensure the successful completion of a number of key tasks. Thus, the method was more a measurement and control methodology designed to ensure that the project was proceeding as it should and that every facet of it was completed. But the process was very technically focused. It applied strictly to the physical design and development of the product (it was not cross-functional, excluding marketing and operations people). It did not specify what actions should be taken in each stage, nor were best practices a part of the process. And some people found it very time-consuming.

Today's *second-generation processes*, the Stage-Gate process described in the last two chapters, evolved from the phased-review process of the 1960s. It too consists of identifiable and discrete stages preceded by review points or gates, but that is where the similarities with the first generation end. Stage-Gate overcomes many of the objections found with first generation processes. Stage-Gate is cross-functional, with no department owning any stage. The gates are also cross-functional: Marketing and operations are now integral parts of the process, there is alignment of senior people on project priorities, and it is more holistic. This process puts greater emphasis on the front end (up-front homework and a stronger customer input). It specifies stage activities and best practices, and it builds in parallel processing.

Once the second-generation, or Stage-Gate, process has been successfully installed in your business, it naturally evolves into a *third-generation process*. Stage-Gate processes are evergreen processes: They are constantly evolving and improving. Experienced stage-gaters have improved their processes to emphasize efficiency by speeding up an already effective second-generation process and more efficiently allocating development resources. According to the latest PDMA survey, in almost one half of companies that have adopted a Stage-Gate process, it has evolved to include some of the elements of our third-generation process.[1]

The third-generation process features six fundamental F's:

1. Flexibility
2. Fuzzy (conditional) gates
3. Fluidity
4. Focus (project prioritization and portfolio management)
5. Facilitation
6. Forever green—always regenerating and improving.

1. Flexibility.   The process is not a straitjacket nor a set of hard and fast rules. Rather, each project can be routed through the process according to its specific risk level and needs. Stages can be collapsed and gates combined, provided the decision is made consciously at gates, and with a full understanding of the risks involved. The new service process is essentially a risk-management process. Thus, the risk level and the need for information dictate which steps need to be done and which can be left out. Typically, for lower-risk projects some stages, activities, and gates can be omitted on the basis of decisions made at previous gates.

Recall that the Business Banking Division of the Royal Bank of Canada uses a five-stage, five-gate new service process called RPR (Right Projects Right), as shown in Exhibit 4.1 in Chapter 4. Senior management uses a triage approach and has defined three categories of projects based on project scope, investment, and risk level:

- *System change:* Requests, which are relatively minor changes and improvements, often made in response to a request from a major corporate client. These go through a two-stage, two-gate version of the model (in effect, Stages 1 and 2 are collapsed to a single stage, and so are Stages 3, 4, and 5—see Exhibit 6.2).
- *Fast-track projects:* These are medium-cost projects and feature some risk (less than $500,000 development cost, but impact on multiple customers). These moderate-risk projects are tracked through a four-stage version of the model, which collapses the two homework stages into a single stage (a shortened version of Exhibit 4.1).
- *Major projects:* Projects with a cost of over $500,000 are considered higher-risk, and pass through the full five-stage model shown in Exhibit 4.1.

EXHIBIT 6.2   Shortened Process for Low-Risk, Simple Projects

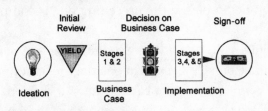

Note that the stages are combined, not omitted.

2. Fuzzy Gates. Here we mean "fuzzy" as in fuzzy logic, a newer form of mathematics; gates, instead of just being binary (open or closed), can have various states in between. Thus, Go decisions can be conditional on the occurrence of some future event, and the Go decision can be made in the absence of perfect information, conditional on positive results delivered later.

> In one major telephone company, if a project is reviewed at a gate and found to be missing one key deliverable (for example, the results of a market study), the decision is to hold the project, awaiting the results of this study. In the faster-paced third-generation Stage-Gate process, the gate decision becomes a "conditional Go." The team moves ahead to the next stage, but is required to report back to the head gatekeeper the results of the missing study. If the gatekeeper is comfortable with the results, the conditional Go decision becomes a full Go. If not, the head gatekeeper calls for a full gate meeting and the project is reviewed again, possibly to be killed or rethought. The point is that the project is not held up for the sake of one piece of information, but there is also a check to ensure that the future information is forthcoming and that results are positive.

3. Fluidity. The process is fluid and adaptable. Activities are not married to specific stages as they are today. Rather, stages overlap: Some activities normally done in the next stage will begin before the previous stage is completed. Long lead-time activities can be brought back from one stage to an earlier one, and the demarcation between stages is more fluid. Stages can overlap: The next stage can begin before the preceding one is complete.

> Here is the rule at GTE's Network System Division: "Long lead-time activities can be brought back from one stage to a previous one. For example, ordering materials or equipment with very long lead times may best be done in an earlier stage even though the project may yet be canceled. The risks of placing the order earlier must be weighed against the extra cost of postponement of the launch."

4. Focus.   The process is focused, functioning much like a funnel. Poor projects are weeded out at each gate, and resources are reallocated to the best projects. This means tough Go/Kill decision points coupled with effective portfolio management, meaning that more than just the merits of the one project under review are considered at each gate. Portfolio management is an important topic to which Chapter 7 is devoted.

> VISA, the credit card company, builds tough gates into its new service process, with clearly defined criteria for Go. Projects must meet these criteria in order to progress to the next stage. At the same time, VISA also has a pipeline management system which considers all the projects in the pipeline. It ensures that the company is focused on the right projects—the right mix, types, and value of projects.

5. Facilitation.   The fifth F is facilitation—a new element we have added since the appearance of the original article on third-generation Stage-Gate processes.[3] To our knowledge, there has never been a successful installation of a Stage-Gate process without a process facilitator in place. In larger companies, this is a full-time position. The role of this process facilitator—often called the key master, process manager, gate-meister, or process keeper—is to make sure that the Stage-Gate process works efficiently and effectively (see Exhibit 5.6 for a job description for process manager). The process manager facilitates every important gate meeting and acts as a referee, ensuring that gatekeepers follow the rules of the game (see Exhibit 5.10) and that a decision is made. He/she coaches the project teams, helping them overcome difficulties and roadblocks, and making sure that all the key deliverables are in place. The process manager updates the process and provides for continual process improvement; trains new employees on how to use the system; and, most important, is the scorekeeper in the game (see "Metrics," page 172).

> At PECO (Pennsylvania Energy Corporation), senior management installed a process manager for their Gateways process even before the

process was designed. She led the task force as it undertook audits of current practice; she chaired the task force meetings as members designed the process; and she shepherded the process through the ranks of senior management to secure approval to implement. Now she is making sure that her Gateways process works—that gate meetings are held, that project teams are ready and deliverables in place, and that decisions get made. Given the size of the organization and the turmoil of deregulation, it is probable that there would be no new service Gateways process within PECO today without the Herculean efforts of this process manager!

No complex process, no matter how good, ever implemented itself. Experienced Stage-Gaters readily admit that the key to success here is not just in the design of the process, but in its implementation, and that if Stage-Gate processes fail, it is usually because of faulty implementation rather than faulty design. So provide for facilitation: Install a full-time "keeper of the process" in your business.

6. Forever green.   Stage-Gate processes are evergreen. They are being constantly renewed, redesigned, and improved, as user companies gain experience with this approach. Some of the general improvements that businesses have made are the six F's listed above. Other companies have adjusted their Stage-Gate processes to suit their specific needs. Some examples:

Telenor, the Norwegian telecommunications company, relies on a Stage-Gate process to drive new services to market. Management has made many improvements to the process, including building in portfolio management methods, changing the locus of decision making to ensure more integrated decisions on individual projects, and incorporating improved methods of screening early-stage projects. Today their process is far better than when first introduced earlier in the 1990s.

PECO (Pennsylvania Energy Corporation) has modified the standard five-stage, five-gate process to accommodate alliance and partnering projects.

The Royal Bank of Canada has adjusted the front end of their Right Projects Right (a Stage-Gate process) to provide a funnel to "suck in" and deal with third-party new services (services developed by other banks and/or software suppliers, that might be available for license, joint ventures, or sale.

The point is that you should be constantly reviewing and reenergizing your process. If you have not updated your current process within the last two years, chances are it is becoming out-of-date . . . time for an audit and an overhaul!

Before moving too quickly to a 6F third-generation process, a word of caution: Knowledgeable Stage-Gaters argue strongly that you should strive first for a basic and effective new service process, perhaps incorporating only some of the elements of our third-generation process (for example, flexibility and some facets of facilitation, the first and fifth F's). Once this process is up and running well, then seek the full-fledged, fast-paced third-generation process. Advancing immediately to a full 6F process has its downside unless your process is in good shape to begin with: You should walk before you run here.

Topic #3. Cycle-Time Reduction

Accelerated development—getting new services/products to market in record speed and ahead of competition—has become key to success and profitability, according to many observers.[4] Time-to-market and cycle-time reduction have been popular topics in recent years—witness the number of books, trade press articles, and consultants' reports on the subject. Indeed, one new product guru, Merle Crawford, notes that the talk around the subject "verges on hype."[5]

Why the Need for Speed: Facts and Myths

Several beliefs underlie the emphasis on speed—some based on myth, others on fact:

1. *First into the market wins.* This is a popular view, but there is conflicting evidence on this. As Crawford points out, there is no hard data to show that "first in wins," except for those cases where the second and third entries have almost identical products. Our own research shows that "first to market" indeed has a positive impact on success rates and profitability, but only marginally so.[4] The real key to success is having a superior service offering, one that fits customer needs and use systems better than the competition: Often the number 2 entrant achieves this, while the pioneer misses the mark.

2. *Speed means higher profits.* A spreadsheet analysis of the profitability impact of time-to-market often reveals startling information. Money has a time value (that is why one uses a discount factor when calculating the net present value, NPV). Thus, deferring profits by even one year can hurt profits considerably. Second, often the highest profit margins are earned in the early phases of a product life cycle—before competition gets intense and price cutting starts. By being slow to market, one misses this early high-margin stage. Finally, many new services have a fixed window of opportunity before they are made obsolete by some other service or technology. Thus, for every month your launch is postponed, you lose one month's revenue from this fixed life cycle.

One often-cited McKinsey & Co. report reveals that a six-month launch delay reduces the new product's profitability by 33 percent over its life.[6] By contrast, being 50 percent over budget in development costs only has a negative impact of 3.5 percent on profitability. But these provocative figures may be overstated. As Crawford notes, the McKinsey data are taken out of context and are for an atypical and highly dynamic market environment (a high-tech industry sector with 20 percent annual growth rate, 12 percent annual price erosion and a short five-year product life).

3. *Speed means faster response and fewer surprises.* The rapid change and competitive conditions found in most markets give the fast-response company the edge. For example, in the car business, consider the advantage that fast-paced firms such as Chrysler and Toyota enjoy (less than three years to develop a new car for Chrysler) versus the traditional five or six years taken by GM or Mercedes-Benz. A lot changes in that market in six years!

Ways to Reduce Cycle Time

Much has been written on cycle-time reduction in product development. The trouble is, there is very little hard evidence on what works and what does not. A few studies have been done on the topic however, and we share their conclusions with you.

One of the problems is defining what is meant by "fast-paced." "When does the clock start ticking?" is one often-heard question. For example, a project may have moved at lightning speed once it was approved for development. Trouble is, it took two years to get to that approval point. So this apparently rapid project actually took forever if you count time from its inception.

A second issue is "fast compared to what"? Two projects may take the same time, but one is simple and the other is much more challenging and complex. The times are the same, but one is fast and the other is slow. In short, project complexity must be factored in when you speak about reducing cycle time. For example, Crawford discovered that one result of the emphasis on cycle-time reduction is a proliferation of small, unchallenging projects— quick market hits that have only a marginal impact on revenue and profits.[5]

One study lowered the microscope on 203 project teams and focused on those that were fast-paced.[4] Two measures of speed that were used are useful metrics for your own projects:

- *On-time performance:* Did the launch occur when it was promised in the business case, i.e., was there a gap between scheduled and actual launch date?
- *Time efficiency:* How long did the project take from development to launch, compared to the time it should have taken ("time it should have taken" was determined in a retrospective analysis of the project—what the time could have been).

Among the 203 projects studied, the fast-paced teams were able to improve cycle time in six ways (see Exhibit 6.3). Note that all are sensible ways to reduce cycle time. They are totally consistent with sound management practice and are also derived from the lessons for success outlined in previous chapters. In short, not only will these six methods increase the odds of winning, but they also reduce the time-to-market!

1. *The use of a truly cross-functional team*—how the project and team is organized—is the number one driver of fast-paced, on-time projects. A cross-functional team comprises players from the

Exhibit 6.3   Impact of Factors on Timeliness and Profitability

	Correlation of Factors			
Factor	*With Timeliness*		*With Profitability*	
Cross-functional Team	0.483	1	0.351	
Up-front Homework	0.408	2	0.366	
Market Orientation	0.406	3	0.440	2
Tech Proficiency	0.316		0.289	
Early Product Definition	0.242		0.413	3
Market Attractiveness	0.215		0.312	
Launch Quality	0.205		0.286	
Product Advantage	0.000		0.530	1

Correlation: a 0–1 measure; 1.0 means perfect 1:1 correlation.

Source: R. Cooper and E. Kleinschmidt, "What Drives Time-to-Market in Product Development." *Research-Technology Management,* 1995.

critical resource departments, is accountable for the project from beginning to end, is dedicated to this project (as opposed to spreading oneself across many tasks), and is led by a strong leader or champion with top management support. This is the strongest determinant of speed to market.

Organize around a cross-functional team with empowerment. "Rip apart a badly developed project and you will unfailingly find 75 percent of slippage attributable to: (1) 'siloing,' or sending memos up and down vertical organizational 'silos' or 'stovepipes' for decisions; and (2) sequential problem solving," according to Tom Peters.[9] Sadly, the typical project resembles a relay race, with each function or department carrying the baton for its portion of the race, and then handing off to the next runner or department (see 5, below).

2. *Up-front homework pays off.* Project teams that spend more time and more effort (proportionately) on the up-front homework and predevelopment tasks actually save time later. Doing this up-front homework and getting clear project definition, based on fact rather than hearsay and speculation, saves time downstream: less recycling to get the facts or redefine the project requirements, and sharper targets to work toward.

Recall what solid homework means: undertaking preliminary technical and market assessments early in the project; executing proficient market studies (user needs and wants studies, market analysis, competitive analysis, and concept tests); and building a business case, complete with financial and business analysis and a clear project definition, based strongly on facts.

3. *A strong market orientation*—building in the voice of the customer—is fundamental not only to new service success, but also to speed to market. Projects for which the marketing tasks are carried out in a quality fashion (indeed, carried out at all) are found to be more time-efficient and tend to stay on schedule. Some of these marketing tasks overlap with the homework in item 2 above, but there are more:

- Building the customer in throughout the development phase (constant iterations with the customer of various facets of the service as it takes shape)
- Rigorous customer tests of the final service (trials, beta tests, preference tests, all based on sound test methodology)
- Trial sell or test market prior to the full launch, where feasible
- A well-conceived, properly resourced market launch.

4. *Do it right the first time*. Project teams that emphasize doing all the project tasks well the first time around not only achieve better results, they also get there faster. Time and again we hear from project leaders statements such as these: "Taking the little extra time to do things well will save all kinds of time later in the projects"; and "The best way to save time is by not having to go back and do everything twice!" The results of project teams that do focus on quality of execution bear these statements out (see Exhibit 6.3). Quality of execution means handling the following in an exemplary fashion:

- marketing tasks (above)
- technical tasks, such as preliminary technical assessment, the actual service development, in-house tests (alpha tests), trial operations, and operations start up
- evaluation activities (e.g., business analysis or pre-launch analysis).

5. *Parallel processing speeds projects to market*. The relay-race approach to service development is antiquated and inappropriate today. Given the time pressures of projects coupled with the need for a complete and quality process, a more appropriate scheme is a rugby game, or parallel processing (discussed in Chapter 3). Recall that the play is a lot more complex with parallel processing than with a series approach, hence the need for a disciplined game plan, such as Stage-Gate.

6. *Prioritize and focus.* The best way to slow projects down is to dissipate your limited resources and people across too many projects. Concentrating resources on the truly deserving projects means that the work will be done not only better but faster. But focusing means tough choices: killing other and perhaps worthwhile projects.

The trouble is that many companies lack the will and the process to kill projects. In one firm, the comment was "We never kill projects . . . we just wound them." This was an admission that management did not have the fortitude to kill projects but merely continued to remove or transfer resources, a few at a time. Focus means killing projects and putting others on hold. That requires tough, disciplined decision making, a rigorous gating process, and the right criteria for making Go/Kill decisions.

There are other techniques that the fast-paced project teams employ:

7. *Outsourcing.* Many service companies find that suppliers and vendors are available to develop much of the service for them. Recall from Chapter 5 the benefits of outsourcing: faster, often more proficient, and frequently less expensive developments, especially if the product/service is an off-the-shelf one (e.g. software). But a word of caution: We have witnessed many outsourced projects where the results were not as promised. Vendors sometimes prove less capable than originally thought. Also, the off-the-shelf product must be integrated into your existing systems and operations, sometimes at great cost and time. The due diligence and appropriate vendor qualification must be done beforehand.

One major financial institution decided that a quick route to a new payroll service was to purchase software from a noted supplier. The cost of the off-the-shelf software was about $500,000, and another $300,000 was budgeted to "lash" the software into the bank's existing systems (customer billing system, management information system, etc.). The trouble was, the payroll service did not have all the functionality required for the bank. The poor up-front homework had led to an incomplete set of project requirements: The U.S.-based payroll software could not handle international payroll situations, and integrating the software into the bank's existing systems proved much more difficult than originally thought. In the end, the "final" service cost the bank over $2,000,000. Ironically, its own IT department could have developed the service faster and cheaper.

When using the services of a third party to develop services/ products, do not throw discipline out the window. Follow most of the steps in your Stage-Gate process, but rely on a modified version (see Exhibit 5.6).

8. *Alliances* are yet another way to save time. Often, a partner provides the skills, resources, and competencies required not only to make the project a success, but also to move it along much faster. Again, some words of warning: An alliance is like a marriage—some are made in heaven, others end in a nasty divorce. Again we recommend the due diligence of following a modified Stage-Gate process, in which partner screening and alliance-building activities are a routine part of the process. If you do not have an internal alliance process, consider putting one in place.

9. *Rapid prototyping* is a speed-to-market technique borrowed from manufacturing sectors. The notion here is that customers do not know what they are looking for until they see it. You can do extensive market research into customer needs, wants, and preferences, but until the customer actually experiences the service offering, you cannot be really sure about customer reaction to it. So let the customer experience the service as early as possible—even before it is developed. This means developing representations of the service, a "protocept," which may be a crude working model, a virtual service, or some facets of the service (e.g., sample computer screens)—and presenting these to prospective users for feedback. By getting creative here, it is possible to put something together that the customer will understand and can react to. This should be done as early as possible, perhaps even before the development stage begins in earnest.

10. *Flowcharting helps.* Here the team maps out its entire project from beginning to end, and focuses on reducing the time of each task in the process. Do a "brown paper exercise": Get a long roll of brown wrapping paper maybe three to nine yards long and tape it to a wall. Show a time scale along the bottom, usually in weeks. Assemble the project team, give them marking pens, and ask them to map out all the key project tasks from beginning to end. Now go back to this time line, lower the microscope on every activity, and ask, "How can we do this activity or task in half the time?" By doing this for every activity on the chart, the team is often able to dramatically reduce the time to market without cutting out key steps.

11. *Rely on a time line, and practice discipline.* Most project teams use computer software to plan their projects in a critical path, or Gantt chart, format. As in the preceding example, the team maps out the critical path. Once established, this time line becomes the team's internal objective: It ensures that tasks are completed and milestones reached by the agreed-on time. The team should meet weekly to review progress. The rules are simple: The time-line is sacred; practice discipline; resources can be added but deadlines never relaxed.

Do Not Become a Speed Freak

There is a dark side to accelerated service development. Remember: Speed is only an interim objective; the ultimate goal is profitability. While studies reveal that speed and profitability are connected, the relationship is anything but one-to-one.

The goal of reducing the development cycle time is admirable.[7] Over the last five years, most firms have reduced development cycle times by an average of about one third.[8] But keep in mind that speed is only one goal. The dominant goal, of course, is a steady stream of successful new services. The PDMA's best-practices study found that the best firms actually took a little longer to develop new products than the average performer—which might indicate that more challenging projects were undertaken. Further, many of the practices naively employed in order to reduce time-to-market ultimately cost the company money. They achieve the interim objective—bringing the product quickly to market—but fail at the ultimate objective, profitability. Two examples:

- Cutting short the early phases of a new service project—the up-front homework and the market studies—only to discover later that the new service design does not meet customer needs, and that the project itself is an ill-conceived one.
- Moving a service to market quickly by shortening the customer test phase, only to incur reliability problems after launch. This results in lost customer confidence and substantial post-launch servicing costs.

There are additional problems with a single-minded quest for cycle time reduction.[5] It leads companies to focus on the faster but mundane projects. They develop trivial services and line extensions, rather than genuine blockbuster products or major revenue generators. Further, excessive emphasis on speed is disruptive to the team concept: Unrealistic time lines are forced on the team, leading to frustrations, anxiety, and reduced team morale. These team problems ultimately result in a less effective team, greater people costs, and wasted resources.

Be careful in your quest for cycle-time reduction: Too often the methods used to reduce development time yield precisely the opposite effect, and in many cases are very costly. They can be at odds with sound management practice.

Topic #4. Metrics: How Well Are You Doing?

Is it too early to start thinking about new service metrics? Certainly not! We strongly subscribe to the view that "you cannot manage what you cannot measure," and "what gets measured gets done." Some firms have made the mistake of not implementing measurement of their new service process until too late.

At a Stage-Gate benchmarking session attended by leading firms, metrics and measures was a hot topic. Each company identified the metrics that it used to capture how well it was doing. The conclusions:

- First, there is no universal view on what should be measured. Each of these leading companies gauged a variety of things. However, there are certain metrics that the majority of businesses use (shown in Exhibits 6.4 and 6.5).
- Next, virtually every business began with a much longer list of metrics than it now uses. The message seems to be to err on the side of too many metrics at the beginning, and over time, you will decide which ones are the most useful to your management group.

The kinds of metrics various firms use fall into two broad categories, *post-process metrics* and *in-process metrics*.

Post-process Metrics. Post-process metrics are used to get answers to the question "How well are you doing at new service development?" They are "post-process" in the sense that they come into play only after the service is launched. These include both short-term metrics, those that are measurable immediately after launch (for example, "the proportion of new services launched on time"), as well as longer-term metrics, which might take several years after launch to determine—for example, "the proportion of launches that became commercial winners." Exhibit 6.4 lists some commonly used post-process metrics.

Data on these post-process metrics are gathered on individual projects but are most often reported as an aggregate: for example, percentage of sales achieved by new services launched in the last three years, or the average variance in on-time performance.

EXHIBIT 6.4   Post-process Metrics: How Well Are You Doing?

Short term (measured immediately)

Timeliness
- Cycle time (months) from Gate 3 to Launch (not too useful; must be a relative measure)
- On-time launch (actual versus scheduled launch date; difference in months)
- Actual time relative to fastest possible cycle time for that project

Development and Capital costs
- Staying within budget (variance)

Longer term (measured much later, say two years into launch, based on latest expected results)

Financial
- Profitability (NPV, IRR, payback period, break-even time)
- Sales (units, dollars, market share)
- Operation costs (actual vs. objectives)
  - –versus objectives set at Gates 3 and 5
  - –versus your company hurdles

Success rates:
- Percent of services launched that became commercial successes (must define "commercial success")
- Percent of Development projects that became commercial successes
- Attrition curves (number of projects surviving at each gate in the process)

Percentage of your sales coming from new services
- Must define "new service"
- Also must define time horizon: e.g., launched in last 3 years

---

These are very important metrics. The trouble is, if these are the only metrics you employ, you might be waiting three or four years to find out how well you are doing—and that is too long to wait in order to take corrective action. So most companies use in-process metrics too.

In-Process Metrics.   These types of metrics answer the question "Is our process working . . . really?" These in-process metrics can be measured almost immediately, and capture how well new service projects are unfolding. For example, they can help determine

EXHIBIT 6.5   In-process Metrics

Some in-process metrics are subjective

Quality of gate meetings (and deliverables)
- Rating cards filled out at gate meetings

Degree of deviation from Process rules
- Degree of change in project specs after Gate 3
- Number of system change requests (after the "design freeze" in the process)
- Number of gate meetings canceled due to no-shows by gatekeepers

Proportion of projects that are "really in" the process
- A judgment call by the process manager

Some in-process metrics are objective

Timeliness of projects reaching gates
- Percent of projects at each gate that are on time
- Mean variance—actual arrival at gates versus scheduled time (gap in months or percent of scheduled time)

On-budget performance
- Percent of projects that are on budget in each stage
- Mean variance in budgets by stage (as a percent of total project budget)

---

whether projects are on time at gates and whether deliverables to gates are in good shape. Obviously, achieving high scores on these metrics is not the ultimate goal, but results are immediate. Think of these as intermediate metrics and early warning signals about ultimate results. Exhibit 6.5 lists some good examples of in-process metrics.

One company uses its "red-green" chart as a visual metric to spot projects in trouble, or gates and stages in trouble (Exhibit 6.6). Here the various gates in their Stage-Gate process are shown across the top of the grid, while the projects are listed down the side. Inside each box is the expected date for the gate meeting. The actual date is also shown. When a project is "on time," color the box green; when it is late, color the box red.

In the grid in Exhibit 6.6, the shaded boxes represent missed gate review dates. As you read across the rows, you can spot

EXHIBIT 6.6   "Red-Green" Monitoring Chart

	Gate 2	Gate 3	Gate 4	Gate 5	Post-launch Review
Project A	Aug 1/97 Sep 1/97	Dec 1/97 Feb 1/98	Sep 1/98 Sep 1/98	Dec 1/98	—
Project B	Jul 1/97 Sep 1/97	Aug 1/97 Nov 1/97	Dec 1/97 Feb 1/98	Mar 1/98 Jun 1/98	Jun 1/99
Project C	Feb 1/97 Apr 1/97	Jun 1/97 Aug 1/97	Dec 1/98 Feb 1/98	Jun 1/98 Jul 1/98	Jul 1/99
Project D	Jun 1/97 Jun 1/97	Jul 1/97 Nov 1/97	Feb 1/98 Mar 1/98	Jul 1/98 Aug 1/98	Aug 1/99
Project E	Sep 1/97 Sep 1/97	Nov 1/97 Dec 1/97	Aug 1/98 Sep 1/98	Dec 1/98	—
Project F	Nov 1/97 Dec 1/97	Mar 1/98 May 1/98	Dec 1/98	—	—

◼ Late to the gate by more than 1 month (red)   ◻ On time at gate (green)

projects that are clearly in trouble. Projects B and C are clearly off course. Stage 2, the Detailed Investigation stage, which precedes Gate 3, appears to be the most problematic stage in the process.

Red Flags

How does management spot projects that are off course? The prospect of a monthly review of all projects, complete with presentations by project teams, certainly is not very inviting. At the same time, one wants to avoid the situation where a well-intentioned, self-managed project team careens down a path paying little heed to all the danger signals that their project is heading for trouble.

The dilemma faced by many organizations is the desire to maintain flexibility, freedom, and creativity while at the same time avoiding the situation whereby projects take on lives of their own and become out of control, "loose cannon" projects. Red flags are the flexible control system that some companies have employed. The method is very simple, but it works. These companies have developed a list of red flags that signal problems. For example, if the project is significantly behind schedule, or if the business and financial projections change by more than X percent, a red flag is raised. Exhibit 6.7 provides a list of red flags used by a company in the telecommunications and software business.

Whenever a red flag is raised, the project leader is required to call for an immediate project review. This review might be in the form of an immediate gate review, or perhaps a more informal

---

EXHIBIT 6.7   Red Flags

New service projects sometimes encounter problems. Often, original estimates are revised, which renders the project less attractive. One company has developed a list of danger signals, called "red flags," so that gatekeepers can be kept apprised of potential problems. When any one of the following occurs, the project leader must inform the gatekeepers at the next monthly project review or gate meeting:

1. *Project schedule:* If the project falls behind the agreed-to time line by more than 30 days.
2. *Project budget:* If the project development budget goes over budget by more than 5 percent at this point (versus milestone projections), as defined in the plan approved at the previous gate.
3. *Resources:* If any major functional area is unable to meet ongoing resource commitments according to the time line agreed to.
4. *Project cost:* If any change in the expected project cost occurs which is greater than 5 percent above cost estimates provided at Gate 3.
5. *Sales forecast:* If any change greater than 10 percent occurs in the forecast sale, or if any change occurs in the configuration ratios (product mix) which impacts margin by more than 3 percent.
6. *Business case:* If any change occurs that impacts significantly on the business case and financial outlook for the project (more than 5 percent impact).
7. *New service/product specs:* If the new device design or requirements are revised in a way that impacts negatively on meeting a customer need.
8. *Service:* If a change in the service and support planned for the new service occurs in a way that impacts negatively on a customer need or requirement.
9. *Quality:* If quality metrics fall outside 0.3 sigma value.

review with the functional head, depending on the seriousness of the red flag.

Winning at New Services

There are two ways to win at new services. The first is by doing projects right. That is what the last three chapters have been about: how to improve the effectiveness of the way you conceive, develop, and launch new services. The Stage-Gate process, outlined in Chapters 4 and 5, promises significant improvements in success rates, profitability, and time-to-market, provided you implement it properly. The additional features we introduced in this chapter—e-commerce, third-generation approaches, cycle-time reduction methods, and metrics—complement your Stage-Gate process and make it work even better.

The second way to win at new services is by doing the right projects. In the next chapter, we shift gears from *doing projects right* to *doing the right projects*—project selection and portfolio management.

7

Portfolio Management: More Than Just Project Selection

A vital question in new service development is how the corporation should most effectively invest its technology resources.[1] That is where portfolio management comes in: It helps you allocate resources to achieve your business's new service objectives. Portfolio management is more than simply project selection. It examines the entire mix of projects and related investments. Note that project selection deals with the "fingers" (Go/Kill decisions on individual projects), whereas portfolio management deals with the fist (the entire set of project investments). Most of this book has focused on the fingers: developing a good process to manage the development of individual projects. This chapter introduces the concept of the fist: portfolio management and how it interacts with a well-designed Stage-Gate process.

Much like a stock-market portfolio manager, the senior manager who succeeds at optimizing investments by selecting the winning projects, achieving the ideal balance of projects, and building a portfolio that supports the business's strategy will win in the long run.

Portfolio Management Defined

Portfolio management is about resource allocation: Which of the many potential projects should the corporation fund with

179

technology, capital, and all other types of resources, including people. Which projects should receive top priority and be accelerated to market? Portfolio management is also about business strategy. Today's portfolio of new services decides tomorrow's service/market profile of the business. It is also about balance: What is the optimal investment mix of risk versus return, maintenance versus growth, and short-term versus long-term new service projects?

Portfolio management is defined as follows:[2]

> Portfolio management is a dynamic decision-making process whereby the list of active projects is constantly updated and revised. New projects are prioritized; existing projects may be accelerated, killed, or de-prioritized; and resources are allocated and reallocated to active projects. The portfolio decision-making process is characterized by uncertain and changing information, dynamic opportunities, multiple goals and strategic considerations, interdependence among projects, and multiple decision makers and locations. The portfolio decision-making process encompasses or overlaps with a number of other decision-making processes within the business, including periodic reviews of the total portfolio of all projects, Go/Kill gating decisions on individual projects on an ongoing basis, and the crafting of new service development strategy for the business, complete with strategic resource allocation decisions.

At first glance, portfolio management may seem like a mechanistic exercise of decision making and resource allocation (budgeting). But there are many unique facets of the problem that make it perhaps the most challenging of the decision-making tasks faced by the modern businessperson:

- Portfolio management deals with future events and opportunities. Thus, much of the information required to make project selection decisions is at best uncertain and at worst very unreliable.

- The decision environment is dynamic. The status and prospects for projects in the portfolio are constantly changing as new information becomes available.
- Projects in the portfolio are at different stages of completion, yet all projects compete against each other for the same resources. Comparisons must be made among projects, even though the quality of information may vary widely from project to project.
- Resources to be allocated across projects are limited. A decision to fund one project may mean that resources are taken away from another. Further, resource transfers between projects are not totally seamless.

Why Portfolio Management Is So Important

Portfolio management is a critical senior management challenge, according to our recent best-practices studies of project selection and portfolio management.[1] Note how important the topic is rated by senior company executives as well as by technology managers (see box, page 183). Also note that better-performing businesses tend to rate the importance of portfolio management much higher than poorer performers (see Exhibit 7.1).

Portfolio management is important to your business for three main reasons:

1. A successful new service development effort is fundamental to business success as you move into the next century. More than ever, senior management recognizes the need for new services, especially the right new services. This logically translates into portfolio management: the ability to select projects today that will become winners tomorrow.

2. New service development is the manifestation of your business's strategy. One of the most important ways you operationalize strategy is through the new services you develop. If your new service initiatives are wrong—either the

EXHIBIT 7.1   Importance of Portfolio Management

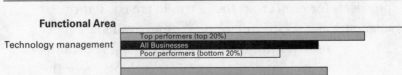

All differences between top and poor performers are significant at the 0.001 level.

Rank-ordered according to mean scores (highest scores at top of exhibit).

Source: R. Cooper, S. Edgett, and E. Klienschmidt, "Best Practices for Managing R&D Portfolios," *Research-Technology Management* 41, 4 (1998): 20–330.

wrong projects or the wrong balance—then you fail at implementing your business strategy.

3. Portfolio management is about resource allocation. In a business world preoccupied with value to the shareholder and doing more with less, resources are simply too scarce to allocate to the wrong projects. The consequences of poor portfolio management are evident: You squander scarce resources on the wrong projects and as a result starve the truly deserving ones.

Top performers emphasize the link between project selection and business strategy. They downplay the need to be careful and avoid failures as a reason for the importance of portfolio management.

Three Goals in Portfolio Management

There are three principle ways to steer the portfolio process, and the goal you choose to emphasize will influence your choice

Eight Key Reasons Why Portfolio Management Is a Vital Management Task[1,4]

1. Financial: To maximize return, to maximize technology productivity, to achieve financial goals.
2. Competitive: To maintain the competitive position of the business, to increase sales and market share.
3. Resources: To properly and efficiently allocate (budget) scarce resources.
4. Strategic: To forge the link between project selection and business strategy. The portfolio is the expression of strategy; it must support the strategy.
5. Focus: To keep from doing too many projects for the limited resources available, and to adequately resource the great projects.
6. Balance: To achieve the right balance between long- and short-term, high-risk and low-risk projects consistent with the business's goals.
7. Communication: To better communicate priorities within the organization, both vertically and horizontally.
8. Objectivity: To provide better objectivity in project selection so that bad projects are weeded out and good ones are nurtured.

of portfolio-management methods (to be discussed in detail below):

1. *Value maximization.* The goal is to allocate resources to maximize the value of your portfolio in terms of a business objective (such as long-term profitability, return on investment, likelihood of success, or some other strategic objective).

2. *Balance.* The principal concern is to develop a balanced portfolio in terms of a number of parameters, for example, long- and short-term projects, or high- and low-risk ones. Or you might seek balance across various markets, technologies, and project types or between resources and number of projects.*

---

*Although the focus here is on portfolio management for new services, to the extent that technology resources used in new services are also required for other types of projects, portfolio managers must consider the fact that new service projects compete against infrastructure developments, maintenance projects, and even platform projects for both people and money.

3. *Strategic direction.* The main goal is to ensure that, regardless of all other considerations, the final portfolio of projects truly reflects the business strategy. The breakdown of spending across projects, areas, markets, etc., must be directly tied to the business strategy, and all projects must be "on strategy."

What becomes clear is the potential for conflict between these three high-level goals. For example, the portfolio that yields the greatest NPV or IRR may not be a very balanced one: It may contain a majority of short-term, low-risk projects, or it might be overly focused on one market. Similarly, a portfolio that is primarily strategic in nature may sacrifice other goals, such as expected short-term profitability. Even though you may not explicitly state that one goal takes precedence over the other two, the nature of the portfolio management tool that you elect to use will indicate a hierarchy of goals. This is because certain portfolio approaches are much more applicable to some goals than others. For example, visual models such as portfolio bubble diagrams are most suitable for achieving a balance of projects; scoring models, on the other hand, may be poor for achieving or even showing balance, but most effective if the goal is maximization measured against an objective. Thus, the choice of portfolio approach depends on which goal your business has explicitly or implicitly highlighted.

Points for Management to Ponder

Take a moment and reflect on how your organization handles portfolio management. Do you have in place a method to ensure that you are achieving the three main goals in portfolio management? Have you been able to overcome the potential for conflict among these three goals?

Remember, the three goals are the following:

1. To maximize the value of the portfolio
2. To achieve the right balance of projects
3. To ensure that projects are "on strategy" and that spending breakdowns mirror the business's strategy

---

Which methods do companies find most effective to achieve the three portfolio goals? The next sections outline the methods and discuss their strengths and weaknesses.

Goal 1: Maximizing the Value of the Portfolio

A variety of methods can be used to achieve this goal, ranging from financial models to scoring models. Each has its strengths and weaknesses. The end result of the chosen method is a rank ordered list of "Go" and "Hold" projects, with the projects at the top of the list scoring highest in terms of achieving the desired objectives (the value in terms of that objective is thus maximized).

Expected Commercial Value. This method is used by those who seek to maximize the commercial value of their portfolio, subject to certain budget constraints. The Expected Commercial Value (ECV) is one approach to determine the value of each project to the corporation. ECV uses basic decision-tree analysis to create a single value for each project, considering the future stream of earnings from the project, the probabilities of commercial and technical success, and commercialization and development costs. This single value can be used to compare different projects against each other. Let's look at an example of how ECV could be applied.

First, the ECV is calculated for each project. This is a financial calculation that considers the present value (PV) of future earnings of a project, along with the probabilities of technical and commercial success. Exhibit 7.2A shows Company X's ECV decision tree and its formula (note: a two-step decision process is assumed). In order to arrive at a prioritized list of projects, Company X considers the constraint of scarce resources. In this case, systems resources are thought to be the constraint because many of Company X's projects are systems-intensive. (Other companies may choose as the constraining resource technology people, calculated in work-months, or technology funds.) Company X takes the ratio

EXHIBIT 7.2A   Determination of Expected Commercial Value of Project

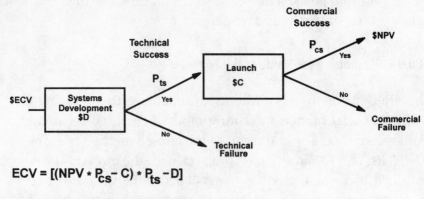

$$ECV = [(NPV * P_{cs} - C) * P_{ts} - D]$$

ECV = Expected commercial value of the project
P_{ts} = Probability of technical success
P_{cs} = Probability of commercial success (given technical success)
D = System development costs remaining in the project
C = Commercialization (launch) costs
NPV = Net present value of project's future earnings (discounted to today)

of what it is trying to maximize—namely the ECV—divided by the constraining resource, namely the systems cost per project (see Exhibit 7.2B). Projects are rank-ordered according to this ECV-to-Systems Dollars ratio until the total systems budget limits are reached. Projects at the top of the list are considered a Go, while those at the bottom (beyond the total available resource limits) are placed on hold. This method ensures the greatest bang for the buck: The ECV is maximized for a given systems budget.*

This ECV model has a number of attractive features: It recognizes that the Go/Kill decision process is an incremental one (the notion of purchasing options on a project); all monetary amounts are discounted to today, not just to launch date, thereby appropriately penalizing projects that are years away from launch; and it

*This decision rule of rank order according to the ratio of what one is trying to maximize divided by the constraining resource seems to be an effective one. Simulations with a number of random sets of projects show that this decision rule works very well, truly giving "maximum bang for the buck"!

EXHIBIT 7.2B   Rank-ordered List of Ratios of ECV/to System Development Cost

Project Name	ECV	Systems Development Cost (Dev)	ECV/Dev	Sum of Dcv
Beta	19.5	5	3.9	5
Echo	15.7	5	3.14	10
Alpha	5	3 limit	1.67	13
Foxtrot	15.5	10	1.55	–23
Delta	1.5	1	1.5	14
Gamma	2.1	2	1.05	15

Criterion: Ratio of what you are trying to maximize divided by constraining resource (yields maximum "bang for buck").

Total System Development budget of $15 million

deals with the issue of constrained resources by attempting to maximize the value of the portfolio in light of this constraint.

The major weakness of the method is the dependency on financial and other quantitative data. Accurate estimates must be available on future streams of earnings for all projects: for their commercialization (and systems) expenditures and other development costs, and for probabilities of success. But these estimates are often unreliable or simply not available early in the life of a project. One seasoned executive took great exception to multiplying two very uncertain probability figures together, noting, "This will always unfairly punish the more venturesome projects!" A second weakness is that the method does not look at the balance of the portfolio, whether it has the right balance between high- and low-risk projects, or across markets and technologies. A third weakness is that the method considers only a single criterion—the ECV—for ranking projects.

Productivity Index. The productivity index (PI) is similar to the ECV method described above and shares many of ECV's strengths and weaknesses. The PI tries to maximize the financial value of the portfolio for a given resource constraint. British Nuclear Fuels, for example, uses this approach.

The productivity index is calculated by means of this formula:[5]

$$PI = ECV \times P_{ts} / R\&D$$

Here, the definition of expected commercial value is different than that used by Company X above. In the productivity index, the ECV is a probability-adjusted NPV (net present value). More specifically, it is the probability-weighted stream of cash flows from the project, discounted to the present, assuming technical success, less remaining development costs.* P_{ts} is the probability of technical success, while R&D is the development expenditure remaining to be spent on the project (note that development funds already spent on the project are sunk costs and hence are not relevant to the prioritization decision). Projects are rank-ordered according to this productivity index in order to arrive at the preferred portfolio, with projects at the bottom of the list placed on hold.

Dynamic Rank-ordered List. This next method overcomes the limitation of relying on a single criterion—such as ECV or PI—to rank projects. It can rank-order according to several criteria concurrently, without becoming as complex and as time-consuming as the use of a full-fledged, multiple-criteria scoring model. These criteria can include profitability and return measures, strategic importance, ease and speed of execution, and other desirable characteristics of a high-priority project. The four criteria used by Company G in the telecommunications sector are the following:

1. *Strategic importance* of the project, namely, how important and how aligned the project is with the business strategy.

---

*There are various ways to adjust for risks or probabilities: via a risk-adjusted discount rate used to determine the NPV; or via applying probabilities to uncertain estimates in calculating the NPV; or via Monte Carlo simulation to determine NPV.

This is gauged on a scale of 1 to 5, where 5 = critically
  important.
2. *NPV (net present value)* of the future earnings of the project,
   less all expenditures remaining to be spent on the project.
   Here the NPV has built in the probabilities of commercial
   success by multiplying sales revenues, margins, etc. by
   probabilities to account for uncertainties.
3. *IRR (internal rate of return)* is calculated using the same data
   as the NPV, but gives the expected return as a percent.
4. *Probability of technical success,* as a percent. Some projects
   in Company G are very speculative technically, so technical success probabilities are often less than 100 percent.

How are projects prioritized or ranked on four criteria simultaneously? Simple. First, the IRR and NPV are multiplied by the
probability of technical success to yield an adjusted IRR and NPV
(Exhibit 7.3). Next, projects are ranked independently on each criterion: adjusted IRR, adjusted NPV, and strategic importance (see
numbers in parentheses). The final, overall ranking—the far right
column—is determined by calculating the average of the three
rankings. Project Alpha is at the top of the list. It scored first on
strategic importance and second on both IRR and NPV. The average of these three rankings is 1.67. Simple perhaps, but consider
the list of projects in Exhibit 7.3, and try to arrive at a better ranking yourself—one that maximizes all three criteria!

The major strength of this dynamic list is its simplicity: Rank-
order your projects on several criteria and take the average of the
rankings. Another strength is that the model can handle several
criteria concurrently without becoming overly complex. The
model's major weakness is that it does not consider constrained
resources (as did the ECV or PI methods above, although conceiv-
ably Company G could build this into its rank-ordering model). In
addition, like the ECV and PI models, it is largely based on uncertain, often unreliable financial data. Finally, the dynamic list fails
to consider the balance of projects.

EXHIBIT 7.3 Company G's Dynamic Rank-ordered List

Project Name	IRR*PTS	NPV*PTS	Strategic Importance	Ranking Score
Alpha	16.0 (2)	8.0 (2)	5 (1)	1.67 (1)
Epsilon	10.8 (4)	18.0 (1)	4 (2)	2.33 (2)
Delta	11.1 (3)	7.8 (3)	2 (4)	3.33 (3)
Omega	18.7 (1)	5.1 (4)	1 (6)	3.67 (4)
Gamma	9.0 (6)	4.5 (5)	3 (3)	4.67 (5)
Beta	10.5 (5)	1.4 (6)	2 (4)	5.00 (6)

Both IRR and NPV are multiplied by probability of technical success (PTS).

Projects are ranked by IRR (return %), NPV, Strategic Importance, Numbers in parentheses show the ranking in each column.

Ranking Score is the mean across the three rankings. This is the score that the six projects are finally ranked on. Projects are rank-ordered until no more resources are available.

Scoring Models as Portfolio Tools. Scoring models have long been used for making Go/Kill decisions at gates. (See Chapter 5 for more information on scoring models.) But they also have applicability for project prioritization and portfolio management. (Telenor uses a scoring model as an early screen to get projects into the portfolio.) Projects are scored at gate meetings, and the total project scores become the basis for developing a rank-ordered list of projects.

> One division at Sprint uses a very straight-forward approach to scoring and ranking projects. Projects are evaluated on the basis of three main criteria in a scoring model: strategic fit, NPV, and technical capability (skills available and new technology).

Scoring models generally are praised in spite of their limited popularity. Research into project selection methods reveals that scoring models produce a strategically aligned portfolio that reflects the business spending priorities. These models also yield effective and efficient decisions and result in portfolios of high-value projects.[6] But there are some pitfalls as well when using scoring models as a tool to prioritize projects:

- *Imaginary precision:* Using a scoring model may imply a degree of precision that simply does not exist.
- *Halo effect:* A high score on one criterion tends to mean the project scores high on many of the rest. This was a concern of managers at the Royal Bank of Canada, which over the years has reduced its list of multiple criteria in their scoring model to five key criteria.
- *Inefficient allocation of scarce resources:* A missing ingredient in scoring models is that they do not always result in a list of Go projects that achieves the highest possible scores for a given total expenditure. For example, a feature of one firm's scoring model was that much larger projects tended to rise to the top of the list. If the ranking criterion had been "project score/project cost" instead of just "project score," then some smaller but efficient projects—ones that required much fewer resources—would have risen to the top.

Goal 2: A Balanced Portfolio

The second major goal sought by some businesses is a balanced portfolio of development projects in terms of a number of key parameters. The analogy is that of an investment fund, where the fund manager seeks to balance high-risk and blue chip stocks and across industries to arrive at an optimum investment portfolio.

Visual charts are favored to display balance in portfolios. Such representations include portfolio maps, also called bubble diagrams (Exhibit 7.4), and more traditional pie charts and histograms.

Portfolio Maps: Bubble Diagrams. A casual review of portfolio bubble diagrams will lead some to observe, "These new models

Points for Management to Ponder

The value maximization methods outlined above have much to commend them. Specific weaknesses—obtaining data, reliability of data, overreliance on financial criteria, dealing with multiple objectives, imaginary precision, and halo effects—have been outlined. As a group, their greatest weakness is that they fail to ensure that the portfolio is strategically aligned and optimally balanced. For example, the portfolio of projects generated via any of the methods above might maximize profits or some project score, but yield an unbalanced list of projects (for example, too many short-term ones) or fail to mirror the strategic direction of the business. These goals—balance and strategic alignment—are highlighted below.

In spite of these weaknesses, maximization of the portfolio's value is still a very worthwhile objective. You can argue about balance and philosophize about the strategic direction of your portfolio, but if the projects in the portfolio are poor ones—poor profitability, low likelihoods of success, or poor attractiveness scores—the portfolio exercise is simply academic. First and foremost, the portfolio must contain "good" projects, and the maximization methods outlined above excel in prioritizing these projects. One cannot ignore these methods; they must be part of any repertoire of portfolio management methods.

are nothing more than the old strategy bubble diagrams of the seventies!" Not so. Recall that the BCG strategy model, and others like it, such as the McKinsey/GE model, plotted business units on a market attractiveness versus business position grid.[7] Note that the unit of analysis was the SBU, an existing business, whose performance, strengths, and weaknesses were all known. By contrast, today's portfolio bubble diagrams plot projects, or future businesses—*what might be.* As for the grid's parameters—the "market attractiveness" versus "business position" axes used for existing SBUs—may not be as appropriate for new service possibilities, so other axes are extensively used.

What parameters to consider. What are some of the parameters that your business should plot on these bubble diagrams in order

EXHIBIT 7.4   Risk-Reward Bubble Diagram for Company B

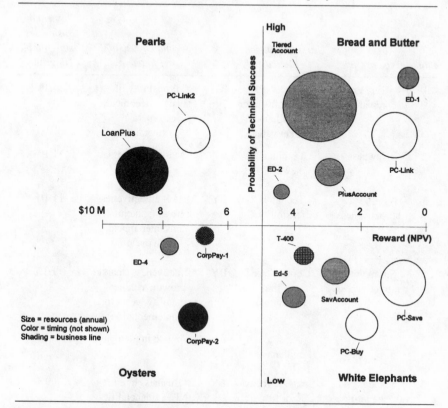

Source: Adapted from SDG model.

to seek balance? Different pundits recommend various parameters and lists, and even suggest the "best plots" to use. Exhibit 7.5 provides a list of the most popular bubble diagram parameters from our study of portfolio practices.[8]

No two companies agreed on the best plots for senior management meetings. So in the following section, we will share with you some examples from leading companies, and leave it to you to decide which might be best for you. Later in the chapter, we will present some recommendations.

Risk-reward bubble diagrams. The most popular bubble diagram is a variant of the risk-return chart (see Exhibit 7.4). Here one axis is

Exhibit 7.5   Popular Bubble Diagram Plots (Rank-ordered by Popularity)

Rank	Type of Chart	First Dimension Plotted		Second Dimension Plotted	Percent of Businesses Using Bubble Diagrams
1	Risk vs. reward	Reward: NPV, IRR, benefits after years of launch, market value	BY	Probability of success (technical, commercial, overall)	44.4%
2	Newness	Technical newness	BY	Market newness	11.1%
3	Ease vs. attractiveness	Technical feasibility	BY	Market attractiveness (growth, potential, consumer appeal, life cycle)	11.1%
4	Strength vs. attractiveness	Competitive position (strengths)	BY	Attractiveness (market growth, technical maturity, years to implementation)	11.1%
5	Cost vs. timing	Cost to implement	BY	Time to implement	9.7%
6	Strategic vs. benefit	Strategic focus or fit	BY	Business intent, NPV, financial fit, attractiveness	8.9%
7	Cost vs. benefit	Cumulative reward	BY	Cumulative development costs	5.5%

some measure of the reward to the company, the other is a success probability.

One approach is to use a qualitative estimate of reward, ranging from "modest" to "excellent."[9] The argument here is that too heavy an emphasis on financial analysis can do serious damage, notably in the early stages of a project. The other axis is the probability of overall success (probability of commercial success times probability of technical success).

In contrast, other firms rely on quantitative and financial gauges of reward, namely the probability-adjusted NPV of the project.[10] Here the probability of technical success is the vertical axis, as probability of commercial success has already been built into the NPV calculation.

A sample bubble diagram for Company B is shown in Exhibit 7.4, in which the size of each bubble shows the annual resources spent on each project (in Company B's case, this is dollars per year; it could also be people or work-months allocated to the project). The four quadrants of the portfolio model are the following:

Pearls: These are the potential star products—projects with a high likelihood of success which are also expected to yield a very high reward. Most businesses desire more of these. Company B has two Pearls, and one of them has been allocated considerable resources (denoted by the sizes of the circles).

Oysters: These are the long-shot project—projects with a high expected payoff but with low likelihoods of technical success. They are the projects where technical breakthroughs will pave the way for solid payoffs. Company B has three of these; none is receiving many resources.

Bread and Butter: These are small, simple projects that have a high likelihood of success but bring a small reward. They include the many fixes, extensions, modifications, and updating projects of which most companies have too many. Company B has a typical overabundance of these projects (note that the large circle here is actually a cluster of related renewal projects). More than 50 percent of spending goes to these Bread and Butter projects in Company B's case.

White Elephants: These are the low-probability and low-reward projects, and inevitably they are difficult to kill. Every business has a few of these, but Company B has far too many. One third of the projects and about 25 percent of Company B's spending falls in the White Elephant quadrant.

Given that Company B is a star business seeking rapid growth, a quick review of the portfolio map in Exhibit 7.4 reveals many problems. There are too many White Elephant projects (it is time to do some serious pruning), too much money is spent on Bread and Butter projects, not enough Pearls are being funded, and Oysters are underresourced.

One feature of this bubble diagram is that it forces senior management to deal with the resource issue. Given finite resources (a limited number of people or money), the sum of the areas of the circles must be a constant. That is, if you add one project to the diagram, you must subtract another; alternatively you can shrink the size of several circles. The elegance here is that the model forces management to consider the resource implications of adding one more project to the list—that some other projects must pay the price.

Also shown in this bubble diagram, by means of shading, is the business line that each project is associated with. Company B also uses color to indicate timing (not shown in our black-and-white map). Red means "imminent launch" and blue means "an early-stage project." Thus, this apparently simple risk-reward diagram shows a lot more than simply risk and profitability data. It also conveys resource allocation, timing, and spending breakdowns across business lines.

Variants of Risk-Reward Bubble Diagrams: Dealing With Uncertainties.   There are many styles of risk-reward bubble diagrams. We present the following approaches to illustrate how several leading companies have come up with innovative approaches to measuring and displaying risk-reward. Although these companies are not from the service industry, the diagrams could easily be used in any industry.

3M's ellipses. One problem with the bubble diagram employed by Company B is that it requires a point estimate of both the reward (namely the probable NPV) as well as the probability of success. Some businesses at 3M use a variant of the bubble diagram to effectively portray uncertain estimates.[11] In calculating the NPV, optimistic and pessimistic estimates are made for uncertain variables, leading to a range of NPV values for each project. Similarly, low, high, and likely estimates are made for probability of technical success. The result is illustrated in Exhibit 7.6, where the sizes and shapes of the bubbles reveal the uncertainty of projects: here, very small bubbles mean highly certain estimates on each dimension, whereas large ellipses mean considerable uncertainty (a high spread between worst case and best case) for that project.

Monte Carlo simulation. A Monte Carlo simulation is one where thousands of scenarios are computer-generated (hence the name Monte Carlo, a reference to thousands of spins of the wheel). Procter & Gamble uses a Monte Carlo simulation to handle probabilities. P&G's portfolio model is three-dimensional, created by CAD

EXHIBIT 7.6   3M's Risk-Reward Bubble Diagram Showing Uncertainties

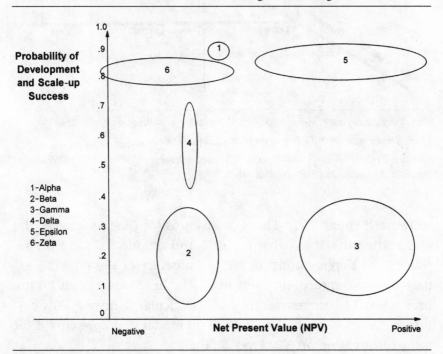

Larger circles and ellipses denote more uncertain estimates.

Source: Adapted from "New Product Investment Portfolio" by Dr. Gary L. Tritle, and other internal 3M documents. Used with permission.

EXHIBIT 7.7   Procter & Gamble's Three-Dimensional Risk-Reward Bubble
Diagram

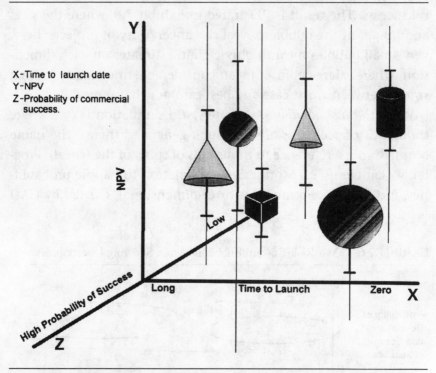

Shapes denote degree of technological fit with company (spheres are high; cubes low).

I-bars denote range of NPV (based on Monte Carlo simulation).

Source: Developed by Tom Chorman, finance manager, Corporate New Ventures, Procter & Gamble. Used with permission.

software (Exhibit 7.7).* The X axis stands for time to launch (the longer the time, the higher the risk, and the more distant the reward). The Y axis stands for NPV, a measure of the project's expected reward (probability-adjusted). The line Z axis stands for the probability of commercial success, as calculated from P&G's customized version of the NewProd 2000 model (see Appendix B for more information on NewProd 2000).

---

*This unique 3-dimensional portfolio diagram is still (at the time of writing this book) experimental at P&G, and is being developed by Corporate New Ventures.

In order to account for commercial uncertainty, every variable—revenues, costs, launch timing, and so on—requires three estimates: high, low, and likely. From these three estimates, a probability distribution curve is calculated for each variable. Next, random scenarios are generated for the project using these probability curves as variable inputs, and the result is a distribution of financial outcomes. From this, the expected NPV and its range are determined. The final NPV figure has all commercial outcomes and their probabilities figured in. P&G shows this range of NPVs as an I-beam drawn vertically through the geometric symbols (see Exhibit 7.7).

Traditional Charts for Portfolio Management.   There are numerous variables across which one might wish to seek a balance of projects, and there is also an endless variety of histograms and pie charts that help to portray portfolio balance. Some examples:

Timing. Timing is a key issue in the quest for balance. One does not wish to invest strictly in short-term projects, nor totally in long-term ones. Another timing goal is for a steady stream of new service launches spread out over the years: constant "new news" and no sudden logjam of service launches all in one year. The histogram in Exhibit 7.8 captures the issue of timing and shows the distribution of resources to one company's different projects according to year of launch. For example, 35 percent of funds are allocated to four projects all due to be launched in year 1. Another 30 percent of resources are being spent on four projects whose projected launch date is the following year, and so on.

Cash flow. Cash flow is another aspect of timing. The desire is to balance one's projects in such a way that cash inflows are reasonably balanced with cash outflows. Thus a chart is designed that produces a timing histogram portraying the total cash flow per year from all projects in the portfolio over the next few years.

Project types. Project type is yet another vital concern. How much do you spend on different types of projects: genuine new

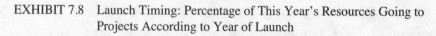

EXHIBIT 7.8   Launch Timing: Percentage of This Year's Resources Going to
               Projects According to Year of Launch

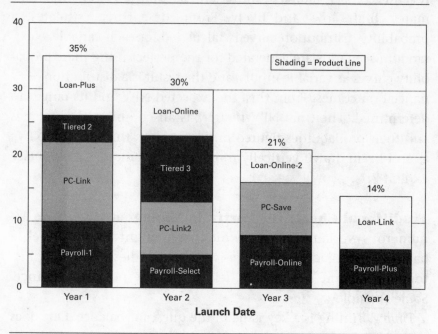

service initiatives, renewals (improvements and replacements), platforms, extensions, maintenance, cost reductions, and process improvements? And what should it be? Pie charts effectively capture the spending split across project types. Exhibit 7.9 shows actual versus desired splits.

Markets, business lines, and technologies. These provide another set of dimensions across which managers seek balance. The question is, do you have the appropriate split in spending across your various business lines? Or across the markets or market segments in which you operate? Or across the technologies you possess? Again, pie charts are good at capturing and displaying this type of data.

There is much to be said for achieving the right balance of projects in the portfolio. In other words, there is more to life than simply achieving a high-value portfolio. Balance is also an issue. The trouble is that achieving balance—or selecting an appropriate

EXHIBIT 7.9   Breakdown of Resources Spent by Business Line, Market
Segment, and Project Type

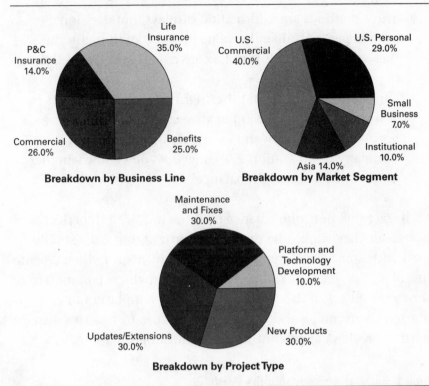

Breakdown by Business Line   **Breakdown by Market Segment**

Breakdown by Project Type

tool to help achieve balance—is easier to conceptualize than to
put into practice. In spite of the many intricate and ingenious
methods and diagrams, there remain problems with the quest for
balance:

- Some of the more popular bubble diagrams have the same
  weakness as the maximization models previously outlined:
  They rely on substantial financial data, when this financial
  data is often either unavailable or highly uncertain.
- Information overload can overwhelm. "Maps, endless
  maps!" was the complaint of one exasperated executive as
  she leafed through more than a dozen maps plotting

everything versus everything in her business portfolio method.

- These methods are information displays, not decision models per se. Unlike the value maximization methods, these methods' result is not a convenient rank-ordered list of preferred projects.

- Often it is not clear what the "right balance" of projects is. You can stare all you want at various charts, but unless a portfolio is obviously and extremely out of balance (like Company B's in Exhibit 7.4), how does one know whether or not one has the right balance?

The fact that portfolio balance methods are far from perfect does not mean they should be dismissed outright, but they should be used with some forethought: The choice of maps (which axes to use in the plots, for example) and charts (which parameters to show) must be well thought out. Avoid the temptation of portraying too many maps and charts. And be sure to test their use in portfolio reviews or gate meetings before adopting them.

Goal 3: Building Strategy into the Portfolio

Strategy and resource allocation must be intimately connected. *Strategy begins when you start spending money!* Until you begin allocating resources to specific activities—for example, to specific development projects—strategy is just words in a strategy document.

The mission, vision, and strategy of the business is made operational through decisions on where to spend money. For example, if a business's strategic mission is to "grow via leading-edge new service development," this must be reflected in the number of innovative and aggressive projects under way—projects that will lead to growth (rather than simply to defend) and projects that really are innovative. Similarly, if the strategy is to focus on certain markets, services, or technology types, then the majority of spending must be focused on such markets, services, or technologies.

One business unit's senior executive claimed, "My SBU's strategy is to achieve rapid growth through product leadership." Yet when we examined his breakdown of project spending, the great majority of resources was going to maintenance projects, modifications, and extensions. Clearly this was a case of a disconnect between stated strategy and where the money was spent.

Approaches to Linking Strategy to the Portfolio. Two main issues arise in the desire to achieve strategic alignment in the portfolio of projects:

Strategic fit: Are all your projects consistent with your business strategy? For example, if you have defined certain technologies or markets as key areas to focus on, do your projects fit into these areas? Are they in bounds or out of bounds?

Spending breakdown: Does the breakdown of your spending reflect your strategic priorities? If you say you are a growth business, the majority of your spending ought to be in projects that are designed to grow the business. In short, when you add up the areas where you are spending money, are these totally consistent with your stated strategy?

There are two ways to incorporate the goal of strategic alignment. The *bottom-up* approach builds strategic criteria into project selection tools. Strategic fit is achieved by including numerous strategic criteria into the Go/Kill and prioritization tools. The *top-down* approach uses the Strategic Buckets method. This begins with the business strategy and then moves to setting aside funds, or "buckets" of money, destined for different types of projects.

Bottom-up—strategic criteria built into project selection tools. Scoring models not only are effective ways to maximize the value of the portfolio, but they can also be used to ensure strategic fit. One of the multiple objectives considered in a scoring model, along with profitability or likelihood of success, can be to maximize strategic fit, simply by building into the scoring model a number of strategic questions.

> In one organization's scoring model, of the 20 criteria that they have developed to prioritize projects, six, or almost one third, deal with strategic issues. Thus, projects that fit the business strategy and boast strategic leverage are likely to rise to the top of the list. Indeed, it is inconceivable how any "off strategy" projects could make the active project list at all; the scoring model naturally weeds them out.
>
> Similarly, another company subjects all projects at gate meetings to a list of must-meet criteria before any prioritization consideration is given. At the top of this must-meet checklist is strategic fit. Projects that fail this criterion are knocked out immediately. Next, a set of should-meet criteria is used by means of a scoring model. Again, the project is knocked out if it doesn't get a certain minimum score. Embedded within this scoring model are several strategic-direction criteria.

Thus, checklist and scoring models can be used at the project level to introduce strategic criteria so that "off strategy" projects will not pass the gate, whereas projects with good strategic fit will receive a high score (see examples in Exhibits 5.8 and 5.9).

Top-down strategic approach—Strategic Buckets model. Strategic fit can be assessed by means of a scoring model, but the only method designed to ensure that the eventual portfolio of projects truly reflects the stated strategy for the business—that where the money is spent mirrors the business strategy—is a top-down approach.

The Strategic Buckets model operates from the simple principle that implementing strategy equates to spending money on specific projects. Thus, setting portfolio requirements really means setting spending targets.

The method begins with the business strategy and requires senior management to make forced choices along each of several dimensions about how they wish to allocate their scarce money resources. This creates "buckets of money." Existing projects are categorized into buckets; then it is determined whether actual spending is consistent with desired spending for each bucket. Finally, projects are prioritized within buckets to arrive at the ultimate portfolio of projects, one that mirrors management's strategy for the business.

It sounds simple, but the details are a little more complex. Senior management first develops the vision and strategy for the business. This includes defining strategic goals and the general plan of attack to achieve these goals, a fairly standard business strategy exercise. Next, they make forced choices across key strategic dimensions: On the basis of this strategy, the management of the business allocates technical and marketing resources for new services across categories on each dimension. Some common dimensions are the following:

- *Strategic goals:* Management is required to split resources across specified strategic goals, for example, defending the base, diversifying, extending the base, etc.
- *Business lines:* How much to spend on business line A? Business line B? C? In one firm a plot of business line locations on the product life cycle curve was used to help determine this split. Many banks allocate technology resources across product groups to ensure that each group has an appropriate budget.
- *Project type:* What percent of resources should go to new service development? To maintenance-type projects? To process improvements? To platform development? Pie charts, as in Exhibits 7.9 and 7.10, depict this desired split.
- *Familiarity Matrix*: What should be the split of resources to different types of markets and to different technology types in terms of their familiarity to the business? One method is to use variants of the "familiarity matrix"

proposed by Roberts—technology newness versus market newness—to help allocate resources (see Exhibit 7.11).[12]

The Star method (see Exhibit 7.10) is a Strategic Buckets approach that uses a simple project type split. The leadership team of the business begins with the business strategy and divides the resources into three categories: platform development projects that promise to yield major breakthroughs and new technology platforms, new service developments, and maintenance (technical support, improvements and enhancements, etc.). Management rates and ranks projects against each other within each of these categories, thus ensuring that it is spending money according to the strategy.

After going through the strategy exercise, management develops the categories that will be its Strategic Buckets. Here the various strategic dimensions (above) are collapsed into a convenient hand-

EXHIBIT 7.10   Star Method of Portfolio Management

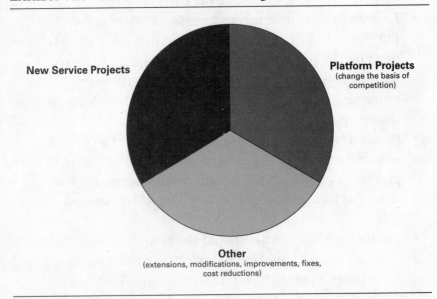

The business's strategy dictates the split of resources into buckets; projects are rank-ordered within buckets, but different criteria are used in each bucket.

EXHIBIT 7.11   Familiarity Matrix: Technology and Market Newness

	Market Newness	
Technology Newness	Existing/Base	New
New Step Out	Step Out Service Development	New Businesses and New Ventures
New But Familiar	New Service Items (existing lines)	Market Development
Base	Defend and/or Penetrate	Market Expansion (Customer Application Projects)

Resources are split across project types via the familiarity matrix.

ful of buckets. A sample group of buckets for a particular company might be the following:

- Service development projects for business lines A and B
- Cost-reduction projects
- Renewal projects for business lines C and D.

Next, the desired spending by bucket is determined: the "what should be." This involves a consolidation of desired spending splits derived via the strategic allocation exercise above (see Exhibit 7.12). Next comes a gap analysis. Existing projects are categorized by bucket, and the total current spending by bucket is added up (the "what is"). Spending gaps are then identified between the "what should be" and "what is" amounts for each bucket.

Finally, projects within each bucket are rank-ordered, using either a scoring model or financial criteria (Exhibit 7.12). Portfolio adjustments are then made either by immediate pruning of projects or by adjusting the approval process for future projects.

The major strength of the Strategic Buckets model is that it firmly links spending to the business strategy. Over time, the portfolio of projects and the spending across strategic buckets will

EXHIBIT 7.12   Four Strategic Buckets, Desired Resource Allocations Across Buckets, and Ranking of Projects Within Buckets

New Services: Business Line A Target Spend: $8.7M	New Services: Business Line B Target Spend: $18.5M	Maintenance: Business Lines A & B Target Spend: $10.8M	Cost Reductions: Business All Lines Target Spend: $7.8M
Project A 4.1	Project B 2.2	Project E 1.2	Project L 1.9
Project C 2.1	Project D 4.5	Prolect G 0.8	Project M 2.4
Project F 1.7	Project K 2.3	Project H 0.7	Project N 0.7
Project L 0.5	Project T 3.7	Project J 1.5	Project P 1.4
Project X 1.7	**Gap = 5.8**	Project Q 4.8	Project S 1.6
Project Y 2.9		Project R 1.5	Project V 1.0
Project Z 4.5		Project V 2.5	Project AA 1.2
Project BB 2.6		Project W 2.1	

Projects rank-ordered within columns according to a financial criterion: NPV * Probability of Success, or ECV, or a scoring model.

equal management's desired spending levels across buckets. At this point, the portfolio of projects will truly mirror the strategy for the business.

Another positive facet of the strategic buckets model is the recognition that all development projects that compete for the same resources should be considered in the portfolio approach. For example, development projects must compete against cost reduction projects, because both utilize technology resources.

Finally, different criteria can be used for different types of projects, so one is not faced with comparing and ranking very different types of projects against each other—for example, major new projects and minor modifications. Because this is a two-step approach (first allocate money to buckets, then prioritize like projects within a bucket), it is not necessary to arrive at a universal list of scoring or ranking criteria that fits all projects.

The major weakness of the approach is the burden it places on senior management of the company: This is a very time-consuming, arduous exercise. Further, making forced choices on resource splits in the absence of considering specific projects may be a somewhat hypothetical exercise. Finally, there are often too many dimensions across which resource splits must be made.

One way to avoid this problem is to focus on only a few of the most relevant dimensions, as defined by your strategy (and these will vary by business area, even within the same corporation).

> The head of strategic planning at one company prefers not to split spending along every possible dimension as illustrated above. Rather, the secret is selective breakdowns: "The key is to define the areas of strategic thrust of the business. A business must have its strategy clearly defined . . . whether it be in terms of markets or business lines, or technology areas. For example, if a particular strategic initiative is to 'grow via development of new services aimed at market X,' then 'services aimed at market X' is the definition of an area of strategic thrust. Then the leadership team must define how much effort [or money] it wishes to spend against each area of strategic thrust. . . . That's the essence of portfolio management!"

Top-down and bottom-up: a combined approach. In an attempt to overcome the deficiencies outlined in the top-down (Strategic Buckets) and bottom-up methods, some firms adopt hybrid approaches. For example, a business division at Sprint uses a bottom-up analysis of the projects and a top-down approach for the total dollars. At first glance, the approach is similar to the Strategic Buckets model:

- The hybrid method begins with the business's strategy: mission, strategic arenas, and priorities.
- Next, flowing from this strategy, tentative target breakdowns of spending splits across different categories are developed, for example, across business lines, or markets, or technologies, or project types, or some or all of these.

So far the method closely resembles a top-down approach. Now the method moves to a bottom-up approach:

- All existing or active and all on-hold projects (potential projects) are rated and ranked. This ranking is achieved via a maximization method such as a scoring model or some other criterion outlined earlier in this chapter. Some companies use the scores, ratings, or data from the most recent gate meetings to do this. Others re-score all projects.
- This exercise yields a single prioritized list: a ranking of all projects and potential projects that are in the pipeline. The projects near the top of the list are obvious Go projects; those near the bottom (or below the cut-off line) are obvious Kills—at least on this first iteration.

The final step is to merge top-down and bottom-up outcomes. Note that frequently the list of projects generated by the bottom-up ranking yields splits in resources that are inconsistent with the top-down tentative spending splits. So the two methods do not coincide on the first iteration:

The strategic planning exercise used in Bank A is fairly typical. Bank A uses a scoring model to rate and rank projects. One check that the firm has built into its scoring technique to ensure that project spending is linked to strategy is their "StratPlan" exercise.

StratPlan is a macro-level strategic planning exercise. Each of 12 product groups are assessed via a strategic exercise, resulting in strategies for each. StratPlan scores these 12 product groups and classes them according to a McKinsey-style grid: Stars, Cash Cows, Dogs, and Question Marks.* The map yields a tentative spending split across the product groups.

Independently, all active and on-hold development projects are scored and rank-ordered by means of a scoring model. The cutoff point on the rank-ordered list is the point where total spending

---

*Bank A uses somewhat different nomenclature than the standard model, but the meaning of the four quadrants is the same.

equals the total budget: Any project above this cutoff line is a "first-cut Go." These Go projects are then broken down by product group, and the product group's total proposed expenditures as a percentage of revenue are calculated. The groups' percentages are compared, and inconsistencies of each product group's strategy—gaps between spending levels per group and the desired spending—are identified. For example, if a product group is classified as a "maintain and defend" product line, yet receives a rather large percentage of development spending via the scoring model, a gap exists.

A second round of project prioritization ensues, and some projects that were Go are now removed from the Go list. This moves the portfolio closer to the one dictated by the StratPlan exercise. Several rounds are required before the final list of Go projects is agreed to: At this point, the prioritized list contains very good projects, according to the scoring model; and the spending allocations correctly reflect the strategies of the various product groups.

This top-down, bottom-up method checks that the resulting list of projects and their spending breakdowns is indeed consistent with the business's strategy and with the tentative desired spending breakdowns. At the same time, the method fully considers what projects—both active and on hold—are available, and their relative attractiveness.

This StratPlan exercise resembles the Strategic Buckets model in that desired spending levels per area (in this example, by product group) are decided, gaps identified, and the portfolio of projects is arranged accordingly. However, the method reverses the order of steps: Projects are prioritized first, and then spending splits are checked for consistency with strategy. It is also somewhat easier to implement and is less demanding on senior management.

Moving Toward an Integrated Portfolio Management Process

The challenge now is to integrate portfolio management decisions with decisions made at the gates. There are two fundamentally differently ways to approach this, with the key difference being which decision framework will dominate resource allocation:

Method 1: The gates act as the principal decision process. If the project has merit, resources are assigned. Portfolio meetings are held periodically and serve largely as a check mechanism that the gates are working well.

Method 2: The portfolio meetings dominate. Usually an early gate meeting is combined with the portfolio review and, say, a "mass Gate 2" meeting is held. At this review meeting, all new and existing projects are reviewed and prioritized against each other. Approvals are granted and resources are assigned. Subsequent gate meetings act merely as checkpoints or project review meetings.

Which portfolio management process is right for you? This is not an easy question, for it has no single right answer. But what follows are some recommendations based on our best practices studies, what appears to work, and management views on the various methods.

Method 1: Gates Dominate

An integrated portfolio management process where the gates dominate consists of three decision processes (see Exhibit 7.13).* Each is linked to the other, and all three decision processes must work in harmony if the objective of effective portfolio management is to be met.

1. *Strategy development at the business unit (BU) level.* Ideally the BU's strategy also includes a new service strategy, which specifies goals (for example, percentage of revenues to be derived from new

---

*For more detailed information, see R. G. Cooper, S. J. Edgett, and E. J. Kleinschmidt, *Portfolio Management for New Products* (Reading, Mass: Perseus Books, 1998).

EXHIBIT 7.13   The Total Portfolio Management Process, Linking Strategy,
Portfolio Review, and Stage-Gate Model

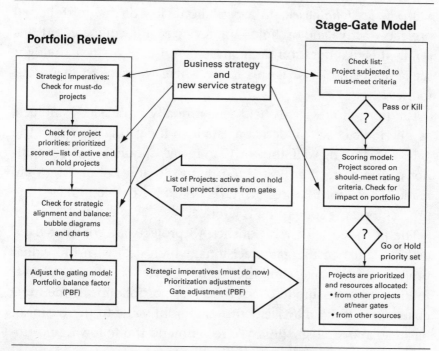

The portfolio review feeds the Stage-Gate model, and the Stage-Gate model feeds the portfolio review. Both models are in sync and driven by strategy.

services), arenas of focus (for example, the markets, technologies, and areas where new services will be developed), and even attack plans and relative priorities (for example, the desired breakdown of spending across markets, technologies, and project types).

2. *The BU's Stage-Gate™ model.* The formal process that guides projects from idea to launch is part of an integrated portfolio management system. Real-time portfolio decisions are being made here. The gates are where Go/Kill decisions are made on individual projects, and hence where resources are allocated.

Recall from Chapter 5 that prioritization takes place at the gates, as resources must be allocated. Resource allocation is made by comparing the proposed project at that gate to the active projects already in the pipeline, as well as to those that are on hold, awaiting resources.

3. *The portfolio review.* In a periodic review of the portfolio, all projects—active and on hold—are reviewed and compared. At this point, the vital question for management is: Do we have the right set of active projects? Is this really where we want to spend our money?

The portfolio review is held semiannually or quarterly and acts as a periodic check on decisions made in the gating process. If the gates are working well, the portfolio review should be merely a minor course correction. But if too many Go and Kill decisions are made at this portfolio review, take a hard look at your Stage-Gate process, because something is wrong.

The portfolio review is holistic: All projects are considered together. Think of the gate decisions, which deal with individual projects, as the fingers and the portfolio review as the fist. At portfolio reviews, be sure to check that your portfolio meets the three goals of portfolio management: maximum value to the business, balance, and strategic link. We recommend the following portfolio models for use at this portfolio review:

To achieve maximum portfolio value: The gate scoring model (see Chapter 5, pages 130–132) is an excellent way to rate and rank projects, not only at gates but also at the portfolio review. This yields a prioritized list of the best projects. Consider using criteria similar to those highlighted in Chapter 5 and in Appendix B.1—they are proven and they work! Alternatively, if your business is very financially driven, and if financial projections for new services are quite predictable, use a financial index or other metric to rank projects, such as the ratio of ECV to project cost.

To achieve balance: Balance is best shown by the various types of charts:

- Use bubble diagrams to show reward versus risk. If there are other goals besides financial ones, and if financial estimates are uncertain, place less reliance on financial numbers and use a bubble diagram whose axes are derived from a qualitative assessment of reward. Otherwise, use the standard Risk-Reward bubble diagram (see Exhibit 7.4).
- Use pie charts and histograms to capture split of spending across markets, technologies, project types, and launch timing (see Exhibit 7.9).

To achieve strategic alignment: Consider using the Strategic Buckets approach in order to pre-allocate funds to various buckets, across project types or across markets, technologies, or business lines. Many senior managers seem to like the Star method shown in Exhibit 7.10. Or use the top-down, bottom-up approach to ensure that the spending breakdown mirrors strategic priorities. In addition, be sure to build in strategic criteria—fit and importance—into your gate scoring model in order to drive "on strategy" projects toward the top of the list.

Method 2: The Portfolio Review Meetings Dominate

This approach still incorporates the three decision processes described in method 1 and Exhibit 7.13—strategy development, a Stage-Gate process, and portfolio reviews—but now the portfolio review meetings dominate the allocation of resources. Resource decisions are *not* made at the gates.

How does this method work? Simple. A project enters the portfolio process usually after the first or second stage is completed. Therefore, some data are available about the project and preliminary screening has removed the more obviously undesirable projects.

Points for Management to Ponder

1. Ensure that your business has an effective gating process in place (the right side of Exhibit 7.13). Do not rely on portfolio reviews to correct problems created by a broken gating process!

2. Gates should have clearly defined, consistent, prespecified and visible criteria for Go/Kill and prioritization decisions, as outlined in Chapter 5.

3. Gates achieve portfolio balance and strategic alignment in three ways:

    • By means of Strategic Buckets or Target Spending Levels
    • By building strategic criteria into the scoring model used at the gate
    • By using the prioritized scored list and various bubble diagrams and charts (maps and lists that show other projects in the portfolio, and the impact of adding the current project) at gate meetings

4. Portfolio reviews are held to serve as a check that the right group of projects has been selected—as a check on the gate decisions.

A combined portfolio review meeting and a mass Gate 2 meeting now takes place. All new projects that have completed Stage 1 and are ready for Gate 2 are reviewed and prioritized. All other active projects that have previously passed Gate 2 are also reviewed. (You could also conduct this mass meeting at Gate 3 instead of Gate 2, if you believe it is too early and not enough information is available.)

This portfolio/Gate 2 review can occur as many times a year as necessary. However, experience suggests that four times a year is enough. Any more meetings and you are having too many; and any less, projects are being delayed. Although this is a periodic process—not exactly real-time—the frequency of the meetings makes it almost real-time. Remember, at these meetings, all active

EXHIBIT 7.14   Method 2: The Portfolio Management Process, Linking
              Strategy, Portfolio Review, and Stage-Gate Model

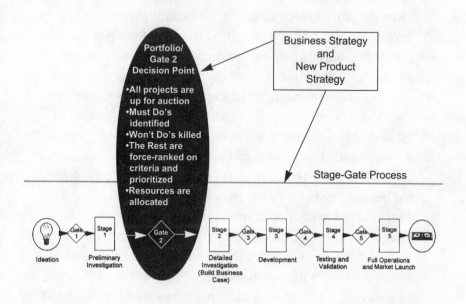

projects can be killed or reprioritized, and resources are allocated here, not at the gate meeting.

This shift in emphasis to allocating resources at the portfolio/ Gate 2 meeting is the principal difference between methods 1 and 2. In method 2, gate meetings after Gate 2 become mere checks or review points for the project. These subsequent meetings check to ensure projects are on time, on course, and on budget. They also become the quality control checkpoints to ensure that the gate deliverables meet acceptable standards. Subsequent gates also are used to ensure that the project's business case and the project itself are still in good shape. Projects can still be killed or recycled at these meetings.

What is the format for this portfolio review/Gate 2 meeting? Here is a suggested approach:

1. The business strategy and new service development strategy is reviewed, as are the resulting target resource splits—Strategic Buckets.
2. Must-do projects are identified. These are automatic Go's, or "untouchables," which are put at the top of the prioritized list. This group usually includes projects that are very important to the company and/or projects that are in the late stages of the development process and are still sound (they could also be compliance in nature). This identification of must-do projects removes resources from the resource pool.
3. Projects that should be killed are identified, discussed, and killed. These are either projects that should not pass Gate 2 for business reasons or projects in later stages that are no longer attractive. This shortens the list of projects seeking resources and frees up resources from killed projects.
4. The portfolio review team then proceeds to review and vote on the remaining projects . . . those in the middle.
5. Projects are rank-ordered until resources are fully allocated.
6. The final step is to review the list to ensure it appears right—the right balance and strategically aligned. Very often, at this stage, steps 4 to 6 are repeated to get the correct mix of projects.

An advantage of method 2 over method 1 is that it is easier to prioritize projects when the management teams look at all the projects at the same time rather than individually (at gates). Further, some executives criticize the approach method 1 takes in allocating resources at the gate meeting. They suggest that it is difficult to allocate resources to a project without knowing what resources other projects are using: "In order to approve resources to a project, one has to be able to take them away from another project. We have no uncommitted resources." Another advantage of method 2 is that projects are reprioritized on a regular basis. Only the must-do projects are sacred.

There are also some disadvantages to method 2. To kill a project at the meeting you need reliable up-to-date information, so the project teams need to be present with updated business cases. This makes more work for project teams and increases the time needed to conduct the meetings. (One company holds these portfolio review meetings over a two-day period four times a year.) One way to reduce work for the project teams is to not have every project team present an update: Only those projects that are in trouble would be reviewed.

Points for Management to Ponder

In addition to a sound development process with effective gates, a company needs periodic portfolio reviews (see Exhibit 7.13). Recall that gates look at individual project., the fingers, whereas portfolio reviews look at all projects together and in aggregate, the fist. Here are the important steps in the portfolio review:

1. Check for strategic imperatives—must-do-now projects.
2. Check project priorities: Use the prioritized scored list and spot inconsistencies.
3. Check for balance and alignment: Use the recommended bubble diagrams, charts, and maps.
4. If using method 1, identify the needed adjustments to the gating process.
5. If using method 2, conduct the project reviews and prioritize the projects.

   Recommended charts and maps to use at portfolio reviews include the following:

   - The risk-reward bubble diagram (NPV versus probability, or nonfinancial reward versus success probabilities).
   - Pie charts showing splits in resources (Strategic Buckets approach).

Recap: The Portfolio Management Process

The portfolio review is a holistic review of all projects in the portfolio. It is held periodically and is staffed by the leadership team of the business. If method 1 is used, this review monitors the decisions made at gates and makes needed adjustments both to the portfolio of projects and to the gating decision process. If method 2 is used, portfolio review meetings are held more frequently and are where the actual Gate 2 Go/Kill decisions are made.

Regardless of which approach is right for your organization, three critical elements must work in harmony (see Exhibit 7.13): the business strategy and the defined spending splits, the development process with its gates in place and working well, and the portfolio review with its various charts and lists. The result should be a portfolio of projects that deliver economic payoffs to the business, that mirror the business's strategy and direction, and that achieve the business's new service goals. If any piece of the process is not working—if there is no clearly defined new service strategy for the business, or if the development process and gating process is broken—the results are less than satisfactory.[13]

New services are the leading edge of your business strategy. The choices you make today determine what your business service offerings and market position will be in three years. Making the right choices today is of paramount importance: Portfolio management and project selection is fundamental to business success. Make sure that your business has what you need to make these choices: an effective portfolio management process.

8

Defining, Designing, and Implementing Your New Process

Development of new services is one of the most important business challenges management faces in the new millennium. But the design and implementation of a new service development process is one of the most difficult tasks, both conceptually and operationally, that an organization will face.

Putting in place a new service development process is very much like developing and launching a new service. The difference is that you are developing a new management process and the customer is now internal—your company—rather than external.

How can an organization get started designing and implementing a new service development process? First is the realization that process change is one of the most difficult types of organizational change, because it affects company culture. Second is the realization that this is a major undertaking that requires the help and input of many people in your organization, including the organization's leadership team. Once the support of key individuals has been secured, most companies that have successfully developed new processes follow the three steps that form this chapter's three main sections (outlined in Exhibit 8.1): defining the process requirements, designing the process, and implementing the process.

EXHIBIT 8.1   The Key Stages in Implementing a Stage-Gate™ Process

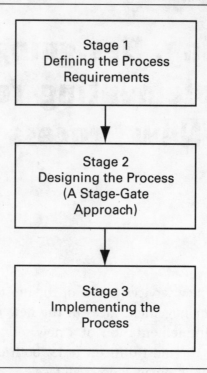

In this chapter we describe each step in detail and lay out a game plan that draws on the learnings and experiences of other companies that have instituted new development processes.

Step 1: The Foundation–Defining the Process Requirements

Step 1 involves defining the requirements for an effective new service development process. This is a first and necessary stage, and one that is often skipped by the process team. Understanding a problem is the first step toward a solution. Too often a well-intentioned task force will rush toward a solution in the belief that they know what the problem is and what the solution ought to be. Unfortunately, when they present their "solution," they are often surprised by the lack of buy-in by their colleagues. Shortly thereafter the process dies a slow death. Why? Because the team did not do the needed up-front homework to gain an understanding of the needs and problems within the company that the new process must address. This failure is analogous to developing and launching a new service without first gaining valuable insights and input from potential customers.

The purpose of this definitional step is twofold:

- To understand the problems and issues facing the business regarding new service development needs; in short, to identify what needs fixing.
- To map out the specs for the development process: what the process must be and do, how it must function, and what its requirements should be.

In an electric utility, an in-depth audit of a new service development process revealed several critical deficiencies. First, although a development process did exist, there were no clearly defined gate criteria for making Go/Kill decisions; nor was the process being adhered to, owing to a lack of agreement as to which projects should go through the process. Second, projects tended to proceed even though backed up by very little business analysis—financial and market information. Third, there was no standard list of activities to be conducted at each stage in the process. As a result, development teams were skipping many of the proven drivers of success in a rush to get to market—they were defining their own levels of work. Fourth, too many projects were reaching the pre-launch decision point, only to have senior management pull the rug out from under the project team, usually for strategic reasons. There were too many eleventh-hour Kills, often after many months of work and too many dollars had gone into the projects.

With these problems uncovered, the requirements for a new service development process for this business became clear:

1. The process must involve senior management earlier in the life of a project, during the predevelopment decision points. Re-

views of active projects in the pipeline should also involve senior people so there would be no eleventh-hour surprises.

2. Senior management must lead: They are the generals and their
obligation to the business is to develop strategy. In our first session with the executive group, they committed to fleshing out
their business strategy and moving toward a new service strategy for the business, which would involve identifying defined
arenas, priorities on these areas, and target spending levels.

3. Stages and gates should have visible activities and defined criteria and there should be agreement on which projects are in the
process. The key tasks in Step 1 are described below:

Assemble a Task Force.   The design of a company's new service development process is beyond the capabilities of one or even
a few people. This is not an easy task, and assigning it to one person to handle will not lead to success:

> One person has too narrow a view of the problem. Different perspec-
> tives are required to fully illuminate the role and implications of new
> service development in the business.

> There will be a lack of buy-in on the part of those who must use the
> process.

We recommend that you assemble a new service development
task force charged with executing the steps outlined below, leading
to the design and implementation of your new process. Carefully
select the task force members. They should be thought leaders in
the company (although not necessarily senior management), with
experience in new services; they should be representative of various
functions and businesses in the corporation; they should be people
with time made available to do the work. The task force should
have strong senior executive sponsorship (with a designated execu-

tive sponsor) and the task force should be given a leader who is respected and is passionately committed to the task at hand.

Define and Seek Concurrence on the Mandate.   The task force, together with the executive sponsor or sponsoring group, should develop a mandate statement that sets out what the task force is charged to do, what it should not do, and what deliverables are expected by the sponsoring group. The sponsoring group should sign off on this mandate, agree on their own role, and declare their availability to the task force.

Hold a Kickoff Session.   Consider inaugurating the task with a kickoff seminar/workshop. The session might be a one- to two-day event and be billed as a "best practices in new service development" seminar, focusing on best-practice techniques (see Chapters 2 and 3). Invite a fairly large group, essentially those in your business who will become the users of the new process, such as project team members, project leaders, and their immediate bosses. Senior management should also be brought into the loop, either at the kickoff or via a session tailored for them. An event like this helps in three ways.

First, it creates awareness of the need for improvement. Observing best practices in other organizations is an excellent start. Further, the workshop is the venue where the executive sponsors reiterate the business's new service goals and strategy, which usually points to the need for a change of direction. The executive sponsors also announce the new process initiative at the workshop and introduce task force members to the attendees.

Second, such a workshop can be used to help identify the problems in developing new services within the business. For example, a "problem detection" exercise can be built into the workshop. Thus, the workshop can double as a "town hall meeting," enabling a wide audience to air their views, concerns, and suggestions.

Finally, a kickoff workshop helps generate organizational buy-in. Remember, obtaining organizational buy-in to new methods and practices is a formidable task, and organizational buy-in must begin in the first few days of this initiative. Use this kickoff event to begin the buy-in process. You might build in a "what's the path forward" team exercise toward the end of the kickoff event, so that participants can provide direction to the task force on what's needed for the next steps. The task force members are the hosts at this workshop, and they must use it to full advantage to seek input and agreement for the road ahead.

Do a Literature Review.   Task force members should conduct a thorough literature review to find out what others have said and done. There is no sense reinventing the wheel. Authors and pundits have been writing about new service/product development since the 1960s. Chapters 1–3 provide a quick review and many key references you might wish to look at. Require that the task force members immerse themselves in these and other writings.

Benchmark Other Firms.   The suggestion to benchmark other firms is made with some caution. First, thorough benchmarking takes a lot of time. Second, some of the better-practice firms have been benchmarked so often that they are now resisting such overtures (or acquiescing but not providing full support). Finally, task force members are not usually specialists in business research, hence they are likely to do a mediocre job of benchmarking. Task force members often set out with great zeal to benchmark others, but lose their enthusiasm when they quickly realize it is not so easy, and they are not learning all that much. We offer two suggestions:

Seek some professional help here, especially in the design of your benchmarking methodology. Numerous suppliers exist who are experienced and capable at benchmarking exercises.

Turn to the literature. Chapters 1 to 3 of this book provide results of a fairly comprehensive benchmarking of industry best practices. Your literature search may also turn up other reports of company practices.

Conduct Internal Audit of Current Practices.   Undertake a study of current practices and deficiencies in your own company. This internal audit poses fewer problems than external bench-marking, and should be an easier task. Surprisingly, many task forces skip this step, largely because they think they already know the answers. Wrong! Every internal 3-P (*practices, performance, and problems*) study we have been involved with has resulted in major revelations. The findings of the studies go far beyond the initial knowledge and understanding of the task force, and there definitely were new learnings that the task force had to deal with. Do not skip this task. Here are some suggestions:

- *Undertake a 3-P study:* A 3-P study focuses on practices, performance, and problems. We have developed a method-ology, called *ProBE*—for *pro*duct *b*enchmarking and *e*valuation[1]—to help you with this effort. Our *ProBE* methodology is a questionnaire-based internal audit of your business's new service practices, performance, and problems (see Appendix A). *ProBE* then compares your or-ganization's practices and performance against, the aver-age business and against the top 20 percent. The method and database are based on our benchmarking study of a large sample of businesses. Alternatively, you can develop your own benchmarking questionnaire using individual interviews, e-mail surveys, or focus groups within your business to uncover current development practices and de-ficiencies—to discover what needs fixing and what seems to be working.
- *Focus on individual new service projects:* Dissecting a reason-able sample of past projects—both winners and losers—provides valuable insights into current strengths and weaknesses in your existing development practices. More specifically, require that project teams from already com-pleted projects undertake a postmortem of their projects.

That is, dissect each project, focusing first on mapping out the activities that occurred during each stage of development from idea to launch. Then lower the microscope on each of the key decision points in the process—how the Go/Kill decisions were made, who made them, what information was available (or should have been available), and what criteria were used.

Define the Steps for Your Process. Integrate your many findings and conclusions from Step 1 (defining the process requirements) into a set of specs and requirements for the new process and write them up. This document might start: "Our new service development process must . . .

- encourage the inception of creative ideas and aid in getting innovative and creative new services to market
- foster the amplification or plusing of ideas—making ideas bigger
- provide team leaders with a clear game plan, outlining the types of activities required at each stage in the development process
- promote objective Go/Kill decision making using common criteria based on facts, and yielding consistency and continuity in decision making
- improve resource allocation by means of better focus, sharper prioritization, and the right people on projects
- define a work plan for Step 2 (designing the process).

That final step will be to map out a detailed work plan for the next phase of the effort, namely the design of the various elements of the process. For example, if your business lacks an effective gating process, then its development becomes a major part of the work plan.

Concurrence from Sponsors and Selected Users.   The specs of the process and the proposed work plan are now presented to senior management for their concurrence and sign-off. This "gate" marks the end of the homework, or audit, phase, and the beginning of Step 2 (designing the process). Selected knowledgeable people who will be the eventual users of the process can also act as sounding boards at this point. While you might be tempted to hold a "town hall meeting" and get everyone who attended the initial kickoff event to review your specs and work plan, unfortunately you really have very little of interest to show people at this point. You begin your presentations to users when you have a first draft of the process in Step 2.

Points for Management to Ponder

Before you charge ahead, be sure to spend time defining the requirements of your new service development process. Remember: Understanding the problem is the first step to a solution. So take a little extra time here and lay the foundation carefully. Tasks you might consider in this Step 1 definitional phase include the following:

- Assembling a task force for the job
- Defining the mandate and seeking concurrence from the executive sponsor or sponsoring group
- Holding a kickoff session—this builds buy-in and also solicits useful input
- Undertaking a thorough literature review (don't reinvent the wheel)
- Benchmarking other firms (with caution)
- Undertaking a thorough internal audit of current development practices in your business
- Defining the specs and requirements for your process—what needs fixing
- Gaining the sponsors' concurrence regarding your process specs and the proposed action plan

---

The tasks outlined above are not easy, nor can they be done overnight. However, when done well, they provide an excellent foundation for the design and implementation work that lies ahead.

Step 2: Key Actions in Designing the New Service Development Process

The homework has been done, the problems identified, and the requirements of the ideal new service development process have been defined—what your process must be and do. Senior management acceptance has been obtained. Now it is time to begin designing the process in earnest.

Designing a new service development process involves much more than merely sketching out a stage-gate diagram. Here are some of the elements:

1. First, map the process. Create a flow diagram similar to Exhibit 5.1, with your stages and gates identified. Label each stage and gate with a name that indicates what the stage or gate does or stands for. Briefly describe each stage and gate.

2. Define the purpose and spirit of each stage and gate. Here is one company's description of Stage 1:

Purpose of Stage 1

Stage 1 amounts to a quick and inexpensive set of activities to gain a better understanding of the idea; that is, to identify which are the best ideas, to assess market potential and technical feasibility, to identify possible show-stoppers, and to determine the need for further work. The spirit here is to make professional assessments and "best educated guesses"—a first cut—often with very limited data and in a very short time period. Detailed assessments and studies are not expected in Stage 1. The Stage 1 work effort varies by project, but the order of magnitude is typically about 5–10 person-days of work, with elapsed time about one calendar month.

3. For each stage, identify the key tasks, actions, or activities and also the resulting deliverables from these actions. Try to build in best practices here, such as sharp, early project definition; strong market and customer orientation; solid up-front homework; and so on (see Chapter 5 for more detailed stage descriptions). For problematic actions and deliverables, or for unfamiliar ones, you may wish to develop guides, templates, or examples for users. Some firms also define accountability for each stage, specifying who is accountable for seeing that these tasks are completed.

4. For each gate, define who the gatekeepers are, the Go/Kill and prioritization criteria, and the gate outputs—what happens next. Exhibits 5.8 and 5.9 provide a good starting point for both must-meet (yes/no) and should-meet (scored) criteria for Gate 3. Early gates conveniently use a subset of these. For example, Gate 1 may use only the must-meet items as criteria for weeding out inappropriate ideas; Gate 2 may use the must-meet and a handful of should-meet items. Gates 3–5 can use the full list of criteria in Exhibit 5.9.

5. Capture the behavioral and organizational issues: team structure and leadership; the gatekeepers' role, and responsibilities and the rules of the game; how gate reviews are to be conducted; rewards and recognition; and the need for and job description of a process manager.

6. Identify other peripheral but vital elements: what projects are "in the process"; flexibility and fast-tracking projects; designing an IT support system to track projects and keep vital statistics on each; improving idea generation and solicitation; developing an "open" idea vault and a convenient idea handling system; integrating the process with other company processes, for example, the technology allocation process; and so on.

7. Deal with and decide on some of the issues and challenges raised in Chapters 5–7:

- How firm are the resource commitments that are made at gate meetings?

- How should you overcome the problem of imaginary precision?
- At what gate should the portfolio management process kick in?
- How should you correctly incorporate financial analysis methods into the gate and gate criteria?
- How does one spot projects in trouble—use red flags? (See sample list in Exhibit 6.7.)

An Iterative Process.   Designing the process is a difficult task; it can't be done all at once, but requires ongoing input and continual revisiting of the decisions made. To carry out the difficult design phase, we recommend that your task force set aside blocks of time so that you can meet regularly in two-day sessions, roughly two to four weeks apart. Meeting an hour here and two hours there usually results in a lack of dedicated effort with too many people missing too many meetings. Rather, block out time slots months ahead, and get out of the office. The two to four-week intervals are suggested because this is approximately how long it takes to pull together the conclusions from each two-day session, disseminate them to team members, share them with others in the organization, and obtain the necessary feedback. Fur-

---

Making Task Forces Work: Checklist

- Executive sponsorship secured
- Membership carefully selected
- Strong, respected leader in place with passion for the task
- Mandate developed and signed off on by sponsors
- Homework done (Step 1, audit)
- Goals for process defined and a work plan signed off
- Arrangements made to get off premises
- Blocks of time set aside
- Outside facilitator and/or expert in place
- Feedback sought from users

---

thermore, subgroups of the task force will be undertaking off-line activities that often take a few weeks to complete.

A word of warning: The toughest job by far is not the design of an effective process on paper, but getting it implemented! So implementation must be a primary concern all the way through this Step 2 design phase. One fundamental truth is that people who have not had a hand in crafting something will invariably resist its implementation. Thus, the goal here is to involve as many of the potential users of the process as possible in its design. Clearly, a committee of one hundred makes no sense, but feedback sessions are one method to encourage organizational buy-in long before formal implementation begins.

When Northern States Power designed its new Stage-Gate process, the task force scheduled a series of two-day meetings, about four weeks apart. Each session had a facilitator/outside expert, specific goals, and an agenda. After each meeting, one person pulled together the material and wrote up a draft of the newest version of the design of the Stage-Gate process and sent it to each task force member for critical review. In addition, a PowerPoint presentation was developed and e-mailed to all task force members, so that they in turn could make oral and visual presentations of the process to their colleagues, subordinates, and superiors.

Feedback from the presentations and the written document were solicited and discussed at the next meeting. With military discipline, the task force moved from one draft design to the next, each one better than the last. But most important, by the time the new Stage-Gate process was rolled out to the user community, *each user had seen it several times*, and had had ample opportunity to critique it and suggest improvements. The end result was a much better process than if the task force had designed it in isolation. The critical buy-in had already begun!

The process in Step 2 is very iterative. A task force meeting is held; the outcomes are written up; this write-up is fed forward to potential users and senior management; feedback is sought; and the task force meets again to integrate the feedback and move ahead on the design of the process.

Top Management Is Part of Step 2.   Top management involvement is critical throughout this entire design phase. The executive sponsor should stay very close to the task force, show up at many of the meetings (though not for the full two days), and closely review the outcome of each session with the task force leader. The role of top managers goes beyond membership in the sponsoring group, however. They must also take an active role in the design of the process:

- The development of a new service strategy for the business is one area where senior management's views, decisions, and approvals must be sought. Ideally they should lead the charge.
- Another top management input is the development of decision criteria for use at the gate meetings they attend.
- Similarly, the development of rules of the game at gates (see Chapter 5) should be led by top management, or at least their concurrence should be sought.

Off-line Activities.   Much work also goes on in the intervals between the two-day task force sessions. This "off-line" work is undertaken by task force members working alone or perhaps in small groups on specific tasks defined by the task force. Some larger task forces establish subgroups with leaders to accomplish certain tasks, such as the following:

- A subgroup to investigate and define IT needs
- A subgroup to start designing appropriate documentation
- A communications subgroup to handle communications and "press releases" to other parts of the company
- A subgroup to liaise regularly with the executive sponsors
- A subgroup to work with the finance department to define

the appropriate financial models, calculations, spread-sheets, and so on.

The point is that there is much work to be done and not all can be accomplished in a set of two-day meetings. Organize to do some work between meetings.

An Implementation Plan.   The final action in Step 2 is the design of an implementation plan for the process, which is also a deliverable for Step 3, Implementation. This plan deals with challenges such as the following:

- Communicating the new Stage-Gate process to users and seeking buy-in at all levels (documentation, events, in-company media)
- Providing training to teams and gatekeepers
- Piloting some projects through the first few gate meetings or stages
- Bringing existing projects into the process
- Gathering data on all existing projects to kick-start the process
- Developing an IT support system for the gating framework and process and project management
- Putting a process manager in place
- Defining metrics—measures of new service performance (How well are we doing at new services?), and measures of the performance of various components of the process (Are gates working? Are projects prioritized correctly?)

Results of Step 2

There are two deliverables at the end of Step 2:

- A new service development process design that has been reviewed by both users and management and meets their needs and demands (buy-in has already begun)
- A detailed implementation plan

Points for Management to Ponder

Step 2 is designing your new service development process. The Stage-Gate new service process needs stages and gates to be defined, complete with a set of identified deliverables to gates, gate criteria, and gatekeepers defined.

Consider structuring your task force so that it meets in two-day sessions off premises, roughly two to four weeks apart. There is much work to be done between sessions, including sharing the evolving process with users and sponsors, and seeking their feedback and suggestions. Buy-in has already begun. Remember: There is an important role for senior people to play in this design phase.

A deliverable from Step 2 is a new service development process on paper that has been reviewed a number of times by user groups and senior management, and that has had considerable input from each group. An implementation plan is also a deliverable from Step 2.

These two items are presented to the sponsoring group for final approval and approval of resources needed for implementation. Assuming concurrence is obtained, then it's on to Step 3, implementation!

Step 3: Implementation of the Process

Implementation of the process is perhaps the most challenging phase. Unfortunately, the challenge is often underestimated. The key tasks of implementation are as follows:

Install a Process Manager.   No process, however excellent its design and concept, ever implemented itself. And committees or task forces, no matter how well intentioned, have a history of being poor at implementation. They may do an excellent job on the design of the process, but once that task is finished, task force members seem to drift off to other work and fail to see the implementation through. To prevent this, one person must be charged with making the process happen: the process manager, or process keeper, or gate-meister. Ideally this person is selected from among the task force members, and is designated before implementation begins. His/her job is to ensure that the process is implemented, that the steps laid out below are indeed executed.

Secure Senior Management Buy-in.   The process is doomed to failure unless senior management buys in and commits totally to it. In spite of the fact that senior management has sponsored the process initiative, and in spite of their apparent sign-off on the process on paper (Step 2), in almost every organization we have worked with, there is still some hesitancy around total buy-in to the principles and methods of the process: They *talk the talk*, but they are not quite ready to *walk the walk*. The dilemma is that in principle, senior management agrees with the concept of a gating process with discipline and tough gates, with stages that deliver fact-based information, all driven by a new service strategy. What they do not quite realize is that the biggest change in behavior must occur at the top. Effective gate meetings demand quite different behavior on the part of senior people than they are used to: The gatekeeper rules of the game bring a certain discipline that is foreign to some senior groups. All projects must be subjected to the same scrutiny so that even the general manager's pet projects come under the microscope.

Here are some ways we ensure senior management buy-in:

- First, involve senior management in the design of the process. For example, during Step 2, ensure that a senior management session is built in where they help design the gates, perhaps the prioritization criteria, and even map out the rules of the game.
- Early in the implementation phase, run some pilot sessions such as a mock gate meeting with senior management as participants.
- Provide a gatekeeper training session, where senior people can not only learn about the process but also can be briefed on expected behaviors and the rules of the game.

When PECO introduced their Stage-Gate process, executives took part in the training workshop. This two-day training session laid out the details of the process, spelled out the gate criteria (which they had helped to craft), and outlined the gatekeepers' rules (which they had already accepted). Then, a mock gate meeting took place, using a real company case. It was an interesting as well as instructive day!

Develop User-Friendly Documentation. Most documentation in support of new management processes is not very user-friendly: It is heavy reading, too long, and not very inviting. So guess what: Most such manuals are never read! Too bad, because no doubt a lot of thought and hard work by some well-intentioned task forces went into their preparation. We recommend that you take a look at some of the manuals and guide books that have been developed for computer software programs in recent years. They certainly are a far cry from the deadly ones of the mid-'80s. Learn from these examples. We are not suggesting that you develop a guide that reads like *New Service Development for Dummies,* but a few ideas from this style of guide might be appropriate.

One way to handle the documentation is to develop several pieces, or booklets, with different levels of detail. Here are two that we often use:

Brochure: A 2- to 4-page glossy four-color brochure can be created that outlines the concept and purpose of the process. It looks much like a sales brochure—and that is what it is. First impressions count! Some companies also use such a brochure as a selling tool with their customers and their alliance and outsourcing partners. It provides a clear outline of how their new service development process works.

Guide/Manual: Typically this is a 10- to 25-page guidebook that provides an in-depth description of the process, for example, details of each stage and gate, the prioritization criteria, and so on. A separate appendix usually contains examples, illustrations, and templates. This guide is designed for a project leader of a new service project to refer to as she moves a project forward.

Some firms provide limited-circulation copies of their process manuals (numbered copies, much in the tradition of ISO 9000). Other companies have no hard copy of their manuals at all: The entire process is on the server or PC. A PC-based manual has the advantage of convenient and timely updates; and it can make use of hypertext (that is, there is a drill-down capability built right into the guide).

Undertake Internal Marketing. Earlier in this chapter, we noted that rolling out a process is a bit like developing and launching a new service. So do not forget the marketing and selling! Here are some common marketing and promotional approaches:

Have an "announcement event" to roll out the process. This might coincide with some other company event. The goal here is to have the sponsor or executive group place their blessing on the new process and announce that "effective March 1, this process is in place." Next, the task force presents some of the details of the process and outlines what will happen as the rollout proceeds, for example, training, bringing existing projects in, etc.

Use internal company communications such as your company newsletter, or magazine or even e-mail. It is excellent practice to keep the rest of the company informed of your task force's progress all the way through Step 2. Sometimes there is a long pause between the initial kickoff event and eventual rollout of the process, so you should be considering "press releases" and news articles all the way along, and not just as rollout begins. Someone on the task force can be appointed "communications manager."

Provide Training.   Most companies underestimate the need for training when they roll out a new service process. The assumption seems to be that "all this Stage-Gate stuff is pretty obvious and anyone ought to be able to handle it by reading the manual." Wrong! First, many people don't read. Second, learning via reading is not everyone's forte. Third, this "Stage-Gate stuff" is considerably more complex than you might expect. Finally, recall that buy-in is a critical goal. People will not use something new if they either fear it or do not understand it, no matter how loud the boss screams. So take every precaution to ensure that people appreciate the benefits of the new process (no fear) and that they fully understand how it works. Training is essential for organizational buy-in.

You might consider varied levels and types of training for different groups of people:

- *For project teams and leaders:* Typically a one- to two-day course is developed for about 25 to 30 attendees per session. The seminar involves lectures or "show and tell" sessions to explain how the process works, as well as teams working their way through a stage of a real company case, or attending a mock gate meeting.
- *For gatekeepers (the senior people):* They require the most training, because their behavior must change the most. Unfortunately, life at the top is rushed, so one day is typically allotted.
- *For peripheral players and resource providers:* For people who are not on project teams, but nonetheless are associated with new service projects (working in, say, finance, legal, or regulatory affairs departments), usually a shorter training session suffices—enough to outline the essence of the process.

Bring Existing Projects into the Process.   First, assemble a list of the projects to be included (this should be available from Step 1, where you had already undertaken a total review of the existing portfolio). For each obtain and/or update data that are needed to characterize and describe each project (name, leader, project type, market, etc.) as well as data needed for the determination of approximately what stage of the Stage-Gate process the project is in.

The next challenge is ensuring that all projects pass through a gate review. Hold gate reviews soon. Note that some of the required data might be of doubtful validity. Also, some data needed in certain stages—for example, project scores from previous gate reviews—may not be available. This gate review should be done as early as possible. An effective approach here is to have a series of "welcome gates" to ensure that all existing projects pass through at least one gate within the first months of rolling out the new process. These welcome gates are somewhat gentler than actual gates and require that the project leader declare in advance what stage he/she is at in the process and what he/she will deliver to the welcome gate. It is understood by gatekeepers that not all the desired deliverables will be available for the welcome gate. One output of the welcome gate is a decision as to what and when the next "real" gate will be, and what deliverables will be available at that time.

Another approach is to begin with some pilot projects. This can start in Step 2 once a skeleton process is in place. Pick a handful of projects whose project leaders are willing to participate in a pilot program to test-drive the Stage-Gate process. (Ideally these project leaders might even be members of the task force). These should be typical projects, perhaps at differing stages. Start running these projects through the gating process to test it, and in particular, to test the gate criteria and gate procedures. And start to test the IT system and database with a limited number of projects.

Develop or Acquire an IT Support System. There are several facets of an IT (information technology) system you may wish to consider to support your process. Often, off-the-shelf software can be used as the shell, but usually there is some original, custom programming or setup required. Here are the types of IT support that firms use:

- Database software used to store all the vital stats and characteristics of projects. This information is important for tracking projects and also for gauging performance (metrics). These data are usually generated and collected at gate reviews.
- Software to display portfolio charts, such as pie charts, histograms, and especially bubble diagrams.
- Software that provides easy access to documentation of the gating process or entire process, for example, a server-based process manual complete with hypertext.
- Software-based tools:
    - screening and diagnostic tools such as NewProd 2000
    - project management tools incorporating timelines and Gantt charts, such as Microsoft Project or Primavera or Live NPD
    - financial analysis tools such as spreadsheets and Monte Carlo simulation packages (e.g. At Risk; Crystal Ball)
    - compiled, pre-formatted spreadsheet for project financial analysis (supplied by the Finance Department)
    - information exchange software such as Lotus Notes so that team members can share information, or two remote parties can work on a common document, or people outside the project can review its progress
    - software to facilitate idea submission, dissemination, and feedback
    - IT to support gates such as wireless voting machines and PC-based meetings-facilitation software.

Develop Metrics.   You cannot manage what you have not measured. Metrics, or performance measures, are required in order for the process to be effectively managed. Recall that there are two types of performance metrics: in-process and post-process (see Exhibits 6.4 and 6.5). Metrics should be designed in Step 2 and be part of the implementation plan.

Points for Management to Ponder

The toughest phase by far is Step 3, implementing the process. Don't underestimate the challenge here. Listed below are some tasks you should consider including in your implementation plan to help pave the way for smoother adoption of the process:

1. Put a Process Manager in place—someone who is charged with implementing the process on a day-to-day basis.
2. Seek senior management buy-in, ensuring senior managers walk the walk.
3. Develop user-friendly documentation such as a brochure and a guide/manual.
4. Do internal marketing. Don't forget, you're introducing a new concept here, so market it!
5. Develop and provide training for project team members and leaders, senior people, and resource providers.
6. Get projects into the process quickly—don't let projects linger.
7. Develop an IT system to support the process.
8. Define metrics to measure how well the process and new services are doing.
9. One more suggestion: Read "Ten Ways to Fail at Process Design and Implementation" (Exhibit 8.2).

The task of designing and implementing a systematic process is not an easy one. And yet, new services are the future of your business. How you manage your new service resources will dictate how well your business does in the years ahead. So make the extra effort that's needed here.

Work with Project Teams. Once the training sessions are finished, do not just leave project teams to fend for themselves. There is much work to be done as teams bring their projects into the process and get ready for their first few gate meetings. Coach the teams—help them through this challenging period. Usually the process manager assumes this coaching role, working and

EXHIBIT 8.2   Ten Ways to Fail at Stage-Gate Process Design and
Implementation—Based on Experiences at Real Companies

1. Design the process on your own, in your own office, and in a vacuum. You know best. Task forces are a waste of time!
2. Don't do any homework or auditing (Step 1). You already know what the problem is in your company, so jump immediately to a solution.
3. Don't bother looking at other companies' approaches, models, charts, criteria, or scoring models, etc. Again, you have nothing to learn here.
4. If you do assemble a task force, meet over several months in private. Then present "your grand design" and assume everyone in the company will applaud, even though they have not been involved in the design.
5. Don't seek outside help: Just read the book and design your process based on the generic one. It's a piece of cake! If you do seek help, hire a reengineering consultant who knows nothing about new service/product management.
6. Don't waste time testing and seeking feedback from others in the company as your task force designs the process. After all, you're the task force, what do these "outsiders" know? Your "process design" is likely to be near perfect!
7. When others do have questions or criticisms, treat these people as "cynics" and "negative thinkers." Refuse to deal with these objections, and never, never modify the process. It's yours and cast in marble.
8. Don't provide training. Most of this "process management stuff" is obvious. Anyone ought to be able to do it just by reading the manual.
9. Speaking of manuals, make sure the process guide is thick, full of checklists and forms. If in doubt, overwhelm the reader and user.
10. Don't bother installing a process manager. The process is so good it will implement itself.

helping project teams to ensure that their projects are on time and in good shape.

There is much work involved in the implementation of a process. There are also many pitfalls along the way. (Exhibit 8.2, "Ten Ways to Fail at Process Design and Implementation," is our tongue-in-cheek list of don'ts.) We could continue with the warnings and cautions, but we think you get the point. Before you proceed, think through the design and implementation of a new process carefully, and be prepared to make a major commitment to its success. But at all costs, do proceed, because the costs of doing nothing are just too high.

Winning at New Services

There are two ways to win big at new services: doing the *right projects* and doing *projects right*. That is what this book is about. New services are the leading edge of your business strategy. The choices you make today determine what your new service offerings and market position will be in the future. The management challenge is to create a process that will truly enhance the organization's ability to create winning new services.

An essential component of developing successful new services is a process that provides a road map to follow as you take a project from idea through to launch in a timely and efficient manner. In this book we have presented a game plan—Stage-Gate™—that provides this road map. Stage-Gate is a carefully designed and successfully implemented stage-and-gate development process that provides discipline, focuses on quality of execution, builds in the up-front homework, is strongly market-oriented, and is backed by appropriate resources. No process by itself can guarantee success, but innovation is too important to be left to chance. *A winning new service development process is the first step toward winning!*

APPENDIX A:

THE PROBE DIAGNOSTIC TOOL

How well are you doing at new service development? And how do your methods and approaches compare with industry best practices? ProBE is a diagnostic tool that helps provide answers to these vital questions. (*ProBE* stands for *Pro*duct *B*enchmarking and *E*valuations. It was developed jointly by Jens Arleth of U3 Innovation Management, in Copenhagen, Denmark, and Robert Cooper and Scott Edgett of the Product Development Institute, Inc., www.prod-dev.com.)

ProBE was originally developed in response to repeated requests by companies whose managements wanted to compare their scores to scores of companies in our database. Recall the benchmarking results presented in Chapters 2 and 3. Some of these results are drawn from our extensive databases on new service development.

ProBE enables your business to compare its performance and practices for new service development to those of companies in the database. This is a questionnaire-based method, where a number of people in your organization answer a detailed, tested questionnaire. The questions are relatively simple ones using 0-to-10 scales with anchored phrases that seek subjective opinion from these knowledgeable people. Questions cover many topics in your business, from culture and climate to whether your new service process is functioning well, and even how well important activities are executed in typical new service projects.

Using our ProBE software, we analyze your questionnaire data and produce an initial report—essentially a set of bar and pie charts—that pinpoints your strengths and weaknesses and helps identify areas that need fixing. Exhibit A.1 shows a sample output page (there are 14 such pages of output). ProBE benchmarks your practices and performance against industry averages, and also against the top 20 percent of best firms.

Next, the ProBE consultants conduct a diagnostic session with you and your people. They review the results and identify the causes of substandard performance. Finally, they develop a plan of action with you to correct the causes.

ProBE is an ideal way to begin your internal audit of your existing process. So before you embark on a major overhaul or redesign of your new service development process or new service efforts, consider using ProBE or a similar structured technique to pinpoint what needs fixing. Remember: The beginning of a solution is understanding the problem!

ProBE is commercially available from a number of sources. For more information, see the Product Development Institute's Web page: www.prod-dev.com, or contact the authors directly.

In Chapter 2 you had an opportunity to answer a number of questions about your new service development process. Use Exhibit A.1 to compare your answers with those of other companies in our database.

EXHIBIT A.1   Benchmarking Your Organization's New Service Development
Process

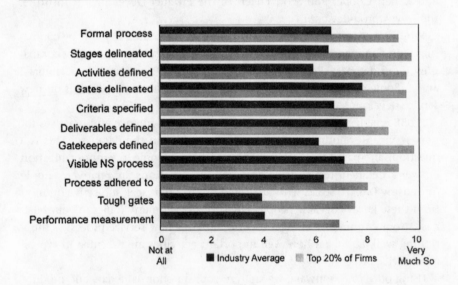

APPENDIX B:

NEWPROD™ 2000–
A DIAGNOSTIC TOOL

NewProd™ 2000 is a management tool for screening, evaluating, prioritizing, and diagnosing new service/product projects. It is designed for use relatively early in the new service/product process—at the idea screening, preliminary investigation, and business justification stages—before a formal development program is begun, and when relatively little is known about the project.

NewProd 2000 can be used as a screening tool, to identify the strengths and weaknesses of a new service/product project, and even to arrive at an estimate of the project's likelihood of success. But most users find that the *real value* of NewProd 2000 is diagnostic, helping the project team to . . .

- share knowledge, and gain a common vision and understanding of their project.
- identify the project's strong points and deficiencies.
- map out a course of action on how to resolve the problems.
- develop team consensus on their project.

NewProd 2000 is based on the fact that a new service/product project's profile is a reasonable predictor of the strengths and weaknesses of the project, and the project's eventual commercial outcome.

Using the NewProd 2000 questionnaire, evaluators rate the project on a number of key questions. The NewProd 2000 model is used to analyze their inputs and compare the profile of the project to the profile of past projects whose outcomes are known.

NewProd 2000 pinpoints the strengths and weaknesses of the new project, and indicates the likelihood of commercial success.

The NewProd 2000 model was derived from a study of projects resulting in approximately two thousand new services and products that were launched into the market, and whose financial results are known. The model has been replicated and validated within a number of companies, and also in different settings.

NewProd 2000, based on the statistical model, has a predictive ability of about 84 percent, meaning that it can correctly predict winners and losers approximately 84 percent of the time.

Thus, NewProd provides a number of benefits to users:

- The NewProd 2000 system brings together a multifunctional group of managers for project evaluation. It enables managers to focus on the key issues and items that have been found to be key to success.
- The model identifies areas of major disagreement between managers, pointing to the need for action and better information.
- It highlights critical areas of ignorance, where more homework must be undertaken prior to moving ahead with a full-scale development.
- NewProd 2000 also identifies the project's major strengths and weaknesses, pointing to a path forward to resolve the weaknesses.
- Finally, NewProd 2000 predicts the project's success likelihood—a useful output for making Go/Kill and prioritization decisions.

The questions in the following pages are taken from the NewProd 2000 model (see Exhibit B.1).

Exhibit B.1   The NewProd 2000 Questionnaire
_____

Instructions:

1. For each of the following questions, indicate your level of agreement or disagreement by circling a number from 0 to 10. Read each question carefully! Anchor phrases are provided to help define what is meant by a 10 or a zero.
2. **Answer every question.** Give your best estimate, even though you may not be sure of an answer.
3. Indicate how sure or confident you are about each answer. Do so by writing a number from 0 to 10 in the final "Confidence" column. Here:

   10 = 100% confident; I am certain about this answer.
    0 = no confidence; a pure guess.

4. Use a pen. Circle and write clearly . . . press hard. Try not to cross out answers.
5. Most people take about 15 minutes to answer the questionnaire. New users are advised against agonizing over questions and their exact meaning. Answer quickly . . . during the feedback section you can revise your answers.
6. **Remember: Two answers are required for each question, a rating and a confidence, both 0–10.**

Company _____ Date _____

Product name _____ Ref _____ _____

Please complete and return before _____

Return completed questionnaire to NewProd 2000 Evaluation Manager/Coordinator

_____

Department/address _____ Tel _____ Fax_____

Evaluator's name/title _____

Department _____ Tel _____

Resources required:

The first 8 questions are designed to probe whether our company has the capabilities, talents, skills, resources, physical facilities and experience necessary to undertake the project, assuming that we were to move ahead with the project. The fact that these resources might otherwise be occupied at present is not relevant.

If certain facets of the project are to be carried out by others (e.g., subcontracted development, distribution, etc.), these outside resources should be considered as available to the project. Be careful to be realistic about the availability and quality of these outside resources.

Remember: two answers per question:

- a rating (0–10) of the resource adequacy; and
- your confidence (0–10) in your rating.

	Strongly Disagree	Strongly Agree	Confidence

1. Our company's financial resources are more than adequate for this project (10=far more than adequate; 0=far less). `0 1 2 3 4 5 6 7 8 9 10` _____

2. Our company's new service development skills and people are more than adequate for this project (10=far more than adequate; 0=far less). `0 1 2 3 4 5 6 7 8 9 10` _____

3. Our company's systems, technical skills & people are more than adequate for this project (10=far more than adequate; 0=far less than adequate). `0 1 2 3 4 5 6 7 8 9 10` _____

4. Our company's marketing research skills & people are more than adequate for this project (10=far more than adequate; 0=far less than adequate). `0 1 2 3 4 5 6 7 8 9 10` _____

5. Our company's management skills are more than adequate for this project (10=far more than adequate; 0=far less). `0 1 2 3 4 5 6 7 8 9 10` _____

6. Our company's operations resources or skills are more than adequate for this project (10=far more than adequate; 0=far less than adequate). `0 1 2 3 4 5 6 7 8 9 10` _____

7. Our company's salesforce &/or distribution resources & skills are more than adequate for this project (10=far more than adequate; 0=far less than adequate). `0 1 2 3 4 5 6 7 8 9 10` _____

| | Strongly Disagree | Strongly Agree | Confidence |

8. Our company's advertising & promotion resources & skills are more than adequate for this project (10=far more than adequate; 0=far less than adequate).

    0 1 2 3 4 5 6 7 8 9 10 _____

Nature of Project:

These 3 questions provide some general descriptors of the new service or project.

Here the terms "market," "customer," and "competitor" must be defined. The market is defined both geographically and in terms of applications: think in terms of which users our service is targeted at, the target users, in order to define the "market." Competitive services are those services that these customers now use that our service is intended to replace.

9. Our new service is highly innovative—totally new to the market (10=totally new; 0=a direct copy).

    0 1 2 3 4 5 6 7 8 9 10 _____

10. The new service specifications—exactly what the service will be—are very clear (10=very clearly defined; 0=not defined at all).

    0 1 2 3 4 5 6 7 8 9 10 _____

11. The technical aspects—exactly how the technical problems will be solved—are very clear (10=very clear; 0=not clear, not known).

    0 1 2 3 4 5 6 7 8 9 10 _____

Newness to the Company:

Is this a familiar project to our company or a totally new one to us? These next four questions probe how new or "step out" the project and service are to our company. Again, be sure to define what you mean by "market," "customer," and "competition" (see note before question 9 above).

12. The potential customers for this new service are totally new to our company (10=totally new; 0=our existing customers).

    0 1 2 3 4 5 6 7 8 9 10 _____

13. The service class or type of new service itself is totally new to our company (10=totally new; 0=existing service class for us).

    0 1 2 3 4 5 6 7 8 9 10 _____

14. We have never made or sold services to satisfy this type of customer need or use before (10=never; 0=have done so, or are doing so now).

    0 1 2 3 4 5 6 7 8 9 10 _____

15. The competitors we face in the market are totally new to our company (10=totally new to us; 0=competitors we have faced before).

    0 1 2 3 4 5 6 7 8 9 10 _____

The Final Service:

The next 7 questions probe our advantage. Be sure to think in terms of our service versus competitive services . . . the services or solutions that the customer is now using to solve his/her problem.

16. Compared to competitive services (or whatever the customer is now using), our service will offer a number of unique features, attributes, or benefits to the customer (10=many positive & unique features & benefits; 5=same; 0=fewer).

    0 1 2 3 4 5 6 7 8 9 10 _____

	Strongly Disagree	Strongly Agree	Confidence

17. Our service will be clearly superior to competing services
in terms of meeting customer needs
(10=clearly superior; 5=equal to; 0=inferior to competitors).   0 1 2 3 4 5 6 7 8 9 10 _____

18. Our service will permit the customer to improve his/her
bottom line, when compared to what he/she is now using
(10=major reduction; 5=same; 0=higher costs).   0 1 2 3 4 5 6 7 8 9 10 _____

19. Our service will permit the customer to do a job or do
something that he/she cannot do with what is now available
on the market (10=clearly yes; 5=same; 0=less so).   0 1 2 3 4 5 6 7 8 9 10 _____

20. Our service will be of higher quality—however quality
is defined in this market—than competing services
(10=much higher quality; 5=same; 0=inferior to competitors).   0 1 2 3 4 5 6 7 8 9 10 _____

21. Our service will be priced considerably higher than competing
services (10=much higher; 5=same; 0=much lower).   0 1 2 3 4 5 6 7 8 9 10 _____

22. We will be first into the market with this type of service
(10=first in; 0=one after many).   0 1 2 3 4 5 6 7 8 9 10 _____

Our Market for This Service:

These last 8 questions look at the nature of the marketplace. Again, be sure to define what you mean
by "market," "customer," and "competition" (see note before question 9 above).

23. Potential customers have a great need for this class or type
of service (10=great need; 0=no need).   0 1 2 3 4 5 6 7 8 9 10 _____

24. The revenue size of the market (either existing or potential
market) for this service is large (10=very large; 0=very small).   0 1 2 3 4 5 6 7 8 9 10 _____

25. The market for this product is growing very quickly
(10=fast growth; 0=no growth or negative growth).   0 1 2 3 4 5 6 7 8 9 10 _____

26. The market is characterized by intense price competition
(10=intense price competition; 0=no price competition).   0 1 2 3 4 5 6 7 8 9 10 _____

27. There are many competitors in this market
(10=many; 0=none).   0 1 2 3 4 5 6 7 8 9 10 _____

28. There is a strong dominant competitor—with a large market
share—in this market
(10=dominant competitor; 0=no dominant competitors).   0 1 2 3 4 5 6 7 8 9 10 _____

29. Potential customers are very satisfied with the service
(competitors' services) they are currently using
(10=very satisfied; 0=very dissatisfied).   0 1 2 3 4 5 6 7 8 9 10 _____

30. Users' needs change quickly in this market—a dynamic
market situation
(10=change very quickly; 0=stable needs, no change).   0 1 2 3 4 5 6 7 8 9 10 _____

APPENDIX C:

NSP'S DECISION FORM— GATES 2 TO 4

Exhibit C.1   NSP's Decision Form—Gates 2–4*

Part A—Completed by New Service Development Team Leader

Project Name: _____

Team Leader: _____

Recommendation to Gatekeepers: Go/Kill/Hold/Recycle (select one)

Deliverables

_____ Part C: Gate Criteria (completed)

_____ Preliminary Business Analysis

_____ Action Plan: Detailed for next stage and outlined for remaining stages.
Includes:
  • Timelines   Resources   Budget

Part B—Completed by Gatekeepers

Decision: (select one)

___ **Go**
  • New service development team leader, team (including release time for people if needed) and required resources for the next stage are agreed to.
  • Action plan for the next stage is approved; including timeline, resources, budget and deliverable and date for next gate meeting.

___ **Kill**
  • The project is archived. No work is done; no resources are committed.

---

*The form is adapted from the *Reddy for Innovation* manual. Special thanks to Therese Lavalle and Jean-Robert Cole of Northern States Power.

___ **Hold**
  • The project is put on the Hold list for review at a future date.

___ **Rework**
  • The project is returned to the previous stage for further work by the new service
    development team as specified by the gatekeepers.

Issues/Concerns: _____

_____

_____

Gatekeepers

Name: Signature   Date

_____

_____

_____

_____

_____

Part C: Gate Criteria—Completed by New Service Development Team Leader

Must Meet Criteria (circle Yes or No)

Strategic Alignment

Does the new service fit within an area of strategic focus?	Yes	No

Market Attractiveness

Does the new service satisfy a customer need and increase customer satisfaction	Yes	No
Does the new service provide a competitive advantage?	Yes	No

Opportunity Magnitude

Does the opportunity justify the resources required?	Yes	No

Should Meet Criteria

	Strongly Disagree	Disagree	Neutral	Agree	Strongly Agree
Strategic Fit					
Fits well with the business strategy	1	2	3	4	5
Provides platform for growth	1	2	3	4	5
Synergy					
Leverages core competencies	1	2	3	4	5
Fits with our existing operations and fulfillment capabilities	1	2	3	4	5
Synergy with other services/products and businesses	1	2	3	4	5
Leverages existing customer relationships	1	2	3	4	5
Builds or supports our brand image	1	2	3	4	5
Market Attractiveness					
Clear market need	1	2	3	4	5
Attractive market growth rate	1	2	3	4	5
Significant long-term potential	1	2	3	4	5
Lack of intense competition	1	2	3	4	5
Minimal entry barriers for NSP	1	2	3	4	5

	Strongly Disagree	Disagree	Neutral	Agree	Strongly Agree
New Service/Product Superiority					
Differentiated product features	1	2	3	4	5
New or unique customer benefits	1	2	3	4	5
Excellent value for money for the customer	1	2	3	4	5
Financial					
Acceptable financial risks	1	2	3	4	5
Acceptable financial rewards	1	2	3	4	5
Feasibility					
Technically feasible	1	2	3	4	5
IT can support development and delivery of the service/product	1	2	3	4	5
Operations can support development and delivery	1	2	3	4	5
People with the skills required are available	1	2	3	4	5
Service/product can be launched within the window of opportunity	1	2	3	4	5
Other					
Positive regulatory, social, and political impact	1	2	3	4	5

TOTAL _____

Showstopper: Is there anything now or on the horizon that will squash the success of this service/product (government regulation, an emerging competitive technology, and so on)?

_____

_____

NOTES

The superscript numbers are not necessarily sequential. One passage may be linked to several notes and several passages may be linked to the same note.

Chapter 1–The Stakes Have Never Been Higher

1   Abbie Griffin, "PDMA Research on New Product Development Practices: Updating Trends and Benchmarking Best Practices," *Journal of Product Innovation Management* 14, 6 (1997):429–458.

2   Scott Edgett and Des Thwaites, "The Influence of Environmental Change on the Marketing Practices of Building Societies," *European Journal of Marketing* 24, 12 (1990):35–47.

3   For a more complete review of the literature that pertains to the differences between tangible and intangible products, see Scott Edgett and Stephen Parkinson, "Marketing for Service Industries—A Review," *Service Industries Journal* 13, 3 (1993):19–39.

4   G. Lynn Shostack, "Designing Services That Deliver," *Harvard Business Review* 62, 1 (1984):133–139.

5   Ibid., and Ulrike de Brentani, "Success Factors in Developing New Business Services," *European Journal of Marketing* 25, 2 (1991):33–59.

6   James Carman and Eric Langeard, "Growth Strategies for Service Firms," *Strategic Management Journal* 1 (1980):7–22; Christopher J. Easingwood, "New Product Development for Service Companies," *Journal of Product Innovation Management* 4 (1986):264–275; and Ulrike de Brentani, "Success Factors in Developing New Business Services," *European Journal of Marketing* 25, 2 (1991):33–59.

7   Easingwood, "New Product Development for Service Companies," and Donald Cowell, "New Service Development," *Journal of Marketing Management* 3, 3 (1988):296–312.

8   Easingwood, "New Product Development for Service Companies."

9   Dan R. Thomas, "Strategy Is Different in Service Businesses," *Harvard Business Review* 56, 4 (1978):158–165.

10   Donald Cowell, "New Service Development," *Journal of Marketing Management* 3, 3 (1988):296–312.

11   Thomas, "Strategy Is Different in Service Businesses," and Cowell, "New Service Development."

12   Patrick Murphy and Richard Robinson, "Concept Testing for Services," in J. Donnelly and W. George, eds., *Marketing of Services* (Chicago: American Marketing Association, 1981), pp. 217–220.

13   Thomas, "Strategy Is Different in Service Businesses," and de Brentani, "Success Factors in Developing New Business Services."

14   Valerie Zeithaml, "How Consumer Evaluation Processes Differ Between Goods and Services," in Donnelly and George, *Marketing of Services*, pp. 186–190; and Valerie Zeithaml, A. Parasuraman, and Leonard Berry, "Problems and Strategies in Services Marketing," *Journal of Marketing* 49 (Spring 1985):34–46.

15   Shostack, "Designing Services That Deliver"; and William Warren, C. Abercrombie, and R. Berl, "Adoption of a Service Innovation: A Case Study with Managerial Implications," *Journal of Service Marketing* 3, 1 (1989):21–33.

16   Richard Besson, "Unique Aspects of Marketing Services," *Arizona Business Bulletin* 20 (1972):8–15; Thomas, "Strategy Is Different in Service Businesses"; Eric Langeard and Pierre Eiglier, "Strategic Management of Service Development," in L. Berry, L. Shostack, and G. Upah, eds., *Emerging Perspectives on Service Marketing* (Proceedings Series)(Chicago: American Marketing Association, 1983), pp. 68–72; and Easingwood, "New Product Development for Service Companies."

17   Easingwood, "New Product Development for Service Companies."

18   De Brentani, "Success Factors in Developing New Business Services."

19   Ibid., and Scott Edgett and Kim Snow, "Benchmarking Measures of Customer Satisfaction, Quality and Performance for New Financial Service Products," *Journal of Services Marketing* 10, 6 (1996):6–17.

20   Bernard Booms, Duane Davis, and Dennis Guseman, "Participant Perspectives on Developing a Climate for Innovation of New Services," in W. George and C. Marshall, eds., *Developing New Services* (American Marketing Association: Chicago, 1984), pp. 23–26; Shostack, "Designing Services That Deliver"; Easingwood, "New Product Development for Service Companies."

21   Easingwood, "New Product Development for Service Companies" and de Brentani, "Success Factors in Developing New Business Services."

22   Richard Besson, "Unique Aspects of Marketing Services," *Arizona*

Business Bulletin 20 (1972):8–15; Bernard Booms and Mary Bitner, "Marketing Strategies and Organization Structures for Service Firms," in Donnelly and George, *Marketing of Services*, pp. 47–51; Christopher H. Lovelock, "Strategies for Managing Demand in Capacity-Constrained Service Organizations," *Service Industries Journal* 4, 3 (1984):12–30; Easingwood, "New Product Development for Service Companies."

23   Easingwood, "New Product Development for Service Companies."

24   De Brentani, "Success Factors in Developing New Business Services."

25   Easingwood, "New Product Development for Service Companies"; G. Lynn Shostack, "Service Positioning Through Structural Change," *Journal of Marketing* 51 (January 1987):34–43; Cowell, "New Service Development"; and de Brentani, "Success Factors in Developing New Business Services."

26   Cowell, "New Service Development."

27   De Brentani, "Success Factors in Developing New Business Services."

28   Theodore Levitt, "Marketing Intangible Products and Product Intangibles," *Harvard Business Review* 59, 3 (1981):94–102.

29   Ibid.

30   Leonard L. Berry, "Services Marketing Is Different," *Business*, May–June 1980, pp. 24–29.

31   Griffin, "PDMA Research on New Product Development Practices: Updating Trends and Benchmarking Best Practices."

32   Stephen Drew, *Business Re-engineering in Financial Services* (London: Pitman Publishing, 1994).

33   Scott Edgett, "Best Practices in the Service Sector," Innovation Working Paper Series (Hamilton, Ontario: McMaster University, 1998).

34   C. Easingwood and J. Percival, "Evaluation of New Financial Services," *International Journal of Bank Marketing* 8, 6 (1990):3–8.

35   Adapted from David Leonhardt, "McDonald's: Can It Regain Its Golden Touch?" *Business Week*, March 9, 1998, pp. 70–77.

36   These definitions have been adapted from several sources, including Christopher Lovelock, *Services Marketing*, 3rd ed. (New Jersey: Prentice Hall, 1996); Donald Heany, "Degrees of Product Innovation," *Journal of Business Strategy* (1983):3–14; and Booz, Allen and Hamilton, *New Product Management for the 1980's* (New York: Booz, Allen and Hamilton, Inc., 1982).

37   For more information on portfolio management see R. Cooper, S. Edgett, and E. Kleinschmidt, *Portfolio Management for New Products* (Reading, Mass.: Perseus Books, 1998).

38 For more information see G. L. Shostack, "How to Design a Service," *European Journal of Marketing* 16, 1 (1982):49–63.

39 For an excellent review of the academic literature on new service development, complete with a detailed listing of articles and their content, see A. Johne and C. Storey, "New Service Development: A Review of the Literature and Annotated Bibliography," *European Journal of Marketing* 32, 3–4 (1998):184–251.

Chapter 2–Critical Drivers of Success: Process Factors

1 Parts of this chapter have been adapted from Robert Cooper, "Overhauling the New Product Process," *Industrial Marketing Management* 25, 6 (1996):465–482, and Scott Edgett, "The New Product Development Process for Commercial Financial Services," *Industrial Marketing Management* 25, 6 (1996):507–515.

2 Abbie Griffin, "PDMA Research on New Product Development Practices: Updating Trends and Benchmarking Best Practices," *Journal of Product Innovation Management* 14, 6 (1997):429–458. For more information on the Product Development Management Association see their Website at http://www.pdma.org.

3 Scott Edgett, "Developing New Financial Services Within UK Building Societies," *International Journal of Bank Marketing* 11, 3 (1993):35–43.

4 For research results that examine this issue see S. Edgett, "The New Product Development Process for Commercial Financial Services"; R. G. Cooper and Ulrike de Brentani, "New Industrial Financial Services: What Distinguishes the Winners," *Journal of Product Innovation Management* 7, 2 (1991):75–90; R. G. Cooper et al., "What Distinguishes the Top Performing New Products in Financial Services," *Journal of Product Innovation Management* 11 (1994):281–299; U. de Brentani, "Success Factors in Developing New Business Services," *European Journal of Marketing*, 25, 2 (1991):33–59; ibid., "The New Product Process in Financial Services," *International Journal of Bank Marketing* 11, 3 (1993):15–22; C. Easingwood, "New Product Development for Service Companies," *Journal of Product Innovation Management* 3, 4 (1986):264–275; C. Easingwood and C. Storey, "Success Factors for New Consumer Financial Services," *International Journal of Bank Marketing* 9, 1 (1991):3–10; S. Edgett, "The Development of New Financial Services: Identifying Determinants of Success and Fail-

ure," *International Journal of Service Industry Management* 5, 4 (1994):24–38; ibid., "The Traits of Successful New Service Development," *Journal of Services Marketing* 8, 3 (1994):40–49; S. Edgett and S. Jones, "New Product Development in the Financial Services Industry: A Case Study," *Journal of Marketing Management* 7 (1991):271–284.

5 R. G. Cooper, *Winning at New Products: Accelerating the Process from Idea to Launch*, 2nd ed. (Reading, Mass.: Addison-Wesley, 1993).

6 S. Edgett, "The New Product Development Process for Commercial Financial Services."

7 Cooper et al., "What Distinguishes the Top Performing New Products in Financial Services"; R. G. Cooper, *Product Leadership: Creating and Launching Superior New Products* (Reading, Mass: Perseus Books, 1998).

8 R. Cooper, S. Edgett, and E. Kleinschmidt, *Portfolio Management for New Products* (Reading, Mass.: Perseus Books, 1998).

9 These questions come from a larger set of best benchmarking questions that have been adapted from ProBE, a benchmarking instrument developed jointly by Jens Arleth of U3 Innovation Management (Copenhagen) and Robert Cooper and Scott Edgett of the Product Development Institute Inc. (Hamilton, Ontario). For more information on ProBE, see our Website at www.prod-dev.com or contact the authors directly through our Website.

Chapter 3–Critical Steps for Success:
The Project Factors

1 Much of this database has been published in a number of articles. For more information see R. G. Cooper and S. J. Edgett, "Critical Success Factors for New Financial Services," *Marketing Management* 5, 3 (1996):26–37; Scott Edgett, "The New Product Development Process for Commercial Financial Services," *Industrial Marketing Management* 25, 6 (1996):507–515; R. G. Cooper and U. de Brentani, "New Industrial Financial Services: What Distinguishes the Winners," *Journal of Product Innovation Management* 7, 2 (1991):75–90; R. G. Cooper et al., "What Distinguishes the Top Performing New Products in Financial Services," *Journal of Product Innovation Management* 11 (1994):281–299; S. Edgett, "The Development of New Financial Services: Identifying Determinants of Success and Failure," *International Journal of Service Industry Management* 5, 4 (1994):24–38; S. Edgett, "The Traits of Successful New Service Development," *The Journal of Services Marketing* 8,

3 (1994):40–49; S. Edgett and S. Jones, "New Product Development in the Financial Services Industry: A Case Study," *Journal of Marketing Management* 7 (1991):271–284.

2   Cooper and de Brentani, "New Industrial Financial Services: What Distinguishes the Winners"; Edgett, "The New Product Development Process for Commercial Financial Services."

3   Cooper and de Brentani, "New Industrial Financial Services: What Distinguishes the Winners"; Edgett, "The New Product Development Process for Commercial Financial Services"; and Cooper et al., "What Distinguishes the Top Performing New Products in Financial Services."

4   B. Uttal, "Speeding New Ideas to Market," *Fortune,* March 1987, pp. 62–66.

5   Cooper and de Brentani, "New Industrial Financial Services: What Distinguishes the Winners"; Edgett, "The New Product Development Process for Commercial Financial Services."

6   Cooper and de Brentani, "New Industrial Financial Services: What Distinguishes the Winners"; Edgett, "The New Product Development Process for Commercial Financial Services"; Cooper et al., "What Distinguishes the Top Performing New Products in Financial Services."

7   Cooper and de Brentani, "New Industrial Financial Services: What Distinguishes the Winners"; Edgett, "The New Product Development Process for Commercial Financial Services."

8   Cooper and de Brentani, "New Industrial Financial Services: What Distinguishes the Winners"; Edgett, "The New Product Development Process for Commercial Financial Services."

9   Cooper et al., "What Distinguishes the Top Performing New Products in Financial Services."

10   See Cooper and de Brentani, "New Industrial Financial Services: What Distinguishes the Winners"; and Cooper and Edgett, "Critical Success Factors for New Financial Services."

Chapter 4–Developing a Winning
New Service Development Process

1   Abbie Griffin, "PDMA Research on New Product Development Practices: Updating Trends and Benchmarking Best Practices," *Journal of Product Innovation Management* 14, 6 (1997):429–458.

2   Parts of this section are taken from R. G. Cooper and S. J. Edgett, "Critical Success Factors for New Financial Services," *Marketing Management* 5, 3 (1996):26–37.

3   R. G. Cooper, "The New Product Process: A Decision Guide for Managers," *Journal of Marketing Management* 3, 3 (1999):238–255; ibid., "Stage-Gate Systems: A New Tool for Managing New Products," *Business Horizons* 33, 3 (May–June 1990); ibid., *Winning at New Products: Accelerating the Process from Idea to Launch* (Reading, Mass: Addison-Wesley, 1993).

4   This early work is reported in R. G. Cooper, "Identifying Industrial New Product Success: Project NewProd," *Industrial Marketing Management* 8 (1979):124–135; ibid., "The New Product Process: An Empirically Derived Classification Scheme," *R&D Management* 13 (1983):2–11.

5   Ibid., "Third-Generation New Product Processes," *Journal of Product Innovation Management* 11 (1994):3–14.

6   In a report entitled *Beyond Commodity Status: Responding to the New Mandate for Growth* (Washington, D.C.: The Advisory Board, 1997) of a Council on Financial Competition Study conducted by The Advisory Board, Stage-Gate was cited (pp. 175–198) as a best in-class practice.

Chapter 5—How to Build a Winner:
From Idea to Launch

1   Based on material in R. G. Cooper, *Winning at New Products: Accelerating the Process from Idea to Launch* (Reading, Mass: Addison-Wesley, 1993).

2   R. Sears and M. Barry, "Product Value Analysis^{SM}—Product Interaction Predicts Profits," *Innovation*, Winter 1993, pp. 13–18.

3   For more information on the use of lead users in idea generation, see E. von Hippel, M. Sonnack, and J. Churchill, *Developing Breakthrough Products and Services: The Lead User Method* (Minneapolis: LUCI Press, 1988); C. Herstatt and E. von Hippel, "From Experience: Developing New Product Concepts via the Lead User Method: A Case Study in a 'Low Tech' Field," *Journal of Product Innovation Management* 9 (1992):213–221; G. L. Urban and E. A. von Hippel, "Lead User Analyses for the Development of New Industrial Products," *Management Science* 34 (1998):5, 569–582; E. A. von Hippel, *The Sources of Innovation* (New York: Oxford University Press, 1988).

4   A. Griffin et al., eds., *The PDMA Handbook of New Product Development* (New York: John Wiley, 1996).

5   For an interesting example of using a Product Roadmap see A. Yu, *Creating the Digital Future: The Secrets of Consistent Innovation at Intel* (New York: Free Press, 1998).

6   Based on unpublished work of Dr. Larry Gastwirt, Stevens Institute of Technology, Hoboken, New Jersey.

Chapter 6—Issues and Challenges: New Approaches in the Innovation Process

1   See PDMA best-practices studies by Abbie Griffin, "PDMA Research on New Product Development Practices: Updating Trends and Benchmarking Best Practices," *Journal of Product Innovation Management*, 14, 6 (1997):429–458, and ibid., *Drivers of NPD Success: The 1997 PDMA Report* (Chicago: Product Development & Management Association, 1997). For a thorough description of third-generation new product processes, see R. G. Cooper, "Third-Generation New Product Processes," *Journal of Product Innovation Management* 11 (1994):3–14.

2   G. Hamel and J. Sampler, "The E-Corporation," *Fortune*, December 7, 1998, pp. 80–93; and E. Schonfeld, "Schwab Puts It All On-Line," *Fortune*, December 7, 1998, pp. 94–100.

3   See Cooper, "Third-Generation New Product Processes."

4   R. G. Cooper, "Developing New Products on Time, in Time," *Research & Technology Management,* September–October 1995, pp.49–57.

5   M. Crawford, "The Hidden Cost of Accelerated Product Development," *Journal of Product Innovation Management* 9, 3 (1992):188–199.

6   See B. Dumaine, "How Managers Can Succeed Through Speed," *Fortune*, February 13, 1989, pp. 14–25.

7   R. G. Cooper, *Product Leadership Creating and Launching Superior New Products* (Reading, Mass.: Perseus Books, 1998).

8   See note 1, above.

9   Tom Peters, *Thriving on Chaos* (New York: Harper & Row, 1988).

Chapter 7—Portfolio Management: More Than Just Project Selection

1   Much of this chapter has been adapted from three articles by R. G. Cooper, S. J. Edgett, and E. J. Kleinschmidt: "Portfolio Management in New Product Development: Lessons From the Leaders," Parts I and

II, *Research-Technology Management* 40, 5 (1997):16–28 (Part I), and *Research-Technology Management* 40, 6 (1997):43–52 (Part II); and ibid., "Best Practices for Managing R&D Portfolios," *Research-Technology Management* 41, 4 (1998):20–33.

For more detailed information on portfolio management, see ibid., *Portfolio Management for New Products* (Reading, Mass: Perseus Books, 1998).

2 Ibid., p. 3.

3 A. Griffin, *Drivers of NPD Success: The 1997 PDMA Report* (Chicago: Product Development and Management Association, 1997).

4 R. G. Cooper, S. J. Edgett, and E. J. Kleinschmidt, *R&D Portfolio Management Best Practices Study* (Washington, D.C.: Industrial Research Institute [IRI], 1997).

5 For more information, see David Matheson, James E. Matheson, and Michael M. Menke, "Making Excellent R&D Decisions," *Research Technology Management*, November–December 1994, pp. 21–24; and Patricia Evans, "Streamlining Formal Portfolio Management," *Scrip Magazine*, February 1996.

6 See note 1, above.

7 For more information on these corporate planning models, see, for the Boston Consulting Group's Growth-Share Matrix, B. Heldey, "Strategy and the Business Portfolio," *Long Range Planning* 1977; for the General Electric Approach, see George Day, *Analysis for Strategic Marketing Decisions* (St. Paul: West Publishing, 1986), and La Rue Hosner, *Strategic Management* (Englewood Cliffs, N.J.: Prentice-Hall, 1984).

8 Cooper, Edgett, and Kleinschmidt, *R&D Portfolio Management Best Practices Study.*

9 The Arthur D. Little model is outlined in P. Roussel, K. Saad, and T. Erickson, *Third Generation R&D: Managing the Link to Corporate Strategy* (Boston: Harvard Business School Press and Arthur D. Little, Inc., 1991).

10 On the SDG method, see note 7.

11 Source: from discussions with, and internal 3M documents written by, Dr. Gary L. Tritle, "New Product Investment Portfolio."

12 Adapted from E. Roberts and C. Berry, "Entering New Businesses: Selecting Strategies for Success," *Sloan Management Review*, Spring 1983, pp. 3–17.

13 R. G. Cooper, *Product Leadership* (Reading, Mass: Perseus Books, 1998).

Appendix A–The ProBE Diagnostic Tool

1   ProBE a benchmarking instrument developed jointly by Jens Arleth of U3 Innovation Management (Copenhagen) and Robert Cooper and Scott Edgett of the Product Development Institute Inc. For more information see our Website at www.prod-dev.com or contact the authors directly via the Website.

INDEX